ISLAM AND POLITICS AROUND THE WORLD

ISLAM AND POLITICS
AROUND THE WORLD

Edited by John L. Esposito

AND

Emad El-Din Shahin

OXFORD
UNIVERSITY PRESS

OXFORD
UNIVERSITY PRESS

Oxford University Press is a department of the University of Oxford.
It furthers the University's objective of excellence in research, scholarship,
and education by publishing worldwide. Oxford is a registered trade mark of
Oxford University Press in the UK and certain other countries.

Published in the United States of America by Oxford University Press
198 Madison Avenue, New York, NY 10016, United States of America.

The essays in this volume were originally published in
The Oxford Handbook of Islam and Politics

Library of Congress Cataloging-in-Publication Data
Names: Esposito, John L., editor. | Shahin, Emad Eldin, 1957– editor.
Title: Islam and politics around the world / edited by John L. Esposito
and Emad El-Din Shahin.
Description: New York, NY : Oxford University Press, [2018] | Includes index. |
Description based on print version record and CIP data provided
by publisher; resource not viewed.
Identifiers: LCCN 2018013402 (print) | LCCN 2018015093 (ebook) |
ISBN 9780190900403 (updf) | ISBN 9780190900410 (epub) |
ISBN 9780190900397 (pbk.) | ISBN 9780190900380 (hardcover)
Subjects: LCSH: Islam and politics.
Classification: LCC BP173.7 (ebook) | LCC BP173.7 .I7625 2018 (print) |
DDC 297.2/7209—dc23
LC record available at https://lccn.loc.gov/2018013402

1 3 5 7 9 8 6 4 2
Paperback printed by WebCom, Inc., Canada
Hardback printed by Bridgeport National Bindery, Inc.,
United States of America

CONTENTS

CONTENTS

CONTRIBUTORS

Irfan Ahmad is an anthropologist and a Senior Research Fellow at the Max Planck Institute for the Study of Religious and Ethnic Diversity in Göttingen, Germany.

Abdullah A. Al-Arian is Assistant Professor of history at Georgetown University's School of Foreign Service in Qatar.

Sam Cherribi is Senior Lecturer in the Department of Middle Eastern and South Asian Studies and Director of the Emory Development Initiative at Emory University.

John L. Esposito is Professor of religion and international affairs and Founding Director of the Prince Alwaleed Bin Talal Center for Muslim-Christian Understanding in the Walsh School of Foreign Service at Georgetown University.

Moataz A. Fattah is Associate Professor of Middle Eastern politics and Islamic studies at Cairo University in Egypt and Central Michigan University.

Shireen Hunter is Research Professor at the Prince Alwaleed bin Talal Center for Muslim-Christian Understanding at Georgetown University.

Azzedine Layachi is Professor of government and politics at St. John's University.

Emad El-Din Shahin is the Dean of the College of Islamic Studies, Hamad bin Khalifa University, Qatar Foundation, and a Senior Fellow at Georgetown University.

Leonardo A. Villalón is Dean of the International Center and Professor of political science and African studies at the University of Florida.

The Late **Fred R. von der Mehden** was Professor Emeritus of political science at Rice University.

NOTE ON TRANSLITERATION

Due to variance in usage, rather than attempt to impose a style of transliteration across the entire volume, we have allowed each author to transliterate foreign-language terms according to his or her stylistic preference.

ISLAM AND POLITICS AROUND THE WORLD

Islam and Politics
Around the World

JOHN L. ESPOSITO AND EMAD EL-DIN SHAHIN

In the late 1960s and 1970s, a religious revival swept through the
Muslim world. Common to the resurgence was a quest for identity,
authenticity, and community and a desire to establish meaning and
order in both personal life and society. Many Muslims became more
religiously observant, emphasizing prayer, fasting, dress, and family
values. In the public sphere, Islam reemerged as a religio-political
alternative to failed nationalist ideologies. Governments and Islamic
movements, from moderate to extremist, used religion to mobilize
popular support. Islamic movements sought to address the problems of political and social injustice (authoritarian governments,
repression, maldistribution of wealth, and corruption) while also
seeking to preserve Muslim religious and cultural identity and
values that had been threatened by Western hegemony.

A number of visible crises or failures proved to be catalytic.
The 1967 Arab-Israeli war (Six-Day War), in which Israel decisively
defeated the combined Arab armies of Egypt, Syria, and Jordan—
which led to the Israeli occupation of Sinai, the West Bank and
Gaza, and East Jerusalem—discredited the prevailing ideologies of
Arab nationalism and socialism and transformed the liberation of

Palestine into a transnational Islamic issue. The Pakistan-Bangladesh civil war of 1971–1972 heralded the failure of Muslim nationalism as a unifier in West and East Pakistan. The Iranian Revolution of 1978–1979 proved to be a pivotal event with long-term global impact and implications for the Muslim world and the West. Finally, the continued conflict in Palestine-Israel grew in strength during the 1980s and spawned its own Islamist movements, among them HAMAS and Islamic Jihad.

The resurgence of Islam in politics was intimately tied to relations with the West. Western models of development had failed in many Muslim (and non-Muslim) countries. Arab and Muslim nations found many Western countries to be unreliable allies. And they feared political, economic, and cultural dominance by the West. Many blamed the ills of their societies on excessive influence of and dependence on the West, especially the two superpowers: the United States and the Soviet Union. Efforts to modernize were seen as tools of westernization, secularization, and globalization. Resentment grew against Western "neocolonialism" imposed by the West and Western-oriented elites in Muslim countries. Such efforts, it was feared, would powerfully undermine Muslim religious and cultural identity and values.

In the late twentieth century, while most Islamic movements developed in response to domestic conditions, international issues and actors increasingly played important roles in Muslim politics: the Soviet-Afghan War, the Arab-Israeli conflict, sanctions against Saddam Hussein's Iraq, the "liberation" of Bosnia, Kashmir, and Chechnya, and the rise of Osama Bin Laden and al-Qaeda. In addition, wealthy individuals and countries like Saudi Arabia, Iran, and Libya used their petrodollars and wealth to extend their influence internationally. They promoted their religious and ideological worldviews and politics by supporting government Islamization programs as well as Islamist movements, both mainstream and extremist.

IDEOLOGICAL WORLDVIEW

Islamists blamed the Muslim world's decline on corrupt authoritarian and un-Islamic regimes and excessive political, economic, and cultural dependence on the West. The cure was a return to the faith and values of Islam. Islam, they assert, is a comprehensive framework for Muslim life, public as well as personal. The revitalization of Muslim societies requires the restoration of Islamic law and values. While the westernization and secularization of society are condemned, modernization, as such, is not. Science and technology are accepted; but the pace, direction, and extent of change must be subordinated to Islamic belief and values in order to guard against excessive dependence on the West.

THE QUIET REVOLUTION

In contrast to the 1980s, when political Islam was simply equated with revolutionary Iran or clandestine groups like Islamic Jihad or the Army of God, in the 1990s Islamists began to participate in the electoral process. A quiet revolution had taken place. While a minority of religious extremists sought to impose change from above through terror and violent means, many others pursued a bottom-up approach, seeking a gradual transformation or Islamization of society through words and example, preaching and activism.

Islamic organizations and associations emerged as part of mainstream society. They became forces in civil society, active in social reform, providing educational, medical, dental, legal, and social welfare services. Islamic banks and insurance companies, as well as publishing houses, mushroomed.

This social activism was accompanied by increased political participation. In the late 1980s and 1990s, failed economies, and discredited governmental development policies, led to political crises and mass demonstrations in several Muslim countries. These protests resulted in limited, state-controlled political liberalization. Islamic candidates were elected as mayors and parliamentarians in countries as diverse as Morocco, Egypt, Turkey, Lebanon, Kuwait, Bahrain, Pakistan, Malaysia, and Indonesia. They served in cabinet-level positions and as speakers of national assemblies, as prime ministers (Turkey, Iran, and Pakistan), as a deputy prime minister (Malaysia), and as Indonesia's first democratically elected president. The general response of many governments to the growing political power of Islam was to retreat from open elections. They identified their Islamic opposition as extremist, and they manipulated or simply canceled elections, as in Tunisia, Algeria, Egypt, and Jordan.

ISLAM AND GLOBAL TERRORISM

The majority of Islamic activists and movements worked to bring about change through social and political activism within their own societies by participating in electoral politics and civil society. However, a significant and dangerous minority of extremists— jihadist groups from Egypt to Indonesia, including al-Qaeda and ISIS—have claimed a mandate from God to make radical changes, grounded in the belief that rulers in the Muslim world and their societies are anti-Islamic. For these extremists, those individuals and governments who remain apolitical or resist extremist ideas have been no longer regarded as Muslims but rather as atheists or unbelievers, enemies of God, against whom all true Muslims must raise arms (armed *jihad*).

ABOUT THIS BOOK

This book provides overviews of the development and interaction of Islam and politics across virtually all regions of the globe. Abdullah Al-Arian provides a perspective on Islam's historical presence, development, and legacy in North America. Sam Cherribi addresses what he calls the growing obsession of the political elite and the media that has resulted in patterns of polarization all over Europe. Moataz Fattah offers a panoramic view of the eight different agendas that have resulted in Muslim societies in the Middle East. Shireen Hunter surveys the factors behind the vitality of Islam in Central Asia and the Caucasus. Irfan Ahmad argues against the dominant framework of securitization of Islam with a particular focus on Jamaat-e-Islami in India, Pakistan, and Bangladesh. Fred von der Mehden discusses the complex interaction of religion and politics in the heterogeneous societies of Malaysia, Indonesia, and Brunei. Azzedine Layachi examines the diverse roles of Islam in the Maghreb (Algeria, Libya, Morocco, and Tunisia) in the postindependence period and its relationship to national identities, to the state, and to reformist and revolutionary tendencies. Leonardo Villalón explores the main characteristics that describe the patterns and varieties of political Islam in Sub-Saharan countries.

Taken together, we hope that these essays provide readers with an illuminating overview of the state of political Islam around the world.

Chapter 1

Islam and Politics in North America

ABDULLAH A. AL-ARIAN

Over the past half century, the presence of an Islamic community in North America has been treated as a recent phenomenon in the continent's rich history, exhibited through the lives of mid-twentieth-century Muslim converts such as Malcolm X and Muhammad Ali. In the years leading up to the attacks of September 11, 2001, the focus on Muslims in North America shifted to the recent immigrant community, viewed through the lens of the security challenges posed by a perceived impending confrontation between the Western and Islamic worlds. In both cases, Islam has been presented as an alien faith that is largely out of step with mainstream American culture and traditional values. The following discussion will attempt to shed light on Islam's historical legacy in North America, demonstrating its contributions to the complex mosaic of American life. With a proper understanding of the historical context of Islam's presence in this region of the Western hemisphere, one is better able to explain the recent developments in the Muslim community, including the maturation of its identity and its establishment of prominent political institutions. In light of the Muslim community's recent attempts to secure its civil rights and carve out a place within the broader American public square, these efforts have all the hallmarks of prior struggles, whether by indigenous or immigrant communities, making the story of Muslims in this continent a distinctly American experience.

HISTORICAL BACKGROUND

Recent scholarship on Islam in America has attempted to dispel the traditional notion that dates Islam's emergence on the continent to the Black Nationalist movements of the 1930s. In fact, this literature provides a compelling portrait of a Muslim presence in North America from the dawn of the Columbian era.[1] The Age of Exploration, which began with Christopher Columbus's voyage to the New World in 1492, coincided with the end of Islamic rule in Spain after nearly eight centuries that featured the rise of one of the most advanced multicultural civilizations in history, known as *convivencia*. The era in world history that began with European discovery of the Americas cannot be separated from the key developments taking place within the Old World, namely, the establishment of a Christian empire on the ruins of an Islamic one. The legacy of Islamic Spain appears throughout the expedition by Columbus, who relied on Morisco ship owners, African navigators, and Muslim technology to reach the Americas.

In the centuries that followed, as the trajectory of global power continued to tilt in favor of European kingdoms, often at the expense of Islamic dynasties, Muslims who came to America were brought as slaves from West Africa to serve in the rapidly expanding colonial outposts. There are no reliable estimates on the percentage of African slaves in the Americas who were Muslim in background—much of this research is still in its infancy—but a number of historical accounts have been brought to light. In recent years, an attempt has been made to popularize the experiences of Muslim slaves through books and films devoted to the lives of Ayuba Suleiman Diallo, an eighteenth-century slave whose remarkable journey allowed him to eventually return to his home along the Gambia River in West Africa, or `Abd al-Rahman Ibrahima Sora, an African prince enslaved in the Americas during the early nineteenth century and freed only after the intervention of President John Quincy Adams. In these cases, the Muslim slaves were highly educated, reading and writing in Arabic and exhibiting a strong Islamic identity with knowledge of the Qur'an and the Hadith. In some instances, they ensured that their families continued to practice the religion, even under the most austere circumstances.

In contrast to these exceptional stories, however, the great majority of Muslim slaves in the American colonies suffered the same hardships and indignities as non-Muslim slaves, with almost no avenues to attain their freedom. Most were forced to repress their Islamic identities, and those who continued to practice their faith did so in secret, severely restricting their ability to pass it on to their descendants. It is no surprise then, that in the homogeneous cultural and political climate of colonial America, little remained of the West African slaves' Islamic character in the generations that followed. It was not until the twentieth century, during the early days of the civil rights movement, that some African Americans made a concerted effort to rediscover their Muslim heritage, finding in it a source of empowerment.

In addition to the population of African slaves, a subtle yet ever present undercurrent of Islamic culture developed throughout the course of early American history. In 2006, when the first American Muslim elected to the US Congress chose to take his oath of office on a Qur'an once owned by Thomas Jefferson, many Americans were surprised to learn that one of their founding fathers had kept a copy of Islam's holy book in his private library. Indeed, some of

America's most enduring literary figures, including Edgar Allan Poe and Herman Melville, claim Islamic texts among their influences. In some cases, this curiosity was piqued by Americans embarking on a spiritual quest outside of their dominant religious culture. Such was the experience of Alexander Russell Webb, a journalist and diplomat who became one of the most prominent American converts to Islam before the turn of the century. Recent scholarship has focused on Webb as a foundational figure in the development of a distinctly American Islam.[2] Following his travels abroad and interaction with Muslims in Asia, Webb returned to the United States to establish one of the earliest Muslim institutions in the country. Through his organization and publications, Webb attempted to attract other Americans to Islam, citing the common values and aspirations shared by his cultural background and his new faith.

In the first half of the twentieth century, Islam's presence in America spread at a far more rapid pace, and along several parallel tracks. These divisions represent the background and makeup of these communities, commonly depicted as an indigenous versus immigrant divide. Rising immigration from the Arab territories under Ottoman rule was a sign of the great empire's state of permanent decline. Mostly uneducated and unskilled laborers, Christians as well as Muslims came to North America in search of a new life. They settled mainly in the Midwestern United States, in newly industrialized cities such as Michigan City, Indiana; Detroit, Michigan; and Cedar Rapids, Iowa, home to one of the oldest mosques in America. Further west, immigrants from South Asia began to seek new opportunities in the expanding economy of California. These trends continued steadily until the National Origins Act severely restricted immigration from nonwhite countries for four decades beginning in 1925. Though this era saw the establishment of some of the earliest lasting institutions of the American Muslim community, these mosques and Islamic centers were usually the exception. This wave of Muslim immigration is marked by a far greater tendency toward assimilation into the broader American society, as seen in the number of families in the community who changed their names and ceased religious observances, especially among second-and third-generation immigrants. In both instances, the contributions of this community to its adopted homeland remained constant, with a number of immigrant Muslims serving alongside fellow citizens in the US military during World War II.

The African American experience with Islam in the first half of the twentieth century was vastly different from that of the immigrant community. Continuing to suffer the effects of institutionalized discrimination and inequality decades after the abolition of slavery, African Americans were not granted the same economic opportunities, and therefore did not harbor the same visions of the American dream as many immigrants did. Instead, the African American population engaged in a civil rights struggle and in some prominent circles within that movement, Islam played a significant role as a political, cultural, and spiritual force. Early encounters with Islam in the African American community involved conversion to the faith through particular organizations, such as the Moorish Science Temple or the Nation of Islam. Due to fundamental doctrinal differences, these movements were regarded as conflicting with traditional Islam, but served as an important stepping-stone for many African American converts to mainstream Sunni Islam. Under the leadership of Elijah Muhammad, the Nation of Islam established a number of important institutions addressing the community's needs, including schools, cultural centers, and social service organizations. It also focused on the political demands of the growing African American Muslim community, by creating external avenues for change, rather than encouraging direct political participation.

Though by no means the first, Malcolm X (later, El-Hajj Malik El-Shabazz) was one of the most prominent figures to make the transition from an exclusively African American Muslim group to mainstream Islam. El-Shabazz continued to be a powerful voice for African American rights in the context of the larger Black Nationalist movement, but began to integrate traditional Islamic principles, such as universal equality, in his message. His departure from the Nation of Islam and embrace of traditional Islam in the mid-1960s signaled an important transition in the history of Islam in America.

THE MODERN COMMUNITY AND EARLY INSTITUTIONS

Offering a tribute at the funeral of El-Hajj Malik El-Shabazz in February 1965 was Omar Osman, a Muslim college student of Sudanese background. The tragedy of El-Shabazz's assassination brought together the two constituencies of the American Muslim community, with its indigenous and immigrant components, ushering in a new era of Islam in America, one that featured increased fluidity and interaction among communities and greater appreciation of their cultural diversity. Later that same year, the administration of Lyndon Johnson repealed longstanding immigration quotas, paving the way for increased migration to the United States from countries with large Muslim populations. Perhaps more significantly, this wave of immigration featured a qualitatively different profile than that of previous eras. Whether in the indigenous or immigrant communities, the contemporary American Muslim identity is largely the product of the significant developments that began in the late 1960s.

Hailing mainly from the Middle East and South Asia, the Muslim immigrants to America after 1965 were naturally a reflection of the recent changes in their societies. On the heels of the development policies in such countries as Egypt and Pakistan, they were more highly educated, often in technical fields such as engineering and medicine, and came to pursue advanced degrees in the United States or start their own businesses. Unlike earlier Muslim communities, these immigrants became independently wealthy at a rapid pace and were integrated into a growing American middle class. On a cultural level, they held more firmly to their Islamic identity, embodying the recent religious revival across the Islamic world, as represented by such groups as the Muslim Brotherhood and *Jamā`at-i Islāmī*. The institutions developed during this period signified the growing international character of the American Muslim community, witnessed by the close linkages maintained between local mosques and student groups in the United States and Canada and their counterparts in the Muslim world. It was not uncommon, for instance, for a prominent Islamist figure, such as the Sudanese intellectual Hassan al-Turabi or Egyptian scholar Yusuf al-Qaradawi, to embark on speaking tours across North American universities and Islamic centers.

The Muslim Students Association (MSA), originally established in 1963 to provide local religious services on American campuses, expanded greatly to meet the growing needs of a community that desired to extend its activities beyond fulfilling basic ritual requirements. By the mid-1970s, the MSA had an established national headquarters and was holding regular meetings to address the community's urgent political concerns, such as the recent Soviet invasion of Afghanistan, the fallout from the Islamic revolution in Iran, or the continuing Israeli occupation of Palestine. In later years, the community's great emphasis on international affairs would face internal and external critiques. However, in its time, this activism signaled the first major collective action on the part of the American

Muslim community as a coherent political constituency, and signaled a recognition of the growing role the United States was playing in deciding the fate of fellow Muslims around the globe. Early American Muslim political activism generally consisted of keeping community members informed of important developments overseas, using the pulpits of mosques and a burgeoning Islamic press as their main tools, while establishing charitable organizations to provide support to those suffering from various forms of oppression throughout the Muslim world.

The decade that followed witnessed an important development in the state of the community of recent immigrants. Having settled in North America and enjoyed a considerable degree of professional success, the community set out to form permanent institutions commensurate with its established presence in American life. Out of the MSA, an organization serving the needs of students as they pursued their education, came the Islamic Society of North America (ISNA), a national umbrella organization that includes mosques, community centers, professional associations, educational institutions, and family support groups. In addition, ISNA maintains the North American Islamic Trust (NAIT), an institution that provides financial backing for Islamic projects throughout the United States and Canada. This period featured a boom in the number of mosques and Islamic centers and a significant transition from the use of commercial properties and private homes to freestanding structures built for the sole purpose of serving the community's religious and social needs. Another feature of this period was the founding of Islamic educational institutions across the country. Over two hundred full-time Islamic schools educate thousands of Muslim children, yet another sign that the immigrant community abandoned the "myth of return," that is, the conception of America as a temporary economic haven on the road back to one's homeland. Instead, the community began to invest in the future of its American-born children and the cultivation of an Islamic identity in harmony with American values.

.For the African American Muslim community, the 1970s and 1980s was a period of great transformation as well. Following the death of his father, Imam Warith Deen Muhammad inherited the leadership of the Nation of Islam. Through his education in traditional Islamic studies, Muhammad led the majority of his community into mainstream Sunni Islam and welcomed many new converts into the fold. Until his death in 2008, W. D. Muhammad's nationwide network of mosques and Sister Clara Muhammad schools made him one of the most prominent Muslim leaders in the United States. He is consistently recognized for his role in bridging the gap between the Islam of the Black Nationalist movement and a mainstream African American Islamic identity that seeks to carve out its place within the larger American cultural landscape.

CIVIL RIGHTS AND ELECTIONS: THE EMERGENCE OF AMERICAN MUSLIM POLITICS

American Muslims had explored the possibility of entering the public domain as a political constituency for many years. As early as 1983, a visionary community leader named Mohammad T. Medhi founded the National Council on Islamic Affairs in New York as an effort to encourage Muslims to participate in American politics. Among Mehdi's many accomplishments was the successful campaign to place the crescent and star, Islamic cultural symbols, side by side with Christian and Jewish symbols in official decorations at the White House and the World Trade Center.[3] Internally, however, the broader community had yet to embrace the idea of political participation for a number of reasons, including the lack of institutional support and civic education, and questions as to the religious permissibility of participating in a non-Muslim political system. Moreover, the urgency for engagement in the political process was not yet apparent in the 1980s, as the community's priorities lay in the dual tasks of developing internal institutions and assisting struggles abroad. Early in the next decade, however, all of these challenges would be overcome at a lightening pace.

Just as the Cold War had drawn to a close, the United States led a coalition of nations into the Persian Gulf to force Iraq's withdrawal from Kuwait. It was the first large-scale American military action in the Middle East and signaled the beginning of a significant presence in the region that has solidified over the course of two decades. In the aftermath of the Gulf War, American thinkers and pundits contemplated impending challenges to the nascent unipolar system dominated by US power, the "new world order," as described by George H. W. Bush. Noted scholars such as Bernard Lewis and Samuel Huntington advanced the notion that the world of Islam, stretching from Morocco to Indonesia and comprising over 1 billion people, constituted the key threat to the post-Cold War global order. Raising the specter of "Islam's bloody borders," Huntington predicted a "clash of civilizations" between Islam and the West, laying the foundation for an intellectual project that would gain much currency in American policy-making circles in the ensuing years.[4] Seemingly for the first time since it became organized as a national religious constituency, the American Muslim community was forced to confront a rising challenge that pitted its layered identities against one another.

Whatever internal divisions had existed within the American Muslim community regarding the permissibility of participating in the political process had all but disappeared by the mid-1990s. The

dominant view that emerged from that debate argued that engagement of the political system was the most effective means of defending the community's rights, advancing its interests, and claiming its
place within the broader American political landscape, thereby dis-
pelling the notion that American Muslims stood on the frontlines of
an impending battle between the Western and Islamic worlds.

During the early years of this period, the community met with
a considerable degree of success. American Muslim leaders established several national political organizations with varying points of
emphasis, from promoting civic education in local communities, to
monitoring media coverage and legislation concerning Muslims, to
outright lobbying of lawmakers. Unlike older organizations such as
ISNA that focused mainly on religious and cultural issues within the
community, these institutions maintained an outward orientation
with a decidedly political emphasis. The American Muslim Alliance
(AMA) established nearly one hundred local chapters around the
United States to provide civic education and promote an electoral
strategy that ranged from local to national elections. The Council on
American-Islamic Relations (CAIR) became a prominent fixture in
local and national media to provide balance in the coverage on
issues of concern to the American Muslim community, and also
worked to defend the rights of Muslims in cases of work discrimination or hate crimes.

The American Muslim Council (AMC), based out of the nation's
capital, took on the lobbying efforts necessary to bring about real
change in the community's most pressing issue areas. Its leaders
established strong relationships with top officials in both political
parties and AMC was well on its way to building a permanent
presence in the Washington corridors. Founded in California, the
Muslim Public Affairs Council (MPAC) offers its research and
policy papers to political leaders, members of the media, and the

entertainment industry in the hopes of bringing about more accurate representation of Muslims in the spheres of policy and popular culture. Another organization, the Muslim American Society (MAS), was established out of the activism of the 1980s and traces its roots to the Islamic movement in the Arab world, whose influence was instrumental in the development of the early American Muslim organizations. Active within a large number of mosques across the country and at the national level, MAS provides charitable support as well as social activism within the community. The Council for Good Government (CGG), the political arm of W. D. Muhammad's organization, also made important strides during this period. In 1992, Muhammad became the first Muslim to offer the opening prayers before a session of the US Senate.[5]

Though modest, the gains made by the early American Muslim political organizations were considerable given the community's prior status as a virtually nonexistent force in politics. Many policymakers were intrigued by the rise of a new political constituency, which, if able to harness its high level of education and vast resources, could form a valuable electoral bloc. Some politicians sought to cultivate a strong working relationship with American Muslims in the hopes of providing Washington with a fresh perspective on many of the crucial issues facing the country. Among their successes, American Muslim organizations raised awareness within the Clinton administration of the plight of Bosnian Muslims in the former Yugoslavia and the victims of hate crimes at home. They also educated policymakers on Islam, resulting in annual holiday greetings addressed to the community and Ramadan *iftars* at the White House. In 2001, the United States Postal Service issued a postage stamp commemorating the Islamic Eid holidays.[6]

On the critical issues, however, it became clear that American Muslim leaders lacked the experience and the political clout to bring about real change. In spite of their calls for the United States to take a more evenhanded approach to the Peace Process in the Middle East, American foreign policy in the region continued much in the same direction. The organizations faced critics from within the community and from the society at large. Internally, the community was frustrated with the lack of coordination among the various political organizations, especially the perception of divisions along ethnic and cultural lines. The community's detractors in the political and media spheres charged that its political activism represented foreign interests that were in conflict with US policy. These critics frequently used the backgrounds and past affiliations of many Muslim leaders as proof of their dual loyalties. In the mid-1990s, a new challenge would swiftly shift the landscape of American Muslim political activism, bringing home many of the concerns that had been simmering in the background for some time.

The secret evidence civil rights crisis was the product of the rising concern over terrorist attacks in the United States. In the ongoing discourse regarding a violent confrontation between the Western and Islamic worlds, minority Muslim communities in Europe, Canada, and the United States became a focal point for national security policy. Out of the ashes of the 1995 Oklahoma City bombing, an attack perpetrated by domestic terrorists, Congress passed antiterrorism legislation that focused primarily on the perceived terrorist threat from immigrant communities. Beginning in 1996, federal authorities initiated legal proceedings against a number of individuals, detaining them indefinitely without charges and on the basis of classified information that they could neither see nor confront in court. In all, thirty secret evidence cases were brought in communities around the country. Nearly every case targeted a Muslim immigrant, usually one who had resided in the United States for years with established family and community ties.[7]

In its early stages, the effort to combat the use of secret evidence occurred primarily at the local level, where communities rallied around a particular case, devising strategies to challenge the detention in the judicial, legislative, and public spheres. American Muslim leaders sought to raise awareness of the secret evidence cases in their local communities, relying on the news media to investigate the new policy and provide a human face to the story by profiling the victims and their families. Realizing that the community could not wage this civil rights battle alone, American Muslim groups enlisted the help of other organizations, ranging from conservative religious groups to civil liberties organizations. Together, these ad hoc coalitions convened informational lectures, held mass protests, and met with public officials to request an investigation into the use of secret evidence by the Department of Justice and propose a legislative remedy for the problem. They also employed top immigration and constitutional attorneys to challenge the cases in court. The struggle against secret evidence centered on two overarching themes: the constitutional concerns arising from the government's tactics and the singling out of a minority community toward whom these abuses were directed.

It was not long before the struggle to end the use of secret evidence and free those detained by it across the country became a national campaign. Nearly all major American Muslim political organizations prioritized the civil rights crisis facing the community, joining with nearly twenty prominent religious and civil liberties groups in what came to be known as the National Coalition to Protect Political Freedom (NCPPF). The new organization took the three-pronged local strategy to the national level, building on the momentum to educate the public and policy makers on the issue. Two dozen newspapers, including the *New York Times* and *Washington Post*, published editorials decrying the use of secret evidence. In the House of Representatives, a bill to ban its use in court proceedings was sponsored by several congressional allies of the American Muslim community. By 1999, the legislation had received over 130 co-sponsors, representing both political parties. In the House Judiciary Committee, a hearing on the issue was held, featuring the testimony of a constitutional law expert and victims of secret evidence. The bill passed a committee vote by a count of 28–2, paving the way for a vote on the House floor. For its part, the Clinton administration had responded to concerns over its practices by pledging to review all future secret evidence cases at the level of the attorney general, effectively suspending the practice, as no new cases were brought following the announcement.[8] Indeed, by early 2000, it appeared as though the American Muslim community had finally come of age as a political constituency. In the first major test to the community's aspirations in the public square, its institutions successfully transformed a civil rights crisis affecting a segment of their community into a national issue that deserved the attention of policy makers in Washington. As the challenges mounted during the course of this battle, it became clear to American Muslim leaders that in order to earn a seat at the decision-making table, first the civil rights struggle had to be won.

Although it had gained considerable momentum, passage of the congressional bill to end the use of secret evidence was interrupted by the 2000 elections. The American Muslim leadership understood that in order to carry its recent gains forward into the next administration, it must engage in the electoral process. Prior attempts to establish an American Muslim voting bloc had largely ended in failure. As recently as 1996, the national leadership could not agree on the main issue areas affecting the community, often prioritizing foreign affairs at the expense of domestic issues, or vice versa. Furthermore, as a young and unproven community, American

Muslims did not generate much enthusiasm from the presidential campaigns, receiving virtually no attention from Bill Clinton, while Bob Dole's campaign addressed American Muslim leaders as heads of a foreign lobby.[9]

The scene four years later stood in stark contrast to that of the previous election cycle. With the anticipation of one of the closest presidential races in nearly half a century, and the sudden emergence of an active and organized Muslim community in the United States, the campaigns hoped to elicit the support of this new constituency. The leaders of the American Muslim political organizations came together to harness the electoral power of their community, composed of 6 million citizens, according to their own accounts. The American Muslim Political Coordination Council (AMPCC), an umbrella group comprising all the major political organizations, explored the possibility of demonstrating the community's growth and unity by endorsing a presidential candidate and encouraging all American Muslims to cast their ballots in his favor. The immediate goals for the election were clear-cut: develop an internal consensus on the most pressing issues, engage the candidates on those issues, and ultimately endorse the one who appears most responsive to the community's concerns.

The issue of secret evidence, especially within the larger context of civil rights abuses, took on the status of top priority within the American Muslim community. After all, it had been the issue that mobilized the community into political action and galvanized a nationwide lobbying effort. Another focal point of AMPCC member groups was greater inclusion in the political process. President Clinton had made some moves in this regard, including the appointment of Muslims to various government posts, but these were viewed as largely symbolic gestures. Though continuing to be important, foreign policy issues such as the faltering Palestinian-Israeli peace process or the debilitating sanctions on Iraq were relegated to secondary status for the first time in the community's short history of political activism. The American Muslim community had come to the realization that the foundation for these larger issues would be built upon successes in smaller areas; in other words, the fight for civil rights would place the community on the path toward political empowerment.

With only a few weeks remaining until the 2000 election, the AMPCC made its decision to endorse the Republican candidate George W. Bush for president. The combination of the community's interaction with the candidates during the campaign and a close examination of their respective platforms established Bush as the favorite over Al Gore, then the vice-president and Democratic candidate. Whether as a result of taking American Muslim votes for granted (as they had traditionally voted for Democrats), or out of a desire to avoid confronting the community over the Clinton administration's dismal civil rights record, Gore remained inaccessible to the American Muslim community during the duration of the campaign, repeatedly canceling scheduled events or sending low-level representatives in his place. Bush, on the other hand, not only met with American Muslims but also went out of his way to speak with them during his campaign stops. In early October, when Bush stood before the nation during the second presidential debate and declared secret evidence to be a form of racial profiling, and then proceeded to endorse the legislation to end the practice, many American Muslims believed they had found a candidate who understood their concerns. For his part, Gore could only muster a similar statement in response the following day. As a member of the administration responsible for the secret evidence phenomenon, however, American Muslim leaders expected him to take a more forceful stance and possibly take immediate measures to roll back the abuses in the justice system.

The American Muslim community could not have chosen a more critical election in which to make its presence felt as an electoral bloc. When the smoke settled weeks after the election, Bush had won by the narrowest of margins. Across the nation, various exit polls indicated that the American Muslim vote for Bush ranged from 70 to 80 percent. Florida, the state whose twenty-five electoral college votes determined the outcome of the election, was home to one of the nation's most prominent secret evidence cases and an active Muslim community that voted heavily in favor of the Republican candidate, by a margin of 3 to 1.[10] Even within the African American Muslim community, whose leaders refused to join the AMPCC's endorsement, the rate of those who voted for Bush was twice as high as it was among African Americans generally (18 percent to 9 percent). Some Republican leaders were quick to acknowledge the difference made by the Muslim community's participation and an effort was made to continue the dialogue with the incoming administration. American Muslims running for office also experienced unprecedented success, with 153 elected that November to positions at the state and local levels.[11]

For the first half of 2001, the American Muslim community had reached the height of its political empowerment. The last of the secret evidence victims was freed in December 2000, following a victory in court and an unsuccessful eleventh hour attempt by government officials to block his release by appealing to the attorney general. The new administration was hopeful of establishing a strong working relationship with the American Muslim leadership, inviting representatives of all the major organizations to several high level meetings in Washington. A member of the community, Suheil Khan, was appointed to the White House Office of Public Liaison to assist in coordinating activities with American Muslims. Along with Christian and Jewish groups, Muslim organizations were called upon to participate in the Bush administration's Faith-Based and Community Initiative, a government program designed to provide funds to religious groups who offer social services in their local communities. Finally, the Secret Evidence Repeal Act was reintroduced in the new session of Congress and by late summer had regained its momentum.[12] An announcement from the White House supporting its passage was scheduled for September 11, 2001. As fate would have it, the morning's events would drastically alter the political landscape in the United States and reconfigure the place of the American Muslim community within it.[13]

9/11 AND ITS AFTERMATH

In the American Muslim community's quest for political empowerment, there is no question that the September 11 attacks undid years of dedicated efforts. The domestic fallout from the worst terrorist attack on American soil initially served as a reality check to the recent advancements made by the community's political organizations. The successes in the areas of secret evidence and the bloc vote were placed in their proper perspective once the stakes became much higher. Although political leaders from the president on down made strong public statements against painting all Muslims with the brush of extremism, the toxic atmosphere and the dangerous combination of fear and hysteria in the weeks and months after the attacks made association with the community a dangerous prospect for most public figures. Additionally, in the course of its struggle for political empowerment, the American Muslim leadership had engendered a powerful opposition movement intent on maintaining the status quo and those forces were now mobilized to roll back the modest gains the community had achieved in the public sphere.

With reports of anti-Muslim hate crimes on the rise, CAIR and other organizations were flooded with requests by community members to provide legal assistance and help educate local law enforcement officials to dispel myths about American Muslims. More troubling was the possibility that, in addition to criminal acts targeting Muslims, political leaders would advocate policies with major implications for the civil rights of this religious minority. American Muslim groups had recently made considerable progress in shifting public perception of the community from the prism of the national security to that of civil liberties. In the immediate aftermath of 9/11, however, the pendulum swung swiftly in favor of policies that viewed the American Muslim community as a potential threat to US security. The Patriot Act was passed in Congress to anchor the domestic side of the set of policies that made up the "War on Terror." In one of the first major blows to the American Muslim community after 9/11, the legislation did away with the civil rights restored by the end of secret evidence and brought about a new wave of abuses, many of them far more serious than anything witnessed in the previous decade. Thousands of Muslims were detained without charge and many more were questioned by federal agents regarding their religious and political beliefs and associations. Even more troubling to some was the systematic targeting of American Muslim leaders and institutions, resulting in a number of high profile politically charged arrests and prosecutions.

In the shadow of US military action in Afghanistan and Iraq, the American Muslim community stood on a knife's edge, forced to prove its loyalty to the country, while also wishing to exercise its right to condemn abuses in the War on Terror to which Muslims around the world were subjected. The diverse coalitions that proved so essential to the success of the community's activism in the 1990s no longer played an important part in defending the rights of the vulnerable minority, as self-preservation became the order of the day. For its part, the mainstream media helped stoke the flames of suspicion and fear toward American Muslim groups. This appeared to be part of a downward trend, as a Columbia University study of news coverage during the first anniversary of the September 11 attacks concluded that it was "less contextual, less balanced, and more negative and critical of Muslims and Arabs in the United States than in the immediate post-9/11 period."[14] Politically, the community's national organizations were incapable of making the same impact during the 2004 presidential election as they had in 2000. Both political parties made virtually no attempts to reach out to American Muslims and resisted opportunities to meet with community leaders. Moreover, the community's overwhelming support for Democratic candidate John Kerry was not enough to turn the tide against Bush's reelection, diminishing the importance of the electoral bloc built up in the previous election.

As the decade drew to a close, the American Muslim community reached a critical juncture in its history. Its civil rights were under threat of the excesses of the War on Terror, its institutions were under siege and ill equipped to deal with the challenges of post-9/11 America, and it was nearly powerless in the face of the increased perception that the United States was at war with Islam. Nonetheless, out of the adversity of this period came a number of bright spots that should not be overlooked. American Muslims used the opportunity of the US wars to demonstrate the community's loyalty to its country. A fatwa issued by Islamic scholars affirmed the permissibility of American Muslims to serve in the military, even as it went into war in Afghanistan, a Muslim country.[15] Additionally, the 9/11 tragedy brought about an unprecedented level of interest in Islam across the United States, providing the Muslim minority with the challenge to break through the facile stereotypes and act as ambassadors of their community to the society at large. In the face of a burgeoning Islamophobia, campaigns to educate Americans about Islam and Muslims took off in the years after 9/11. The mainstream media, in spite of its frequent negative coverage, also took a greater interest in the community and actually gave positive portrayals of American Muslims in the days after September 11. There was a discernible shift from topical to thematic coverage that included profiles of the community. For the first time in history, publications such as the *New York Times* appointed reporters to an "American Muslim beat" and featured occasional contributions by writers from the community.

Internally, the American Muslim leadership eventually resumed its efforts to unite various elements of the community and close the divisions in its ranks. A broader coalition was built under the banner of the American Muslim Taskforce on Civil Rights and Elections (AMT) that included more organizations than previous umbrella groups. Though it traditionally shied away from participation in political activities, ISNA joined in these efforts. In 2002, its annual convention was held in Washington for the first time in its forty-year history, symbolizing the influential role that the nation's capital played in the lives of American Muslims. Four years later, Keith Ellison became the first community member elected to the US Congress. In 2008, he was joined by Andre Carson, the second Muslim in the House of Representatives. The election of American Muslims to national office was an important milestone for the community, especially in light of the many challenges it faced during the height of the Bush administration's War on Terror. In addition to the political victories, the American Muslim community also celebrated a number of legal victories. In spite of the numerous court cases that ended with tragic results for the community in the climate of fear that had even gripped the nation's judiciary, several attempts to dismantle charities, think tanks, and other essential institutions ended in failure for federal authorities, who faced frequent accusations of targeting the community for political reasons. Discrimination lawsuits, such as the famous "flying imams" case of 2006, which, three years later, ended in victory for the plaintiffs, sought to demonstrate the consequences for the mistreatment of religious minorities.

Ultimately, the American Muslim community demonstrated its resilience in the face of immense pressures that emerged in the wake of 9/11. In spite of nearly eight years of alienation, its leaders resisted the initial urge to retreat to the margins of society, instead maintaining a keen determination to build upon the accomplishments of prior eras and overcome the challenges of the day. It is in that spirit that the community enthusiastically embraced the message of Barack Obama, the 2008 Democratic presidential candidate who ran on a platform of change. Though the stigma of candidates associating with the American Muslim community was still high during that and successive elections, precluding any engagement on the level of that seen in the 2000 campaign, the community's leaders as well as the rank and file were energetic in their campaigning on behalf of a candidate they believed would signal a real break from the climate of fear and suspicion that had marked the American Muslim experience in the post-9/11 era.

Although engagement with the broader Muslim world was declared to be a priority of the Obama administration, the American Muslim community remained in relative isolation from the national political dialogue. Obama did appoint several American Muslims to his administration, including the US representative to the Organization of the Islamic Conference (OIC), but beyond such token gestures, the civil rights issues afflicting leaders and institutions within the community continued unabated throughout Obama's first term and even after his re-election in 2013. When American Muslims did gain prominence on the national level, it was usually only in the context of a major crisis such as the controversy over the Park 51 Islamic center in New York in 2010 or in the aftermath of the Boston bombings in 2012.

FUTURE OUTLOOK

In looking toward the future of Islam's presence in America, a wider perspective and a proper historical context is not only useful but also essential. The American Muslim community has come a long way from the days of West African slaves yearning to return home or factory workers in turn-of-the-century Detroit pressured to adopt Anglicized names to avoid discrimination. The contemporary American Muslim community has come to terms with its identity and has found an accommodation between its religious obligations and the commitment to its nation. The evolution of a distinct American Muslim identity has been part and parcel of the community's projects to develop a *fiqh* for living as a religious minority and leading the latest struggle for civil rights.

As the community sheds the old ethnic and cultural divisions that have marked its institutions in past eras, new organizations have emerged that reflect the changing profile of the American Muslim community. Based in Chicago, the Inner City Muslim Action Network (IMAN) brings together youth of various backgrounds to assist development projects in their local community. American Muslims for Palestine (AMP) has torn down the old activist model on an issue of central importance to the community in favor of an approach that is more inclusive and in keeping with American traditions of political activism. Organizations such as the American Muslim

Civic Leadership Institute (AMCLI) and the Muslim Public Service Network (MPSN) focus on training the younger generation of leaders and provide them with the opportunities and experiences they need to build on prior efforts to bring Muslims into the American public square.

While organizations such as these are a natural extension of the traditional political groups that fall under the AMT umbrella, they are also a signal that the future divisions in the community will not be along ethnic lines, but rather along generational ones. Discouraged by the failures of the older generation, the more highly educated, culturally and politically savvy generation of American Muslim youth has signaled its desire to break with the past and develop a new institutional culture in the community, free from the baggage of their elders. For their part, the established community leaders desire continuity in leadership and for the younger generation to embrace the rich legacy of American Muslim institution building.

Externally, the American Muslim community is likely to continue establishing partnerships with other faith communities and progressive groups. Building upon the experience from the campaign to end secret evidence and the antiwar coalition in the years after 9/11, American Muslim organizations have attempted to broaden their involvement to issues that affect all Americans, such as health care, job creation, and public safety. Members of the community will also continue to raise their political aspirations, not only developing important relationships with policy makers but also seeking to include more American Muslims in public office. In light of its experience with the bloc vote in 2000, the community has since matured enough to recognize the pitfalls of its electoral strategy and hopes to employ a more deliberate and judicious process in endorsing candidates. In time, the fulfillment of this community's political goals will see to it that American Muslims are considered in the same category as other minority groups who have overcome challenges to their status by embarking on a struggle for their rights, and in the process established themselves as part of the American social fabric.

NOTES

1. Examples of these works include Abd-Allah 2006; Dirks 2006; Curtis 2009.
2. Abd-Allah, Umar F. 2006. *A Muslim in Victorian America: The Life of Alexander Russell Webb*. New York: Oxford University Press.
3. Haddad, Yvonne. 2004. *Not Quite American? The Shaping of Arab and Muslim Identity in the United States*. Texas: Baylor University Press.
4. Lewis, Bernard. 1990. The Roots of Muslim Rage. *The Atlantic Monthly*. September; Samuel P. Huntington. 1993. The Clash of Civilizations? *Foreign Affairs*. Summer. Vol. 72, No. 3. pp. 22–49.
5. Muhammad, W. D. In Curtis IV, Edward E., ed. 2008. *The Columbia Sourcebook of Muslims in the United States*. New York: Columbia University Press.
6. Goodstein, Laurie. 2001. U.S. Muslims Push Stamp as Symbol of Acceptance. *New York Times*. U.S. Politics section.
7. Dempsey, James X., and David Cole. 1999. *Terrorism & the Constitution*. Los Angeles, CA: First Amendment Foundation.
8. Al-Arian, Abdullah. 2003. *Soul Survival: The Road to American Muslim Political Empowerment*. MSc Dissertation. London School of Economics.
9. Ali, Tahir. 2004. *The Muslim Vote: Counts and Recounts*. Lima, OH: Wyndham Hall Press.
10. Al-Arian.
11. Interview with Agha Saeed, American Muslim Alliance, October 2001.
12. The bill was introduced as H.R. 1266 on March 28, 2001. The Library of Congress: Thomas. http://thomas.loc.gov/cgi-bin/bdquery/z?d107:h.r.01266 (accessed June 14, 2010).
13. Clines, Francis X. 2001. Muslim Leader Presses Agenda of Understanding. *New York Times*. October 3. U.S. Politics section.
14. Nacos, Brigitte L., and Oscar Torres Reyna. 2007. *Fueling Our Fears*. Lanham, MD: Rowman and Littlefield Publishers.
15. Goodstein, Laurie. 2001. Muslim Scholars Back Fight against Terrorists. *New York Times*. October 12. U.S. Politics section. Full text of this fatwa at: http://www.unc.edu/%7Ekurzman/Qaradawi_et_al.htm (accessed June 14, 2010).

REFERENCES

Abd-Allah, Umar F. 2006. A Muslim in Victorian America: The Life of Alexander Russell Webb. New York: Oxford University Press.

Ali, Tahir. 2004. The Muslim Vote: Counts and Recounts. Lima, OH: Wyndham Hall Press.

Bukhari, Zahid H., Sulayman S. Nyang, Mumtaz Ahmad, and John L. Esposito, eds. 2004. Muslims' Place in the American Public Square. Berkeley: AltaMira Press.

Curtis IV, Edward E., ed. 2008. The Columbia Sourcebook of Muslims in the United States. New York: Columbia University Press.

Curtis IV, Edward E. 2009. Muslims in America: A Short History. New York: Oxford University Press.

Dempsey, James X., and David Cole. 1999. Terrorism & the Constitution. Los Angeles: Beltsville: First Amendment Foundation.

Dirks, Jerald F. 2006. Muslims in American History: A Forgotten Legacy. Beltsville: Amana Publications.

Findley, Paul. 2001. Silent No More: Confronting America's False Images of Islam. MD: Amana Publications.

Gerges, Fawaz. 1999. America and Political Islam. New York: Cambridge University Press.

Haddad, Yvonne, and Adair T. Lummis. 1987. Islamic Values in the United States. New York: Oxford Press.

Haddad, Yvonne Y., Farid Senzai, and Jane I. Smith, eds. 2009. Educating the Muslims of America. New York: Oxford University Press.

Jackson, Sherman A. 2005. Islam and the Black American. New York: Oxford University Press.

McCloud, Amina Beverly. 2006. Transnational Muslims in American Society. Gainesville: University Press of Florida.

Nacos, Brigitte L., and Oscar Torres-Reyna. 2007. Fueling Our Fears. Lanham: New York: Rowman and Littlefield Publishers.

Nyang, Sulayman S. 1999. Islam in the United States of America. IL: ABC International Group.

Smith, Jane I. 1999. Islam in America. New York: Columbia University Press.

Chapter 2

Islam and Politics in Europe

SAM CHERRIBI

INTRODUCTION

The relationship between Islam and European politics at the dawn of the twenty-first century is anything but normal. It is characterized by electric tension in the public sphere. News media outlets, manifestos of political parties, and the discourse of politicians at all levels of European governance show that Islam dominates the political agenda. Despite the official separation between religion and politics in Europe, there is a growing obsession of the political elite and the media with Islam. The continuous and growing claims of Muslims as citizens and their case for more inclusion make Europe's traditionally secular public space and its ironclad separation of church and state highly polarizing, not only for the lay public but for European politics as well. These patterns of polarization all over Europe originated at the local level and have progressed to the national level.

In a long-term historical perspective, these patterns are the products of three factors that have inflamed the contentious relationship between Islam and Europe. First, the process of EU enlargement, as part of a rapidly globalizing world, has resulted in an increased social insecurity and fear of loss of national identity.

Second, the emergence of Islam as a top security issue has linked the Muslims of Europe to the rise of global militant political Islam and terrorism. Third, the increased religious and ethnic diversity in Europe has led Europeans to discover their inability and inexperience in dealing with "new religious pluralism," a common and fairly comfortable condition in the United States, where there is greater tolerance for religion in the public sphere. These three factors allow us to frame how European policies affect the life of ordinary Muslims, communities, organizations, and the perceptions of Islam in European societies (Berger 2007). European policies at the supranational level toward Islam are still apolitical and at the discretion of those who are in charge at the EU commission (who are themselves not elected but appointed), since the various national contexts are eminently important in electing politicians and articulating and implementing political priorities.

ISLAM, EUROPE, AND THE POLITICS OF IDENTITY

Many writers, pundits, journalists, and politicians have asked the question: What is Europe? For some, Europe refers to a geographical entity and a civilization with a common religion: Christianity. To others, Europe is projected as an idea, combining secular values with diverse countries, ethnicities, and languages.

Since 2004, twelve countries have joined the European Union: Cyprus, Malta, the Czech Republic, Estonia, Hungary, Latvia, Lithuania, Poland, Slovakia and Slovenia, Romania, and Bulgaria, while others still knock at the door, including Serbia, Ukraine, and Georgia. Since 1991 and the dissolution of the Soviet Union, Armenia, Azerbaijan, and Georgia have failed to reconnect with Europe despite appeals to do so. Complicating the picture is the fear of Turkey becoming part of the European Union, something it has been attempting for more than forty years. Europe is a success story because it achieved peace and stability through the use of a common currency and by establishing a Court of Justice of the European Communities (ECJ). Beginning in 1999, this single currency helped the emergence of a singular European economy, which is the largest in the world. Europe, however, still struggles with many issues: the European flag does not rally people like the national flag of the individual countries, it has a presidency that rotates every six months, and, as a result, just recently inaugurated a president who was not elected. Also, national interests are still more important than plural European interests and lastly, words like "transparency," "unity," and "cooperation" hide national interests and are just "Euro-prose" as noted by former Euro-commissioner Frits Bolkestein (Bolkestein 2004). In short, the lack of a shared political European identity and agenda weakens Europe.

The European commission's unelected presidents, the French Jacques Delors, the Italian Romano Prodi, and the Portuguese Jose Manuel Baroso have understood the importance of religious expression in the European public space and sought to codify it in policy. In 1992, Delors saw the need to give Europe a soul by creating the Forward Studies Unit (FSU), which he brought to active fruition during his long tenure at the helm of the European Union. In 1999, Prodi continued this theme through the "Group of Policy Advisors" (GOPA). In 2004, Baroso did the same by creating the Bureau of European Policy Advisors (BEPA). All these initiatives tried to include advisors from different religious groups including Islam. Some Muslims were invited to participate along with those of other religious affiliations; however, the problem of representation has never been solved (Silvestri 2009; Massignon n.d.).

ISLAM AND EUROPE: TWO IDEOLOGICAL CONSTRUCTS

In the previous paragraphs, I mentioned the ambiguities surrounding the term "Europe." Islam refers to a religion with varying traditions and orientations, a religion, which spans a variety of countries, ethnicities, cultures, and languages. In Spain, Islam is a minority religion whereas in Eastern Europe, it is quite the opposite. Europe is now home to transplanted guest workers from the Mediterranean region (from Morocco, Algeria, Tunisia, and Turkey) and from South Asia (India and Pakistan). Very often, little attention is paid to the ordinary Muslims living in Europe, even as their experiences and ideologies give meaning to the construction of Islam as practice, religion, and political force (Waardenburg 2004). After the 1960s and the 1970s, a dominant theme of research and politics dealt with the problems of migration, housing, and health but also with family reunification, education, and women's issues. Islam as a political force was not taken into account. From the 1980s to the 1990s, the height of visibility of Muslim immigrants sparked interest in Islam in Europe: European governments and political parties were more interested in the political organization of Muslims and their associations (Waardenburg 2004). Presenting them as a problem provided a political platform and consequently the media was supported in framing Islam as incompatible with Europe.

Both Europe and Islam through the centuries have had many encounters of Islamization and Christianization: Greek philosophy translated into Arabic, Andalusia's Muslim rulers, and the crusades. In colonial times, some European countries, such as France and Great Britain, dominated the lands of Islam. The Netherlands, meanwhile, reigned over the largest Islamic country in the world: Indonesia.

The politics of past controversies around Europe and Islam reduced the two to historical, cultural, social, but mainly ideological constructs because of the political and ideological escalation on both sides. Keep in mind that "politics" refers to activities, practices, and strategies dealing with the act of governance and the quest for political influence and consider that both Europe and Islam have been victims of terrorist attacks in the name of Islam. The backlash against ordinary Muslims of Europe is unprecedented. As the presence of Islam grows with the third and fourth generations of Muslims born on European soil, Islam is increasingly becoming a permanent player and part of the political outlook of Europe's past, present, and future.

"MUSLIM" POLITICIANS AND THE IMPORTANCE OF NATIONAL POLITICAL CONTEXT

If the 1960s and 1970s were characterized by a silence of the guest workers in the public sphere, the 1980s were a catalyst for articulating more identity claims through cemeteries, mosques, schools, and so on. In the 1980s political leaders in some Northern European countries, like the Netherlands and Scandinavia, went to mosques and religious organizations of Muslim migrants to campaign and recruit people for their political parties. But some Islamic countries showed their objection to involving these Muslims in the political affairs of their countries. Muslims welcomed the municipal right to vote granted to noncitizens in the Netherlands, Sweden, and Ireland.

The growing visibility of Muslims in urban areas triggered a new kind of politics: far right, focused on the mishaps of little criminality and the problems of migration in general. The media, even mainstream media outlets, joined this chorus of disenchantment.

The Muslims who joined political parties at the municipal level, national level in some countries, and some few on the pan-European level have had to carefully strike a balance between the pros and cons of Islam. Recently some Muslim members of the party of President Sarkozy in France felt discriminated against and warned the party not to push them toward communitarianism and ethnic and religious allegiance. Many far right parties, such as the National Front in France, Partij voor de Vrijheid (Party for Freedom) in the Netherlands, and the Liga Nord in Italy, campaigned on an anti-European Union and anti-Islam ticket, making a plea for national identity.

Alain Juppé, former prime minister of France, showed his disagreement with the national debate about the *French* identity by saying, "Let's be honest, this is all about Islam and Muslims." The mayor of Bordeaux echoed that on his blog, saying, "The question 'what does it mean to be French?' does not really arise. We know the answer....Add to this that secularism was the French identity."

In the Netherlands, the *kopvoddentax*, constructed by the PVV (Wilders wil "kopvoddentaks") is doing well in the polls (Trouw 2009). It is a means for mobilizing the insecurities of a country that has had two political murders since 2000. The quick enlargement of the European Union and the lack of a cohesive political identity or a tangible European interest make Europe unclear about its relation to emerging new religious identities. Clearly, the religious question in Europe remains unsolved since some countries, like Poland, are highly religious, or, like France, highly secular. Dutch sociologist Abram de Swaan explains that the lack of pan-European media outlets, such as an all-Europe television channel or newspaper, makes it impossible to have a European public sphere with European topics (de Swaan 2007). In addition to the euro as a source of unity, the identification of Islam as a threat has also served to galvanize Europe. It is a fear that knows no borders within the continent. The ban on minarets in Switzerland sits comfortably alongside the ban on the burka in the Netherlands.

Since the birth of the European Union, Europe's former North African colonies have assumed responsibility for their independence. At the time, it seemed that these two cultures had decided— painfully and in some cases violently—to pursue divergent paths, but soon it would become apparent that their fates were inextricably entwined and utterly interdependent. The idea that the Islamic crescent, which stretches across North Africa from Morocco into the Middle East, could keep its distance from Europe separated from it only by the Mediterranean—and by only nine miles of the Mediterranean at the Strait of Gibraltar—is a notion that has never withstood the test of time. In 1683, the Ottoman Empire's forces trudged all the way to Vienna before being forced back. Now, once again, Europe feels it is under a sort of Islamic siege, but this time the siege is primarily social and political, and, most significantly, a siege of Europe's own making. This siege has ramifications not only for Europe but also for the entire West according to far right parties that have been experiencing an exceptional growth as Islam-as-threat has grown in the public mind. Far right parties, such as France's Front National, Italy's Fiamma Tricolore, Sweden's National Democrats, Hungary's Jobbik, Belgium's Walloon National Front, the British National Party (BNP), Faustri's Freedom Party (FPO), and the Netherlands Freedom Party (PVV), saw success in the June 2009 elections for the European Parliament (EP). More than 40 seats out of 736 went to anti-Muslim parties, despite the fact that Article 13 of the Amsterdam Treaty on the European Union prohibits racism and Islamophobia.

More than fifty years since its inception, the European Union now anticipates expanding beyond its current membership of twenty-seven countries to include Turkey with its 83 million majority-Muslim population, but that possible inclusion is the source of much tension in the European Union. Like Turkish delight, the Turkish dilemma is sticky for Europeans. Once welcomed in theory as a strong buffer state between Europe and the East, it is now viewed as an enclave of Muslims, and that is not something that Europe, seeking an identity of its own and increasingly afraid that its identity is being Muslimized, can accept. Ironically, Europe, viewed for so long by Americans as a much older, more sophisticated society, now finds itself awkwardly young—both in terms of its status as the European Union, and in terms of its burgeoning young Muslim population, two factors that are undermining its sense of self and raising the specter of long-feared "Eurabia."

THE DISINTEGRATION OF EASTERN EUROPE: A MUSLIM TRAGEDY

If Islam has been part of Eastern European countries for centuries and has been invisible during the Soviet era, it exploded with the fall of the Berlin Wall and became a source of public contention and political polarization. However, Western Europe, after its colonial experience in Indonesia, India, the Middle East, and North Africa, severed its ties with Islam after the decolonization. Islam started to become an issue again in Western Europe in the 1980s when family reunification of migrant workers became more visible and the weight of numbers in big cities started to matter. These produced pressures on health care, the educational system, and housing, and so on. The openness of some Western European nations to multiculturalism and diversity experienced a backlash with the rise of political Islam and terrorism.

The fall of the Iron Curtain in 1989 made it possible for many Eastern European countries to join the European Union. Some of these, like Yugoslavia and Albania, constituted the biggest historic challenge to the stability of Europe since World War II. In that same year, 1989, Slobodan Milosevic was elected president of Yugoslavia and the country soon faced an accelerated ethnic disintegration centered on Kosovo and its Muslim population. This crisis manifested itself in the lack of a unified European defense identity able to settle conflicts in the neighboring former communist countries. Europeans could not do it alone, so the Americans and North Atlantic Treaty Organization were called upon to stop Milosevic's ethnic cleansing in the Balkans. That eventually led to air strikes in Serbia and Kosovo in March 1999 and thus revealed continued tensions within Europe itself aggravated by hundreds of thousands of refugees—most of them Muslim—fleeing to neighboring countries in the European Union.

The Yugoslav crisis brought with it political turmoil for Europe as a whole and for the Netherlands in particular. In the midst of the Yugoslavian debacle, the massacre of at least 6,000 Muslim men and boys while under the protection of a Dutch-United Nations peacekeeping force at the Muslim enclave of Srebrenica in July 1995 is now seen as a national conscience-crippling experience second only to the betrayal of the Jews who sought refuge in Holland in the Second World War in terms of its long-term psychic impact.

The murkiness surrounding the atrocities committed at Srebrenica was an early sign of a deepening identity crisis and the end of a number of old certainties about the future. The Dutch government asked the Netherlands Institute for War Documentation (NIOD) in 1996 to set up independent research into the events that took place before, during, and after the fall of the enclave. When the NIOD report was finally released on April 10, 2002, after being postponed for more than a year, Dutch Prime Minister Kok announced six days later, on April 16, 2002, that his government would bear full responsibility for the massacre and he and his cabinet subsequently offered their resignations.

The aftershocks of Srebrenica still continue today, though the trauma has now been overshadowed entirely by the fear of Islamic terror in the Netherlands. No one asked if perhaps an Islamic threat were needed to numb the shame of what had happened at Srebrenica, but the threat, needed or not, had already presented itself in the events in New York on September 11, 2001, seemingly absolving many Dutch citizens of something they would rather not think about anyway.

In the Netherlands, national parliamentary elections were held just weeks after the resignation of Kok and his cabinet, on May 15, 2002, which ushered in the new outsider party, the Lijst Pim Fortuyn (LPF) with twenty-six seats, making it the second largest party in the parliament, despite the assassination of its leader by a Dutch animal rights activist just a week before the election. Fully 79 percent of voters cast their ballots, nearly 6 percent more than had voted in the previous national election in 1998.

The Srebrenica investigation findings and Dutch frustration about the challenges to the Dutch educational, health, and welfare system posed by Muslim migrants, which were often the subject of negative stories in the press, was the background against which public discontent deepened in the country as Pim Fortuyn and his new political party LPF moved ahead in the polls, preaching populist politics based on ethnic distinction and exclusion. The patterns of ethnicization of Islam and Muslims, as in the Balkans, though without the physical violence, were duplicated in many European countries without, it seems, any awareness that ethnic distinction was being used in almost the same way that it had been used politically by the Serbs. Europeans were oblivious to the fact that the construction of Islam as a race would have long-term, inescapable, and broad disintegrational effects.

The break-up of Yugoslavia and the ensuing civil war in the mid-1990s had dispersed thousands of Bosnian Muslim political refugees across Europe (as well as to the United States, Canada, and Australia). Those who had been relocated to Western European countries were sent back to Bosnia when the war ended despite their often successful integration—they had learned the local language and sent their children to local schools—and despite some protests from concerned European citizens.

THE RISE OF SINGLE-ISSUE PARTIES

Political parties all over Europe are experiencing a decline in their traditional constituencies. The taken-for-granted identification with the party as a vehicle for political action is past tense. The ideological lines are becoming more fluid and there is more support for issues than for parties (Eik and Franklin 1996). The rise of many parties like LPF (Livable Netherlands), Party for Freedom (PVV), and the Animal Rights Party started as one-issue parties.

Illegal immigration in Europe soon became the top issue among all European leaders, particularly at the European Summit in Seville in June 2002. At the summit, prime ministers from all over Europe agreed that immigration was such a major problem that it could no longer be addressed effectively at the national level and had to be dealt with by the European Union. At the same time, within the discussion of immigration, the alleged lack of integration of legal immigrants, especially Muslim migrants from North Africa and Turkey, and the ways in which they lived in Europe became an increasingly important issue frequently featured in the media. Consequently, Europe in the 1990s and the early twenty-first century saw an emphasis on populist appeals and the growth of support for populist political parties with strong anti-immigrant policies, including Filip de Winter's Vlaams Belang in Belgium, Jorg Haider in Austria, Pia Kjaersgaard's Danish People's Party (DPP) in Denmark, the Republican Party (REP), the German People's Union (DVU), and the National Democratic Party (NPD) in Germany with no dominant leader, Jean-Marie Le Pen's Front National in France, Makis Voridis's Hellenic Front in Greece, Umberto Bossi's Northern League, and National Alliance in Italy, and Pim Fortuyn's LPF in the Netherlands.

Politicians often take their cues from the media and shape public policy accordingly. The increase in public support for far right parties cannot be seen in isolation from the demographic changes in Europe's major cities over the past two decades and the subsequent media coverage of those changes. A recent comparative study of neopopulism in its variety of forms in societies around the world shows how the media are instrumental in the rise and fall of populist parties and leaders. Some researchers have found that there is a connection between support for the far right and one's daily news diet. In particular, there seems to be a correlation with one item on the menu: crime news, a topic easily sensationalized and often linked to the poor and uneducated—a population in Europe that is usually mostly Muslim. In Austria, for example, scholars have established a link between the type of newspaper one reads exclusively and support for far right-wing populists such as Jorg Haider (Mazzoleni 2003).

THE BACKLASH AGAINST THE MUSLIM POLITICAL ELITE

The backlash against Islam and Muslims takes place very often in local politics and then becomes a national, even pan-European event. Not only has the construction of new mosques in Germany,

France, Italy, and the Netherlands triggered controversies vis-à-vis Islam but everything related to Islam (rightly or wrongly) has been subject to polarization: "Honor" killing, discrimination against women, prayers in public, movies, the Koran, sermons, imams, the burka, the veil, the headscarf, minarets, and so forth. Coexistence with Islam is a political impasse. The fear of "neo-Islamic- fundamentalism" poses questions about the limits of religious practice.

Local politics are more complicated than we think. In areas with Muslim majorities like West Amsterdam two Muslims fought for the leadership of the county governance, both from the same party. Competition between Muslim candidates is as intense as in any politics. There are Muslim candidates who are pro-gay, pro-euthanasia and others who are anti-Islam or totally pro-Islam (Muslim political voices that are pro-*Shari`ah* are mainly located in England and not in continental Europe).

The polarization in politics has made it more difficult for Muslim politicians to ensure continuity in their constituencies. And in addition to the media drumbeat, with the rise of political Islam there are many attempts to create Islamic parties like the Islamic Party in Great Britain, Le Party des Musulman de France, the Islamistische Partij in Belgium, and die Islamitische Partij Deutschland. In Eastern Europe, and particularly in Greece where many ethnic parties exist, religion became, after the Balkan war, a mobilizing force.

EUROPE'S DISENCHANTMENT WITH "NEW" RELIGIOUS PLURALISM

The emergence of more religious claims within the public sphere, engaging politics and society in advanced secular societies, is not typically Islamic, but can be seen in all faiths including Abrahamic traditions. In the book *New Religious Pluralism* edited by Thomas Banchoff, a number of scholars argue that religion in general is increasing as a social and political force. Examples of this around the world include the "under God" clause of the American Pledge of Allegiance and the proliferation of displays of the Ten Commandments, the ban on headscarves and other religious symbols in schools in France, blasphemy laws in the United Kingdom, and the ban on minarets in Switzerland. This religious diversity has serious political implications such as declaring a state of crisis for models of integration.

The lack of understanding of the new religious expression of religious groups in the public sphere has led to the politics of disenchantment against the second religion of Europe: Islam. In the 1980s and 1990s, many European governments like that of France, the Netherlands, Belgium, and Germany tried to find ways to organize Muslim representation. These attempts were not always successful but had the benefit of being a good learning experience for both governments and Muslim groups. Governments understood the difficulty in one representative body for all Muslims because of their diversity. Likewise, Muslim groups understood the logic of governments. However, the plethora of policies that varies from one country to another according to the political contexts of different European countries is reflected in the epicenter of the European Union in Brussels. As the highest level of European governance, the EU commission is concerned with finding established and formal ways to interact with Muslim groups seeking representatives for the Muslims in Europe. Muslims themselves are becoming more active in Brussels and actively seek a voice to be heard. Many Muslim groups are inspired by the ways Catholics and Protestants are organized in lobbying the European commission and the parliament.

With 9/11, the Madrid and London bombings, and the killing of the Dutch filmmaker Theo van Gogh by a young Dutchman of

Moroccan descent, Europe woke up to a forgotten dimension of migrants who came to Europe as guest workers: their religion and spiritual well-being.

After the killing of Van Gogh, a Dutch writer of Moroccan descent described how he could not enter a café without being looked at as someone who might be hiding a weapon under his belt. The methodical drumbeat of the media and politicians against Muslims beginning in the aftermath of September 11, 2001 had succeeded in placing Muslim citizens of Europe in the role of an internal threat like that constructed by the media and politicians in America against Japanese Americans during World War II (Cherribi 2013). The result is that "Muslims" have to publicly express their disgust for radicals and their love, affection, and gratitude for the country in which they live in a way not required of others. Despite the fact that the majority of second- and third-generation Muslims have been born and raised in Europe, their loyalty and European identity are constantly subject to doubt. One leader of the guest workers' emancipation in the Netherlands, a Muslim immigrant himself, said, "I refuse to be Islamized" (Cherribi 52:2013). Allowing freedom of expression of religious identity, or the lack of a religious identity, is a privilege of advanced democracies because their foundational tenet of the separation of church and state is intended to provide a shield from manipulation by the religious community, a circumstance that does not exist in most Islamic countries.

When we consider the values of Islam and the values of European societies, the greatest differences can be found in themes of sexual liberalization. With few exceptions, divorce is so socially accepted that it is a nonissue in most European countries, abortion is legal, prostitution is tolerated or state regulated, and individuals are not to be discriminated against on the basis of their sexual orientation. Public attitudes toward gays and lesbians have become much more "liberalized" in Europe as well as in the United States over the past decade. The European Charter of Human Rights and European states' constitutions include protection of religious freedom and nondiscrimination on the basis of gender, race, ethnicity, and sexual orientation. In the context of a discussion about such value conflicts in European societies, it is worth noting that as recently as 1994 the Dutch Parliament passed a constitutional amendment to specifically protect the rights of "minorities" regardless of their religious affiliation including their "ethnic" and "sexual" rights, and implying the freedom not to practice a religion as part of the freedom of religion. However, the Dutch amendment has not been emulated elsewhere in Europe.

Apart from a few recent studies in which immigrant populations in Europe are described in general terms or with reference to particular examples, and primarily in country-based chapters, there is little in the way of research on the different generations of Muslims in European countries. Are younger Muslims in Europe remaining "unchanged" from their traditional parents in terms of sexual mores and values, as Inglehart and Norris suggest? Are they rejecting their parents' values outright and opting for the norms in the countries in which they live? Or are they creating a new set of values and norms? Inglehart and Norris say little about the contribution of Islamic religious leadership to the maintenance of traditional values in Muslim societies, although it is certainly part of the reason young people in Muslim countries today are as traditional in many ways as their parents and grandparents.

NOSTALGIA FOR A FORGOTTEN HOMELAND

Since the 1950s, European countries have allowed or even encouraged immigration from Muslim countries to suit their individual purposes. The United Kingdom opened its doors to Asian Muslims from its former colonized states in India and Pakistan while France brought guest workers from freshly decolonized Algeria, Morocco, and Tunisia; and the Netherlands, though it had no colonial ties to Turkey or Morocco, brought in guest workers from those countries to fill lower-level, menial jobs.

As Europe's establishment became increasingly uneasy regarding what it perceived as the misplaced loyalties of immigrant communities, the status of the mosques was elevated within migrant communities. For the first generation of Muslims, the mosque was seen as a relocated part of their country of origin, the place to heal the *ghorba*, the burning nostalgia of exile. For members of the second and third generations it has become the place where they speak their language of origin, where they read the Qur'an, where they first encounter their own cultural traditions, and where they first experience civic and social engagement.

The most recent generation of Muslims in Europe sees the mosque as a symbol of their own alienated identity. They associate the mosque with distant lands of minarets and *souks*. These lands are not their own, they are their grandfathers', and like the shadowy, foreign countries of all immigrant progenitors, they have become mythologized. These countries—Algeria, Morocco, Tunisia, Turkey, Egypt, Lebanon, India, Pakistan—have become idealized, a place where life, though impoverished, appears across the distance of a generation to have been morally more cohesive and less confusing. With this vision of an Islamic "Promised Land"—a realm defined by ideology rather than actual geographic boundaries—a new leadership fed by this myth and alienation within the European society has emerged even as the original immigrants have aged and died. The result is new social and religious configuration intent upon acquiring and asserting political power, not dissimilar in style to that of the

African American religious leaders who birthed the American civil rights movement. This admiration of the American Civil Rights movement will define the religious makeup of new Muslim leadership in Europe because it, like the African American model, relies heavily upon the personalities and devotion of its leaders.

Despite the anti-Islam political agenda driven by the far right and its amalgam with terrorism, Muslims in Europe are challenging, but also adapting and interacting with, the secular political culture. In many ways, Muslims are engaging in the democratic process (Berger 2007). Either by becoming members of established political parties or by creating their own religious institutions and even political parties, Muslims are engaging in the governing processes. Engaged members of established political parties have shown loyalty to citizens and professionals ranging from the many members of city councils and ministers to national and European parliamentarians. A recent survey of the newer generation of Muslims born and raised in Europe does not see being European, and respecting Europe's secular culture, as contradicting the fact of being devout Muslims. Secular Muslims and devout Muslims equally feel as if they are capable of convincing others of their tolerant and benign nature, despite persistent images of fanaticism in the popular media.

The most successful experience is on the local level in the Netherlands, the United Kingdom, and Belgium, where many Muslims have been elected to municipalities and have become aldermen or even mayors. At the national level, the Netherlands and the United Kingdom remain the most promising examples in including Muslims in the political arena; they are members of parties all along the full political spectrum from Christian Democrats to the communists parties and Greens (and even in the far right party LPF in the Netherlands). France has had the first Muslim national minister of justice, Rachida Dati.

At the European Union level, a new arena for potential Muslim parties is emerging, but ironically, the majority of Muslims in Europe would not vote for an Islamic party even if they send their children to Islamic schools, buy *halāl* food, and wear headscarves. This has to do with the fact that there is still no political tradition within Muslim communities to be mobilized on the basis of religion and ethnicity. In the future, it is likely the new generation of Muslims who experience more segregation and exclusion would opt for an Islamic party just like the Christian Democrats not because of religious reasons but because of problems with issues of identification.

REFERENCES

Arkoun, Mohammed. 2007. *Histoire de L'Islam et des Musulmans en France, du Moyen age nos jours.* Paris: Albin Michel.

Berger, Peter L. 2007. Pluralism, Protestantization, and the Voluntary Principle. In *Democracy and the New Religious Pluralism,* ed. Thomas Banchoff, 203–222. New York: Oxford University Press.

Bolkestein, Frits. 2004. *The Limits of Europe.* Tielt: Lannoo Publishers.

Byrnes, Timothy A., and Peter Katzenstein. 2006. *Religion in an Expanding Europe.* Cambridge: Cambridge University Press.

Cherribi, Sam. 2007. Politician's Perceptions of the "Muslim Problem": The Dutch Example in European Context. In *Democracy and New Religious Pluralism,* ed. Thomas Banchoff, 113–132. New York: Oxford University Press.

Cherribi, Sam. [2010] 2013. *In the House of War: Dutch Islam Observed.* London: Oxford University Press.

de Swaan, Abraam. 2007. The European Void: The Democratic Deficit as a Cultural Deficiency. In *The European Union and the Public Sphere: A Communicative Space in the Making?,* ed. John Fossum and Philip Schlesinger, 135–153. New York: Routledge.

Eik, Cees and Mark Franklin. 1996. *Choosing Europe? The European electorate and national politics in the face of the Union.* Ann Arbor, MI: University of Michigan Press.

Emerson, Michel. 2009. *Ethno-Religious Conflict in Europe: Typology of Radicalization in Europe's Muslim Communities.* Brussels: Centre for European Policy Studies.

Hervieu-Leger, Daniele. 2007. Islam and the Republic: The French Case. In *Democracy and the New Religious Pluralism,* ed. Thomas Banchoff, 203–222. New York: Oxford University Press.

Klausen, Jytte. 2005. *The Islamic Challenge: Politics and Religion in Western Europe.* Oxford, England and New York, USA Oxford University Press.

Lechner, Frank. 2008. *The Netherlands: Globalization and National Identity.* New York: Routledge.

Marechal, Brigitte, Stephano Alievi, Felice Dassetto, and Jorgen Nielson. 2003. *Muslims in the Enlarged Europe: Religion and Society.* Leiden: Brill.

Massignon, Berengere. 2007. Islam in the European Commission's System of Regulation of Religion. In *Islam in Europe: Diversity, Identity and Influence,* ed. Aziz Al-Alzmeh and Effie Fokas, 125–182. Cambridge: Cambridge University Press.

Mazzoleni, Gianpietro, Julianne Stewart, and Bruce Horsfield. 2003. *The Media and NeoPopulism: A Contemporary Comparative Analysis.* Westport, CT: Praeger.

Semetko, Holli A., and Patti M. Valkenburg. 2000. Framing European Politics: A Content Analysis of Press and Television News. *Journal of Communications* 50: 93–109.

Silvestri, Sara. 2009. Islam and Religion in the EU Political System. *West European Politics* 32, no. 6: 1212–1239.

Trouw. Newspaper "Wilders wil 'kopvoddentaks.' " http://www.trouw.nl/nieuws/politiek/article2865224.ece/Wilders_wil__kopvoddentax_.html (accessed September 16, 2009).

Waardenburg, Jacques. 2004. Diversity and Unity of Islam in Europe: Some Reflections. In *Muslims in Europe, From the Margin to the Center,* ed. Jamal Malik. Munster: Lit Verlag.

Watts, Duncan. 2008. *The European Union.* Edinburgh: Edinburgh University Press.

Chapter 3

Islam and Politics in the Middle East

MOATAZ A. FATTAH

This article is set to provide a panoramic view of the landscape of Islam and politics in the Middle East. To be more specific, this article is an attempt to answer the following questions: Who speaks for Islam? And how do they situate politics in their Islamic discourse? As the reader will see that these questions have no simple answers yet, eight different agendas have developed in Muslim societies of the Middle East to account for these two questions.

The reader of this article will encounter several conclusions. First, having several agendas and discourses is not that new to the complexity of the Muslim history. There has always been different *fiqhi madhabs* (jurisprudential schools), philosophical schools, Sufi orders, Shi`a formations, military rulers, and bureaucrats who have existed, and often contested, parallel to the caliphate institution (Esposito 2005; Lapidus 2002; Lewis 2001).

Second, this article demonstrates how different influential opinion leaders, politicians, parties, and Islamic formations adopt different and possibly contradictory discourses that might eventually serve similar agendas without formal or documented coordination. Here one should note the power of the unintended consequences of one's choices and discourses. For instance, there are five groups, as we will see, of Muslims and non-Muslims who all adopt, to different degrees, an agenda of apolitical Islam though their discourses emanate from categorically contradicting interests and assumptions.

Third, the dynamics of these agendas suggest that Islam is very present in the public and political debates in Middle Eastern countries. Some accounts state without qualification that "Muslims are addicted to religion. Thus any attempt to reform Muslims' affairs will fail unless it starts from Islam or at least not to ignore it" (Omara 1998, 28). Thus, it is no wonder that Islamists appear to be the main winners of the so-called Arab Spring (Berman 2013). The real debates, as we will see, are where to locate Islam in modern societies and polities. Should it be limited to the personal lives of its followers? Can it expand from the "personal" to the "public" sphere? How can (or should) it be limited to these two spheres without delving into the political/legislative sphere?

Fourth, though, historically, the *'ulama'* "were the purveyors of Islam, the guardians of its tradition, the depository of ancestral wisdom, and the moral tutors of the population" (Marsot 1972, 149), this is not the case anymore. *'Ulama'*, with official degrees in *shari'ah* are just one group of opinion leaders, albeit so different in their political opinions and positions, and definitely they are now in the minority among so many other producers of political discourse in the name of Islam.

Fifth, these agendas are widespread among Middle Eastern countries. There is no state that is fully dominated by one agenda. There is always vibrant competition and even cutthroat conflict among some of them. Each agenda is challenged by others, which is a positive sign that *ijtihad* is a continuous endeavor and the dialectical process of qualifying positions and reacting differently to common challenges is underway. Yet, there is another negative aspect of this diversity that it reflects plurality more than it reflects tolerant pluralism. Following the analysis of some Arab scholars, there is some type of inter- and intraideological civil war not only between Islamists and secularist but even inside each camp (al-Azmeh 1992; Bishri 1996). We will note in this article that this is not entirely true; warring discourses might, without explicit coordination, end up endorsing common agendas following the famous Arab saying: "My brother and I are against our cousin; and my cousin and I are against strangers." The details will follow.

1. THE APOLITICAL MUSLIMHOOD AGENDA

There is, first, the ritualistic apolitical agenda. This agenda, surprisingly, is adopted by five different discourses that emanate from formations that are highly critical of each other. This agenda limits Islam to the personal domain, depriving it, thereby, of any role as far as legislation and political action is concerned. In other words, Islam according to this agenda should have no impact on the allocation of resources decisions made by the state. Questions of who gets what, when, where, why, and how should be made solely on nonreligious grounds. This is the model of an "Islam" that is locked up in mosques and whose role is limited to matters of faith, ethics, and rituals. This agenda is endorsed by (1) secular Muslims, whether autocrats or pluralists; (2) non-Muslims; (3) a group of modern preachers who do not want to get involved in political affairs; (4) Sufis; and (5) apolitical Salafis.

Religious minorities in the Middle East, for self-serving purposes, advocate secularism and total separation between religion and states and preach full citizenship à la liberal secular models of the United States and Canada, where there is no official religion of the state, or the British and Spanish models, where the official religion has only minimal symbolic relevance. Most Egyptian Copts, Israeli Arabs, Lebanese Christians, Moroccan Jews, Saudi Shi`a, and Iranian Sunnis have been endorsing a secular agenda emphasizing full citizenship irrespective of religious affiliation at the constitutional, legal, and popular levels.

Secular Muslims (headed by a group of intellectuals, leftists, and liberal political parties) along with non-Muslims perceive Islam as a personal relationship between God and his servants. This is the point on which they utterly disagree with Islamists (Baghdadi 1999; Mernissi 1992). This group of secular intellectuals and politicians (Muslims and non-Muslims) are highly influenced by nonreligious education obtained outside the Muslim world or from translated materials.

This agenda typically starts from two compatible assumptions. The first is that religion, and for that matter Islam, does not offer a concrete guide for governance. Holy texts do not tell Muslims much about how to run their political systems. Holy texts are sources of `aqida (creed) and ethics but not politics and economics. Even when they discuss political and economic issues, they emphasize broad principles such as justice, equality, and so forth.

Secularists refuse the Islamists' argument that Islam has an answer to all questions: "Islam is the Solution." They argue that the Prophet told Muslims that they were encouraged to brush their teeth before prayer. Yet he did not tell them how to select his political successor (al-Sa`eed 2001).

The silence of shari`ah regarding many political issues is a sign that Allah wants the human intellect to function and flourish without textual constraints.

The other assumption is that Muslims need to follow the paths of the most advanced societies in order to outdo them. This is exactly what the West did by learning from ancient Muslims and others. The Islamists' slogans about the peculiar and idiosyncratic nature of Muslims have been obstacles rather than catalysts for development and modernization. Secularists, in particular, argue that interaction with and learning from other civilizations is a human necessity, yet it will never succeed until Muslims are emancipated from the hold of "holy" interpretations and traditions that are assumed to come as a package with the holy texts (Arkoun 1994). Actually, they lament, Muslims imprison themselves in the *turath* (old books of the past) whether they are useful or not, while the world around them advances in all fields.

This agenda is reflected in the platforms of most secular Arab parties ranging from the Socialist Union for Popular Forces and Nationalist Party of Istiqlal in Morocco to the Algerian Party for Democracy and Socialism, the Free Egyptians Party, the Republican People's Party and Nationalist Movement Party in Turkey, along with socialist and liberal parties and candidates in Jordan, Kuwait, and Bahrain. It is reflected as well in the debates about the postrevolution constitutions in Egypt, Libya, and Tunisia.

Interestingly, there are other groups of Muslims who advocate the same agenda though they are very critical of each other: Sufis, apoliticized Salafis, and modern televangelist preachers. They focus on creed, rituals, and ethics to create a pious Muslim personality as a step toward a pious society. But, unlike the Muslim Brotherhood and postrevolution politicized Salafis in Egypt and Tunisia, for instance, they do not extend their discourse to mention the goal of creating a Muslim "state." They all avoid the politicization of their discourses. However, one can argue that their apolitical discourse is by itself politicized since it serves the status quo by diverting peoples' attention from the political plights of their societies. One can even argue that they represent a modern manifestation of Marx's depiction of religion as an opium of the masses. Despite the large gulf between them in style and sharp criticisms that they mount against each other, they all try to stay away from direct confrontations with the state. They do not propose themselves as alternatives to the ruling elites; rather they work within the area left to them by autocratic rulers. Modern televangelist preachers have at least one element that distinguishes them from the Sufis and apolitical Salafis. This element is the modern preachers' emphasis on social activism of leading a life of faith and fun, helping the poor, serving society without challenging authority, and gain Islamic knowledge without going to the extreme of being an Islamist with a political agenda (Haenni 2005). In comparison with the patronizing manner of a typical Azhari shaykh or Saudi imam, the amiable and compassionate modern preachers appear "...to be true democrats. For those who had learned to look for shortcuts to knowledge and were trained to be docile learners... [these preachers] are superior sources of wisdom" (Bayat 2007, 154).

As for the Sufis and dervishes and other mystic and ascetic orders, they are generally apolitical and focus on internal *jihad* and usually give oath of allegiance (*bay`ah*) to the ruling power. Estimations vary of how many Sufis are there. Some scholars estimate that there are more Sufis than Islamists in most Muslim countries (Hoffman 1995).

Heads of Sufi orders in Egypt claim that they have around 15 million affiliates. Others, such as the World Christian Database, estimate the total number of Sufis at 237 million in the whole Muslim world. One cannot verify that number given the fact that Sufis are scattered and not centrally organized (Allen 2009).

However, one knows for sure that they exist and are usually supported by autocratic states given the fact that they are the most complacent group with the status quo and least interested in delving into the world of opposition politics (Heck 2007).

The apolitical Salafis are one branch of "Salafism"—a term that typically refers to a number of different flavors of beliefs, most notably, politicized conservatives like the Wahhabi *shaykhs* in Saudi Arabia or Kuwait's Islamist Salafi movement, radical Islamists (or jihadists) such as al-Qaeda, reformers like Muhammad 'Abduh and Jamal al-Din Al-Afghani, and the apolitical preachers and groups such as Said Nursi's faith-based movements in Turkey (Nurcus), supporters of Mohamed's Sunna (Ansar al-Sunna al-Muhammdiyya) in Egypt and several Arab countries, and Tablighi Jama'at in several Arab countries. Popular apolitical Salafi movements identify a lack of spirituality and decline in personal religious observance as the root cause of the Muslim world's problems, and claim that Muslim identity cannot be successfully revived until these deficiencies are addressed. Interestingly, several groups that were typically antidemocracy and antirebellion against autocratic rulers seized the Arab Spring to form political parties and to deal with democracy as a legit form of government as long as it functions under the constraints of Islamic *shari'ah*.

These apolitical Salafi groups, such as Wahabi *'ulama'* in Saudi Arabia, mount sharp criticisms on Sufis and modern televangelist preachers as heretics, heterodox, and innovators. They are critical as well of violent jihadists such as al-Qaeda Islamists' competition in elections and jihadists' propagation of *takfir* against Muslims have been subject to different waves of criticisms from these apolitical Salafis. Typically Middle Eastern countries tolerate the freedom of expression and association for these groups as long as they do not get beyond their purely spiritual and ritual agendas, and when they talk politics, it is in the direction endorsed by the ruling elites.

However, one cannot understand the political impact of this agenda, without understanding how it is instrumentalized by the statist secularreligious agendas, especially before the Arab Spring.

2. STATIST SECULARELIGIOUS AGENDA

Islam is too important as a source of political legitimacy to be ignored by autocrats and too deeply rooted in the hearts and minds of Muslims to be categorically eliminated from the public sphere.

That is why most Middle Eastern ruling elites have adopted an agenda that has been labeled "seculareligious" (Bayat 2007). These elites adopt positions, discourses, and laws with roots in both religious and secular values. Religious symbols and justifications are important techniques for the ruling elites to maintain moral mastery over society and secure political legitimacy but not to the extent that Islam by itself becomes a political constraint on the pragmatic agenda of the ruling elites. That is why they have to act *as if* they were the true representatives of Islam, even if they do not abide by its teachings in their personal lives or political decisions. These rulers concurrently wage raids against political Islam while taking every opportunity to publicly display themselves as the guardian of religious values and morality and supportive of the apolitical Islamic agenda. The regime of Bashar Al-Assad in Syria started to use Islamic symbols in their war against the rebels whom they started to call *kofar*, or infidels.

The seculareligious agenda has a common tendency to include in the constitution an article that states that Islam is the official religion of the state and that Islamic *shari`ah* is a/the (main) source of legislation. Out of the twenty-five countries under investigation in this article, twelve countries declare Islam as the official religion without having such institutional review or control over legal and judicial processes.[1]

Another seven countries officially claim that law making and judicial processes are under the review and control of an Islamic body of scholars and courts.[2] Egypt's 2012 constitution includes an article that enables state's bodies to consult Al-Azhar on issues related to Islamic *shari'ah*.

Only Lebanon, Syria, and Turkey among the Middle Eastern countries, as defined in this article, are the countries that adopt the French *Laïcité* with no religious control over law making and judiciary, nor an official religion (Kuru 2009).

Tunisia throughout its history since independent in 1956 till 2011 provides us with a good example of a secularreligious structure of power where the state fully controls and dominates the Islamic establishment. Habib Bourguiba (1957–1987) claimed that his program of development and progress was more important than observing the ritual of fasting Ramadan. That is why in 1960, he asked the grand mufti of Tunisia (Shaykh abdel-Aziz Gheit) to issue a fatwa for all Tunisians to break their fast during the days of Ramadan. When the mufti refused, Bourguiba fired him and the position remained vacant for two years, singling a message that Muslims can live without official spokesmen of Allah's will. Despite this disguise to Islamic intelligentsia, Bourguiba and his successor did not give away Islam as a source of legitimacy. In the constitution, adopted June 1, 1959, Article 1 declared Islam the state religion, and Article 38 that the religion of the president must be Muslim. Ben Ali, the Tunisian president ousted in the revolution of 2011, used in his inauguration speech (after the November 7, 1987 coup) clear Islamic expressions ushering "reconciliation between Tunisia and its Arab and Islamic identity." Thus, Tunisian TV started airing the calls of prayer since then. Even when the regime cracked down on Islamists in the early 1990s, this was done with the full support of the official Islamic establishment as a mechanism to protect Islam from the misleading frenzy minority that is misusing and misrepresenting Islam (Burgat and Dowell 1993).

Thus, Islam, in this secularreligious agenda, is not only a set of symbolic articles placed in constitutions, laws, and expressions whose main aim is to provide the ruling regime with a religious façade but also a technique to empower the ruling elites against their enemies. Here the ruling elite seeks to benefit from the legitimacy conferred by Islam, but without really abiding by the restrictions of its *shari'ah*. Abd Al-Nasser openly declared his respect for Al-Azhar. In the meantime, he got rid of some of Al-Azhar scholars and even greatly undermined the institution's independence under the pretext that the institution was dominated by obscurantist *shaykhs* who opposed his socialist policies of nationalization and confiscation of private properties. Similar to that is Sadat's assertion in the second article of the constitution that the Islamic *shari'ah* is the principal source of legislation, to sell his proposal to remove the term limits of the president. Intermittently, seculareligious rulers resort to Islamic symbols and rhetoric to garner support. Saddam Hussein wrote Allah Akbar on the flag to boost the morale of his soldiers and people during Desert Storm and Qadafi declared *jihad* on Switzerland and issued a fatwa that any Muslim in any part of the world who works with Switzerland is an apostate, is against Muhammad, God, and the Qur'an.[3] Most Muslims know that Saddam and Gaddafi had no clout from a religious perspective. Yet, at least for their own peoples, the use of Islamic rhetoric is an important source of legitimacy that they cannot ignore.

This agenda and the previous one are strategically linked to each other. For this seculareligious agenda to pay off, three tactics should be used that use the services of the previous agenda:

1. Control of *'ulama'*: After independence of most Middle Eastern states, the *'ulama''*s dependence on the state was intensified since most states nationalized *al-awqaf* (endowments), abolished religious court, and restructured religious education. Thus, most *'ulama'* have become salaried state technocrats.

Imams of mosques either have become appointed by the state or have to get the approval of the ministries of religious affairs to give sermons and preach. Moreover, the states issued their own official Islamic magazines and newspapers. '*Ulama*' who traditionally constituted a distinct status have become, despite internal differentiation (according to seniority and economic status), more preoccupied with their shared common interests in income security and social and spiritual legitimacy. Official '*ulama*' have come under sharp criticisms from Islamic activists for being henchmen of the ruling elite and thus Islamists curtail the '*ulama*''s control over religious discourse.

2. Supporting or at least leaving room for the apolitical discourses of "Muslimhood" adopted by Sufis, apolitical Salafis, and modern preachers who control hundreds of mosques and scores of schools, welfare associations, independent satellite channels, and their own websites. These discourses become complementary to the discourse adopted by state-appointed '*ulama*'.

3. Series of wars (some of maneuver and others of position using Gramscian terms) against political Islamists who produce antiregime political discourses on Islamic grounds as the reader will note when we discuss the partisan Islamist agenda.

The reaction to the secularreligious agenda has come in different formats. Some are militant and others are nonviolent.

3. THE RADICAL MILITANT ISLAMIST AGENDA

A radical militant agenda launched its violent attacks in forms of waves to completely alter, even to destruct the political status quo— because they consider it anti- or un-Islamic. This group of violent

Islamists has many names in public discourses, including fundamentalists, terrorists, and Salafi-*jihadi* groups. This agenda, regardless of the label attached to it, is adopted by some formations that have based their ideologies on their own interpretations of three concepts: *takfir* (declaring unbeliever, or *kafir* [pl. *kuffār*], an individual or a group previously considered Muslim), *hisba* (to claim control of observance of Islamic principles), and *jihad* (understood by them to mean using violence to force Muslims to abide by Islamic *shari*'*ah*). These radical formations share, more or less, a very radical interpretation of the previous three concepts giving themselves the right to declare their opponents non-Muslims, and believe that they can act as *muhtasib*, which entitles them to punish those who do not abide by Islam's teachings, and they do that under the banner of *jihad* against the enemies of Islam who might be any Muslim who does not accept their interpretation of *shari*'*ah* or even non-Muslims who happen to live in Muslim societies. Though they share the previous aspects, they act at different levels: local, regional, and global.

Table 3.1 demonstrates an operational typology with some illustrative examples of different Islamist groups. The main distinction in this table is between nonviolent Islamists who believe in incremental evolutionary change and others who preach and practice radical revolutionary ruptures against their respective regimes, societies, and others.

Islamists working on the local scale do not extend their goals or operations beyond the state they belong to. They might have sympathizers or funders abroad, but they are basically limited to the radical change within their own states. Some examples include the Islamic Salvation Front of Algeria, al-Jama'a Islamiya of Egypt before their recent revisions, and Somalis Union of Islamic Courts, to name a few.

Table 3.1 OPERATIONAL TYPOLOGY OF ISLAMIC FORMATIONS
WITH POLITICAL AGENDAS

	Violent	*Nonviolent*
Global	Al-Qaeda and its supporting groups, such as Jama`at al-Tawhid wal-Jihad (al-Qaeda in Iraq)	Al-Tahrir Party, Muslim Brotherhood*
Regional	Hezbollah (Lebanon, Syria, Iran), Hamas (Gaza, Syria and Iran), Taliban (Afghanistan and Pakistan)	Salafi and Shi`a movements in the Arab Gulf area
Local	Islamic Salvation Front (Algeria), al-Jama`a Islamiya (Egypt), Somalis Union of Islamic Courts, Al-Mahdi Army in Iraq	Yemeni Congregation for Reform, AKP (Turkey), Party of Justice and Development (Morocco), Islamic Constitutional Movement (Kuwait)

*Some allegations and reports have accused Muslim Brotherhood of Egypt to be sponsoring violence after ousting president Mohamed Moursi from office in Egypt on July 3rd, 2013.

Likewise, regional Islamists are limited to their own regions yet with systematic alliance with other state actors within their regions against common enemies. Hamas and Hizbollah have been operating with full support from Syria and Iran against Israel but never went beyond it. Taliban associates who have never fought the North Atlantic Trade Organization troops beyond Afghanistan and western Pakistan are another case in hand. These two types of groups, local and regional, have been called "religious nationalists" who operate within national and regional boundaries and have local, rather than global or cosmic, objectives. These are different from the transnational *Jihadi* networks such as al-Qaeda that have universal agendas (Gerges 2009).

A second important difference between al-Qaeda and other violent Islamists is that al-Qaeda members do not perceive themselves as citizens of separate Muslim countries; rather they are the vanguards of the *ummah* as a whole. That is why they largely flourish in failed states within a power vacuum. Afghanistan's descent into a civil war following the withdrawal of Soviet troops was a good opportunity for the formation of Taliban-al-Qaeda nexus (Ayoob 2008, 147). The Taliban's agenda was primarily domestic, aiming at "purifying" Afghan society, yet al-Qaeda's Arab leaders had their own version of creative chaos.

A third important difference between al-Qaeda and other violent Islamist formations is that al-Qaeda is not a centralized or structured movement; rather it is more of a franchise. Gilles Kepel has pointed out: "Al-Qaeda... [is] less a military base of operations than a data base that connected *jihad*ists all over the world via the Internet... [US politicians] gave it a vivid, reductionist name—al-Qaeda—but this served only to reify the network's fluidity, thereby masking its true source of strength" (Kepel 2004, 37). Al-Qaeda, as such, has a very limited political impact as an alternative for any of the regimes in the Muslim world unless it is linked and supported by local partners. That is when it cannot be described as a political alternative to the status quo; rather it is just an element of destabilization.

However, the link between the local, regional, and global groups should not be obscured. The Egyptian Islamic jihad was disillusioned because of their inability to overthrow the Egyptian secularreligious autocratic regime at home (till the 2011 revolution) and thus decided to make common cause with transnational groups to target the "far enemy"—the West in general and the United States in particular. These groups in support of al-Qaeda see the "far enemy" as the principal supporters of un- or anti-Islamic repressive regimes at home, the "near enemy." Therefore, they believe that hitting the United States or the West would undermine support in America and Europe for authoritarian pro-Western regimes in the Arab/ Muslim world, leading to the collapse of these regimes (Ayoob 2008; Esposito 2005).

However, a deradicalization process took place in several Middle Eastern countries in the past decade. This deradicalization took the shape of "a radical group or individual reverses behavior and ideology to abandon and de-legitimize the use of violence to achieve political goals" (Ashour 2009, 12). Militant Islamist groups in Egypt, Algeria, Saudi Arabia, Iraq, Libya, Yemen, and Jordan have gone through revisionist endeavors based on reinterpreting their attitudes toward the concepts of *takfir*, *hisba*, and *jihad* to be less violent and more in agreement with most classical interpretations that limit the right to declare *takfir* to well-versed *'ulama'*, and to limit the *hisba* to some type of verbal act of enjoining the good and forbidding the evil and violent *jihad* to be a decision that should be made only by the legitimate authority of the Muslim state.

The most important cases of deradicalization were the in Egypt's al-Jama'a al-Islamiya and Al-Jihad group. Al-Jama'a al-Islamiya declared a unilateral ceasefire in July 1997 that evolved into a comprehensive deradicalization process in 2002. This particular group cooperated with the al-Jihad group in the assassination of President Anwar al-Sadat in 1981. The leaders of al-Jama'a al-Islamiya wrote around twenty-five volumes condemning their radical violent approach, criticizing al-Qaeda's claim of monopoly on Islam, refusing the idea of clash of civilizations, calling for peaceful coexistence between Muslims and non-Muslims on the land of Islam, giving oaths of allegiance to whoever acts as the president of Egypt, declaring repentance, and asking Muslims to forgive them for the violent course of action they had taken. These revisionist writings do not mean that they gave up Islamism but rather that they are self-transformed into nonviolent Islamists.

Another equally influential group went through the same revisionist process of deradicalization, namely the Egyptian *jihad* group that has been the early habitat for Ayman al-Zawahri, Mustafa Abu al-Yazid, the al-Qaeda commander in Afghanistan, and Yusuf al-Dardri, the al-Qaeda commander in Iraq.

The revision was mainly championed by the former leader of al-Jihad and one of the mentors of al-Qaeda, Dr. Sayyid Imam al-Sharif (also known as Dr. Fadl). In two books, Dr. Fadl, mounted a sever attack on al-Qaeda's leaders, describing them as ignorant, arrogant, seeking personal gains,...and acting against Islamic teachings.[4] Al-Zawahri defended his ideology based on rational and religious grounds by writing a book entitled *al-Tabra'a* (The Vindication). *Jihad*'s deradicalization process, however, has not been fully successful since numerous factions within the group came up with their own counterarguments.

The Saudi government launched a program of *munasaha* (advising) to complement the efforts of other '*ulama*' who were not affiliated with the state. This effort paid off in the deradicalization of individuals who have been affiliated with al-Qaeda. In Algeria, similar deradicalizing transformations occurred between 1997 and 2009. As was the case in Egypt, the self-declared armed wing of the Islamic Salvation Front (FIS), known as the Islamic Salvation Army (AIS), declared a unilateral ceasefire in October 1997. The demilitarization process included almost all militant Islamists except for the so-called al-Qaeda in the Islamic Maghreb. Unlike the Egyptian groups, however, the Saudi and Algerian militant Islamists did not produce any literature to constitute a new ideology.

Likewise, in Libya, the Fighting Islamic Group, former ally of al-Qaeda, initiated a deradicalization process in 2006–2007. Its commanders in Afghanistan refused to accept the process then. Yet, with the death of Abu Layth in 2008, the process has been reactivated. On September 1, 2009, on the occasion of Muammar Qadhafi's fortieth year in power, a militant Islamist prisoner issued a public apology to the colonel, declaring that the group will abandon political violence and dismantle its secret units.

Iraq has witnessed the disarming of Jama`at Ansar al-Sunnah (or Group of the Followers of Sunnah) that has been fighting the US-led occupation and the elected government led by Nouri al-Maliki. The leaders of Sunni tribes in Anbar gave up their support to this group and started to fight them back after they stroke a deal with the US commanders and the al-Maliki government.

In Yemen, the Houthis declared that they were trying to reverse the political, economic, and religious marginalization of the Zaydi Shi`a community. Yet, the raids from the Saudi troops and Yemeni army forced them to back down, most likely temporarily.

Failure to achieve their goals, selective incentives, government raids, interaction with moderate Islamists, and the political ramifications of the Arab Spring propelled radical Islamists to reexamine their ideologies, revise their strategies, and moderate their tactics. That is why several of these repressive regimes claimed victory and garnered popular support given what they call their capacity to "repress, deter and de-radicalize the misguided groups" as stated by King Abdullah of Saudi Arabia before the Shoura Council on April 14, 2007.

There is some evidence that there is domino effect for the deradicalization process. Deradicalized groups often interact with violent ones and in some cases the former influences the latter, as demonstrated in the militant groups in Egypt, Algeria, Saudi Arabia, Libya, and others (Ashour 2009).

There is no guarantee that this process of deradicalization is sustainable. Reverse radicalization, either for these same groups and individuals or others, is still a possibility given the perpetuation of political repression, ban of these organizations by autocratic regimes, lack of addressing the grievances of Muslims at large, and the support they might get from other regional actors.

4. ARMED RESISTANCE THE ISLAMIST AGENDA

This agenda is adopted by resistance and liberation formations that turn to Islam as their principal instrument for mobilization when secular parties and groups fail to achieve their nationalist goals, be they ending foreign occupation or gaining independence from existing parent states (Ayoob 2008; Esposito 1999). The foremost examples of this phenomenon are Hezbollah in Lebanon and Hamas in the Gaza strip yet there are other examples in Iraq (e.g., the al-Mahdi army under the leadership of Muqtada al-Sadr) and Somalia (e.g., the Union of Islamic Courts). Six characteristics shape this agenda.

First, groups endorsing this agenda emerge because of the failure of other secular groups to achieve the nationalist objectives of liberation and independence. Both Hizbollah and Hamas were born as a result of the Israeli occupation of the Gaza Strip and the West bank and its invasion of Lebanon in 1982. The same goes for al-Sadr's army in Iraq, which emerged only after 2003.

Second, the violence that these groups have engaged in is context specific and principally in the nature of national resistance to foreign occupation. What distinguishes both Hamas and the Lebanese Hezbollah from al-Qaeda and other global Islamist violent organizations is that the former groups' violence is restricted territorially and directed toward specific targets that they consider to be obstructing their goals of achieving national independence or freeing occupied territory. Al-Qaeda and its supporting groups have no respect for national borders or identities. Hamas and Hezbollah work within the parameters of the state system even if they defy the legitimacy of their national opponents.

Third, there is a tendency among these groups not to give up their arms even when they choose to join the national government. All of them continue to be ambivalent regarding their roles in their respective polities, refusing to surrender arms, because they see them as an essential component of their popularity among their constituencies.

Fourth, these groups tend to straddle the violent and nonviolent worlds by having a political wing and a military wing. They field candidates in elections and even gain the majority, such as Hamas's wining the majority in the 2006 elections and al-Sadr's movement, which was key to the efforts of forming the new Iraqi government, winning 39 seats in the 325-seat parliament of the 2010 elections; that is up 10 seats from their previous standing.

These groups have social wings besides their political and military wings. Part of their electoral gains can be attributed to their vast network of social services that cater to the needs of the most underprivileged and vulnerable sections of their societies. However, each has accumulated popularity because of their success in driving Israeli troops from most of southern Lebanon, the Gaza strip and the promised US withdraw from Iraq.

Fifth, Hamas and Hizbollah are foes by proxy to the United States, since they feel the United States is waging a war by proxy against them through their closest ally in the region: Israel. The more the United States associates itself with Israel's policies, the more it is perceived as an enemy on its own merit.

Sixth, having an armed wing is another distinction between Islamists with a liberation agenda and other Islamists with partisan agendas, as we will see in the coming pages.

This resistance and liberation Islamist agenda is driven almost equally by nationalist considerations and religious ones, although they are still Islamists who use Islamic symbols to legitimize their behavior and mobilize their respective constituencies.

5. THE PARTISAN ISLAMIST AGENDA

There is, fifth, a group of Islamists who work as a part of a trend toward moderation and constitutionalism, not violence and extremism. These formations adopt a party-like Islamic platform as an alternative from among others available for electors to choose. This agenda is endorsed by those seeking to win a parliamentary majority where elections are possible. A part of this discourse involves the formulation of a party program that addresses economic, social, and political aspects and offers better solutions to problems that existing parties already suggest solutions for.

Different Middle Eastern regimes have handled the proposed partisan agenda of Islamists differently in the past decade. Five models can be monitored.

First, partial inclusion and partial exclusion of Islamists: The Egyptian case under Mubarak represented this model par excellence. In this model there is a degree of partial assimilation and a degree of partial elimination without clear lines for what is or is not acceptable on the part of Islamists (Bayat 2007; Norton 2005, 157). Practically, the Brotherhood in Egypt was allowed somewhat free participation in national, syndicate, and students' elections, yet, under the condition that they do not win a majority of votes. Otherwise, election results get manipulated or the candidates of the

Brotherhood get administratively excluded or even arrested. One can think of it as freedom of participation but no freedom after participation. The Muslim Brotherhood's credible performance in the 2005 elections indicated that the free and fair elections in Egypt will give more power to Islamists (Rubin 2007; Shahin 2010).

Second, legal assimilation and political neutralization: This model is best represented by the monarchic models of Jordan, Morocco, Kuwait, and Bahrain in addition to the examples of Algeria, Sudan, and Yemen. In this model, Islamists exist legally but no matter how they do in elections, the monarch or president has the ultimate say on the allocation of resources and deciding who gets what, when, where, why, and how. The Islamic Action Front in Jordan, the Movement of Society for Peace in Algeria, the Justice and Development Party in Morocco, the National Islamic Front in Sudan, and the Yemeni Congregation for Reform are all legally assimilated but politically tamed. Thus, they have to work under the iron ceiling determined by their oppressive regimes. In other words, Islamists can oppose (if they are the minority) or administer and manage (if they are the majority) but cannot rule and govern the affairs of their societies.

Third, autocratic exclusion of Islamists: This is the model of elimination of Islamists through legal, political, and police coercion as witnessed in the cases of Tunisia, Syria, and Libya before the Arab Spring. In these three cases, there was no space, legally or politically, for a group of people who might call themselves Islamists. A political Islamist in these countries used to be either in jail, exile, or the grave. This was particularly true for all the leaders of the Tunisian Renaissance Party, the Syrian Muslim Brotherhood, and the Libyan Islamic group before the Arab Spring.

Fourth, the secular democratic assimilation: In this model, which is solely adopted by Turkey, all political formations are assimilated and included in the political sphere as long as they abide by the rules of a secular and democratic state. These powers are carefully monitored by the Supreme Court and the National Security Council that is dedicated to the protection of supraconstitutional rules, that is, rules that no one can agree to break and that no one can seek to change or amend. In an example of how institutions create the culture conducive to them, the Justice and Development Party (AKP) in Turkey has repackaged its platform in a conservative democratic party emphasizing "Muslimhood," similar to the Christian Democrats in Western Europe, while giving up any radical exclusivist Islamist agenda.

Fifth, postrevolution regimes: The overthrow of five authoritarian regimes in the Arab world gave democracy a chance to bloom but at the same time it has also created opportunities for a wide spectrum of Islamist parties to raise demands for applying Islamic *shari'ah*. Though many of the protest movements associated with the Arab Spring in Tunisia, Egypt, Libya, and Yemen appeared to be largely secular in nature, Islamist parties have been winning most elections across the region, causing unease and uncertainty both domestically and abroad. In Egypt, there are roughly twenty-one new parties that have been formed claiming to endorse Islamic principles. Tunisia, Libya, and Yemen are taking the same path. Indeed, there is more space for procedural democracy to expand, yet it is not clear if this kind of democracy would be liberal enough to meet the minimum requirements of consolidated democracy (Recknagel 2013). One cannot fully predict where these countries are heading, but certainly they are not similar to the cases of Saudi Arabia, Iran, or Sudan, where an Islamist political agenda is fully in control.

6. THE RULING ISLAMIC AGENDA

In the name of Islam, three regimes in particular have reached power and continue to control it. Saudi Arabia, Iran, and Sudan are the three states within this region that have three traits in common: (1) they officially declare themselves as Islamic states and always make reference to Islam as their frame of reference in domestic and international affairs; (2) they officially apply Islamic *shari`ah* in personal and penal laws, besides an institutionalized review of their legal and judicial processes; and (3) their ruling elites have based their legitimacy since their inception on applying Islamic discourse. This is true by looking at the discourses of the leaders of these regimes during the unifying war in Saudi Arabia in the early 1930s, the mass revolution in Iran in 1979, and the coup d'état in the Sudan in 1989. In the three cases, the ruling elites have turned Islam from one of many cultural characteristics of societies into the defining element of their identities, institutions, and policies. These regimes work to have full monopoly over the political use of Islam, like other seculareligious countries, yet they seem to be more successful in Iran and Saudi Arabia than they are in Sudan.

Iran is a unique case since there is no other modern example where the *`ulama'* have themselves taken control of a state. The Islamic Republic of Iran is a case of unifying political power with official religious control of Shi`a clerics as it is embodied in Iran's Assembly of Experts. The Assembly of Experts is comparable to the Vatican's College of Cardinals. It is made up of eighty-six elected clerics whose chief responsibilities are the election of the supreme leader and ensuring the compatibility of official acts with Islam. The preamble to the Iranian constitution says that the Islamic Republic reflects the hopes of Iran's "Muslim people" in an assertion that the previous regimes have ignored the Islamic nature of the Iranian people. This new identity has been reflected clearly in the regime's ideology and state institutions.

Saudi Arabia provides another pattern where the family of al-Saud (possessing political power) and the family of Ibn Abd al-Wahab (possessing religious legitimacy) coalesced to form a state following the traditional pattern that first appeared with the Umayyad dynasty. To achieve primacy, Abdel-Aziz al-Saud formed an alliance with Shaykh Abd al-Wahhab and used religion to offset tribal affiliation and social segmentation. To consolidate the Saud's overall hereditary control, Abd al-Aziz and his sons after him formed strong marriage alliances with the Sudairi, Ibn Jelawi, and Shammar tribes, among others.

Unlike the two other examples of the ruling Islamic agenda, the Saud family rarely needed to resort to modern procedures of elected bodies. Domestically, the `ulama' have been the main supporting constituency for the Saud family. Practically, if the umara' (princes) and `ulama' agree, then there is little room for generalized dissent. This has guaranteed the kingdom's stability for the past seventy-five years, although it is stability without democracy. That is why, in Saudi Arabia, the word "democracy" has no tradition of being officially used, misused, or abused. Even the Westernized intellectual elite that looks to Europe and the United States as models of liberal democracy does not think of achieving many liberal reforms in the near future, mainly because of the illiberal Wahhabi religious establishment that holds up its generally nonpluralistic interpretation of Islam as a guide (Korany and Fattah 2008).

Likewise, except for the short transitional period of 1953–1957 during which the Sudan had implemented secular and liberal laws, every single constitution had a clear reference to Islam as the official religion and shari`ah serving as the sole or primary source of legislation with clear reference to the rights of non-Muslims to practice their religions freely.

Since the three major currents of the Ansar (led by the al-Mahdi family), Khatmiyyah (led by the al-Mirghani family), and the Muslim Brotherhood, which comprise the major forces on the contemporary Sudanese political scene, are religiously based,

Sudan's political history has been colored by Islam, and the implementation of Islamic laws is, therefore, a main component of the Muslim Sudanese portion of the population (roughly 70 percent; Hassan and Ray 2009). Following the same path, the current regime, that launched its coup d'état in 1989, has been actively engaging in a process of Islamizing the political and public spheres in the Sudan. In line with the commitment of al-Bashir's regime to Islamic path, the enforcement of *hudud* law was resumed in December 1990 after its suspension following the overthrow of the Numayri's regime in April 1985.

The architect of the 1989 coup d'état, Hassan al-Turabi (who later became a major opposition figure), described the mission of the regime as follows: "It is to Islamise public life—civil, business, police, military, economy and culture in all dimensions. When I say 'Islamise' I mean not only in forms, according to Islamic *Shari`ah*, but also attitude and disposition…Madinah is our model" (Al-Turabi 1993, 9).

However, this assertion of the Islamist identity has been one of the major causes of the two civil wars (1955–1972 and 1983–2005) that have caused the deaths of around 2 million civilians due to the desire of the southern Sudanese to secede. Unfortunately, the three examples of an "Islamic governance" are not of any appeal to harbingers of democracy and liberalism and have ranged from theocracy to fake democracy.

7. LOBBYING ISLAMIC AGENDA

This agenda is adopted by organized groups as well as spontaneous movements pursuing short-term microgoals. One finds it manifested, for example, in demonstrations demanding the prohibition of a certain novel or book that is considered anti-Islamic; objecting to opening up a store that sells alcoholic beverages; and protesting governments' decision or permission to allow interests on loans and bank deposits, show inappropriate movies and music on national television, invite singers (usually known for dressing in revealing clothes), and organize beauty pageants.

Additionally, the lobbying techniques (such as demonstrations) might be used as a show of support for the Palestinians, Iraqis, or Lebanese especially during times of bloody tensions.

In most cases, the proponents of Islamism and Muslimhood explicitly or implicitly find themselves in coalition to achieve these microgoals. In Algeria, for instance, in March 2010, a temporary coalition was formed by Islamists, conservative Muslims, and official *'ulama'* around the grand mufti who accused Louisa Hanoun of being an "enemy of Islam," calling upon her to repent and stay away from issues that she is ignorant about upon her objection to the perpetuation of applying the capital punishment. Hanoun is a veteran, left wing Trotskyite and leader of the country's Worker's Party and an important secularist figure in Algeria.

In some cases, the interests and attitudes of university students and official *'ulama'* converges with the view of the Islamist formations and results in the adoption of a pressing discourse into a specific direction. However, this pressing role is not considered an ideal option by any of the parties involved. For the Islamists it is just a "minimum," for the secularists it stimulates fears about the "theocracy" ghost, and for the state it signifies pressure that it needs to address, either through coercion or through dialogue.

Typically this agenda works well if there are supporters of the cause on the part of the ruling elite. Islamists in Bahrain failed to prevent a female Lebanese singer from entertaining her audience in 2003 despite condemnations and violent protests against the police. Yet, with the support of some members of the ruling family, in coalition with Islamists (Shi'a and Sunni) and the official religious establishment, the parliament passed a law forbidding a private company from organizing a similar musical festival in 2008.

However, it looks as if they were minor successes on the part of Islamists, yet they are important indicators of their success in the Islamization of Muslim *societies* and failure to Islamize several Muslim *states*. This Islamization takes the format of influencing policies in the direction of increasing the communal activity (*da'wa*) within the existing order with the aim of changing it peacefully and gradually. Islamic resurgence (or *al-sahwa*) manifested both on the individual level (religious rituals and accessories) and on the collective level (proliferation of new mosques, religious charitable associations, and religious satellite channels).

Ruling elites in most seculareligious states left some space for this lobbying agenda as long as they are noninfluential regarding macrosovereign decisions of governance (such as relations with the West and Israel). That is why the lobbyist agenda does not openly challenge the powerful institutions of the presidency or the monarch.

However, this Islamization of society has not yet produced Islamization of the state apparatus because of the glass ceiling imposed by the police (Diamond et al. 2003). In almost all Muslim states with seculareligious agendas, an active Islamist cannot join the army, police, minister of foreign affairs, or any position that might empower the Islamist agenda in these pivotal power centers of the state.

8. ECUMENICAL ISLAMIC AGENDA

This survey would not be comprehensive without discussing the intellectual agenda of a group of '*ulama'*, thinkers and intellectuals who theorize an ecumenical foundational agenda that appreciates the diversity of Muslims' agendas and regards Islam as a frame of reference over and above political conflicts of any type; analogically comparable to liberalism that constitutes the foundational framework for the political life in Western regimes. Under this overarching umbrella, diversity exists and should continue to exist as long as it acknowledges the authentic and indisputable (*qat'ai al-dalala* and *qat'ai al-thubout*) verses of the Qur'an and sayings of the Prophet.

They regard these holy texts to be a frame of reference comparable to the American Declaration of Independence or the British Magna Carta, so these texts should constitute jus cogens out of which no one can contract.

To give their discourse more coherence and organize their efforts, some of the champions of this agenda founded the International Union of Muslim Scholars (IUMS), headed by Shaykh Yusuf al-Qaradawi. It has members from almost all Muslim countries. Grand Ayatollah Shaykh Muhammad Ali Al-Taskhiri (Iran), Shaykh Taha Jabir al-Alwani (Iraq), Dr. Haytham Al-Khayyat (Syria), Ahmad Al-Raysouni (Morocco), Shaykh Salman Al-'Udah (Saudi Arabia), Isam al-Din Al-Bashir (Sudan), 'Abd Al-Wahhab Al-Daylami (Yemen), and Selim al-'Awwa (Egypt) are among its leaders.

They argue that the *ummah* has been divided in so many directions without a compass or a roadmap. This agenda wants to emphasize the common grounds of all Muslim and Islamist agendas. That is why they accept all the nonsecular agendas (except for the militant radical ones) and are even ready to accept dialogue with secularists and non-Muslims.

They act as the champions of *wasatiya* (moderation) and against the seeds of sedition between Sunnis and Shiites and extremism against non-Muslims. The World Forum for Proximity of Islamic Schools of Thought in Iran is a manifestation of this agenda.

Having a common agenda does not mean that there are no internal debates regarding some issues. Dr. Yusuf Al-Qaradawi raised the issue of Shiite proselytizing in some Sunni countries, especially Egypt in 2008. However, Ayatollah Muhammad Ali At-Taskhiri rejected the issue as nothing but baseless rumors. Though it was a tough test for the IUMS, they managed to focus their attention on the common aspects of all Muslims such as the situation in Palestine. The IUMS Statement on Zionist Plots against Al-Aqsa Mosque and the Palestinian Issue is a very tough call upon all Muslims, rulers, and ruled, and even upon people of conscious among non-Muslims to save the Muslim and Christian holy shrines from the hands of Israeli occupying troops.

They think that all Islamists and religious Muslims are partners in a grand project of restoring the Islamic civilization (al-Qaradawi 2000). Modern preachers focus on ethics and rituals; Salafis are important yet they fight heterodox ideas and praxis; and armed resistance movements are the natural reaction to occupation. Their support as well goes to the partisan and lobbying agendas as peaceful expression of political demands. Yet, they unequivocally condemn the radical militant groups and they actually do not shy away from calling them terrorists. They are supportive of the rights of the ruled to choose their own rulers in free fair periodic multicandidate elections that they may or may not use the word "democracy" to describe it (al-Qaradawi 2001).

The proponents of this agenda play the role of the *ummah*'s conscience through issuing statements and giving sermons in mosques and media outlets. Yet, their real influence comes from their impact on other political players on the ground.

CONCLUSION

People of this part of the world have always been fascinated with "unity." The Qur'an says: "This is your *ummah*, one *ummah*, and

I am your God . . ." However, this article has demonstrated that Muslims are very remote from unity at this point in their history.

Islam that united Muslims in the past has become an arena for political competition among Muslims nowadays. A fuzzy set of multiple (and even conflicting) agendas have been created on the ground. Each agenda creates its own logic, rhetoric, narrative, and constituents. This plurality is more political than it is religious. In other words, Islam is rarely the sole source of any of these agendas. It is usually used, misused, or abused by various groups of Muslims. Understanding these mixed and multifaceted phenomena is an indispensable step to fully comprehend who speaks for Islam in the Middle East and how different forces situate politics in their Islamic agendas.

NOTES

1. States with symbolic reference to Islam in their constitutions and basic laws are Algeria, Djibouti, Egypt, Iraq, Jordan, Kuwait, Libya, Morocco, Qatar, Somalia, Tunisia, and United Arab Emirates.
2. States with Islamic review of laws are Bahrain, Iran, Mauritania, Oman, Saudi Arabia, Sudan, and Yemen.
3. http://news.bbc.co.uk/2/hi/africa/8537925.stm.
4. Kamal Habib, Another Wave of Jihadist Adjustment: Internal Debates of the Movement, *Arab Insights*, 2, no. 6, (Winter 2009), pp. 21–25. Jarret Brachman, Al Qaeda's Dissident, *Foreign Policy*, December 2009), pp. 19–20.

REFERENCES

al-Azmeh, Aziz. 1992. *Al-'Almaniya min manzour mukhtalif* [Secularism from a Different Perspective]. Beirut: Markaz Dirasat al-Wehda al-Arabiya.
al-Qaradawi, Yusuf. 2000. *Ummatuna Bayna Qarnayen* [Our Nation between Two Centuries]. Cairo: Dar al-Shorouq.

al-Qaradawi, Yusuf. 2001. *Min Fiqh al-Dawla Fi al-Islam* [On the Jurisprudence of the Islamic State]. Cairo: Dar al-Shorouq.

al-Sa`eed, Rif`at. 2001. *Al-`alamnya Bayna al-Islam wa al-Taa'slum* [Secularism between Islam and Fake Islamization]. Kitab Al-Ahali; Cairo: Al-Tagamu` Party in Egypt.

Al-Turabi, Hassan. 1993. "Challenging Times but Medina Is Our Model." *Impact International*, 23, pp. 3–4.

Allen, John L. 2009. *The Future Church: How Ten Trends Are Revolutionizing the Catholic Church*. New York: Doubleday. pp. viii, 469.

Arkoun, Mohamed. 1994. *Rethinking Islam: Common Questions, Uncommon Answers*. Ed. and trans. Robert D. Lee. Boulder: Westview.

Ashour, Omar. 2009. *The De-radicalization of Jihadists: Transforming Armed Islamist Movements*. Contemporary Terrorism Studies. London: Routledge. pp. xv, 205.

Ayoob, Mohammed. 2008. *The Many Faces of Political Islam: Religion and Politics in the Muslim World*. Ann Arbor: University of Michigan Press. pp. xii, 213.

Baghdadi, Ahmad. 1999. *Tajdid al-Fikr al-Dini [Renovation of the Religious Thought]*. Damascus: al-Mada Publishing Company.

Bayat, Asef. 2007. *Making Islam Democratic: Social Movements and the Post-Islamist Turn*. Stanford Studies in Middle Eastern and Islamic Societies and Cultures. Stanford, CA: Stanford University Press. pp. xxi, 291.

Berman, Sheri. 2013. "The Promise of the Arab Spring." *Foreign Affairs*, January/ February, pp. 22–28.

Bishri, Tariq. 1996. *Al-Hiwar al-Islami al-`Almani* [The Secular–Islamic Dialogue]. Cairo: Dar al-Shuruq. pp. 95.

Burgat, François, and Dowell, William. 1993. *The Islamic Movement in North Africa*. Middle East Monograph Series. Austin: Center for Middle Eastern Studies, University of Texas at Austin. pp. xi, 310.

Diamond, Larry Jay, Plattner, Marc F., and Brumberg, Daniel. 2003. *Islam and Democracy in the Middle East*. A Journal of Democracy Book. Baltimore: Johns Hopkins University Press. pp. xxvi, 322.

Esposito, John L. 1999. " 'Clash of Civilizations'? Contemporary Images of Islam in the West," in Gema Martin Munoz, ed., *Islam, Modernism and the West: Cultural and Political Relations at the End of the Millennium*. New York: I.B. Taurist Publisher.

Esposito, John L. 2005. *Islam: The Straight Path*. Rev. 3rd ed. New York: Oxford University Press. pp. xvi, 304.

Gerges,Fawaz A. 2009. *The Far Enemy: Why Jihad Went Global*. 2nd ed. Cambridge: Cambridge University Press. pp. xiii, 386.

Haenni, Patrick. 2005. *L'islam de Marché: L'autre Révolution Conservatrice*. La république des idées. Paris: Seuil. pp. 108.

Hassan, Salah M., and Ray, Carina E. 2009. *Darfur and the Crisis of Governance in Sudan: A Critical Reader*. Ithaca: Cornell University Press. pp. 528.

Heck, Paul L. 2007. *Sufism and Politics: the Power of Spirituality*. Princeton: Markus Wiener Publishers, pp. 197.

Hoffman, Valerie J. 1995. *Sufism, Mystics and Saints in Modern Egypt*. Columbia, SC: University of South Carolina Press.

Kepel, Gilles. 2004. *The War for Muslim Minds: Islam and the West*. Cambridge, MA: Belknap Press of Harvard University Press. pp. 327.

Korany, Bahgat, and Fattah, Moataz. 2008. 'Irreconcilable Role-Partners?: Saudi Foreign Policy between the *'ulama'* and the US', in Ali E. Dessouki and Bahgat Korany, eds., *The Foreign Policies of the Arab States: The Challenge of Change*. Colorado: Westview Press.

Kuru, Ahmet T. 2009. *Secularism and State Policies toward Religion: the United States, France, and Turkey*. Cambridge: Cambridge University Press. pp. xvii, 313.

Lapidus, Ira M. 2002. *A History of Islamic Societies*. 2nd ed. Cambridge: Cambridge University Press. pp. xxx, 970.

Lewis, Bernard. 2001. *The Multiple Identities of the Middle East*. New York: Schocken Books.

Marsot, Afaf Lutfi al-Sayyid. 1972. "The *'ulama'* of Cairo in the Eighteenth and Nineteenth Century," in Nikki Keddi, ed., *Scholars, Saints, and Sufis*. Berkeley: University of California Press.

Mernissi, Fatima. 1992. *Islam and Democracy: Fear of the Modern World*. Reading, MA: Addison-Wesley, 195.

Norton, Augustus Richard. 2005. "Thwarted Politics: The Case of Egypt's Hizb al-Wasat," in Robert W. Hefner, ed., *Remaking Muslim Politics: Pluralism, Contestation, Democratization*. Princeton, NJ: Princeton University Press, xii, 358.

Omara, Mohamed. 1998. *Hal al-Islam Hoa al-Hal?* [Is Islam the Solution?] Cairo: Dar al-Shorouq.

Recknagel, Charles. 2013. "What Happened to the Arab Spring?" *The Atlantic*, January 2013, pp. 13–14.

Rubin, Barry M. 2007. *Political Islam: Critical Concepts in Islamic Studies*. New York: Routledge.

Shahin, Emad El-Din. 2010. "Democratic Transformations in Egypt: Controlled Reforms…Frustrated Hopes," in Nathan J. Brown and Emad El-Din Shahin, eds., *The Struggle over Democracy in the Middle East: Regional Politics and External Policies*. New York: Routledge, xi, 201.

Chapter 4

Islam and Politics in Central Asia

SHIREEN HUNTER

INTRODUCTION

The vitality of Islam in Central Asia and the Caucasus and its emergence in the last two decades as a potent social and political force after a century and a half of Russian and Soviet rule and subjection to policies aimed at its elimination came as a surprise to many observers and analysts.[1] However, for those familiar with these regions' Islamic history, including Islam's central role in their cultural, social, and political life, Islam's emergence and vitality in the post-Soviet era appear quite natural. This phenomenon becomes even more understandable if seen in light of the growing profile of Islam as a sociocultural and political force in the neighboring regions of Iran, Afghanistan, and Pakistan.

FACTORS BEHIND ISLAM'S VITALITY

Many factors account for both Islam's resilience and staying power in Central Asia and the Caucasus, despite being actively undermined, and its current political relevance. The first factor is its deep historic roots. Most of Central Asia and the Caucasus were Islamized during the first centuries of Islam. Parts of Central Asia, notably Bukhara and Marv, became important centers of Islamic learning and Central Asians of both Turkic and Iranian stock such as Abu Nasr al-Farabi (c.872–c.950), Abu Ali Ibn Sina (Avicenna; 980–1037) and Muhammad Ibn Musa al-Khwarazmi (c.780–c.850), among others, greatly contributed to the development of Islamic civilization. A second factor is Islam's central place as an identity marker for the peoples of these regions. Islam's central role as the ethical, moral, legal, and cultural framework for collective life is the third factor. Until the Russian/Soviet control, in Central Asian political entities such as the Emirate of Bukhara and the Khanat of Khiva and Khokand, educational and legal systems were based on Islam. These institutions were severely undermined during the Russian/Soviet rule. Nevertheless part of their legacy managed to survive underground.

Fourth, the inconsistent character of tsarist and Soviet treatment of Islam is an important factor. This inconsistency allowed for periods of relative tolerance of Islam, which enabled it to retain some aspects of its traditional role. Certain requirements of the Soviet Union's foreign policy as early as the 1930s led the Soviet regime to periodically allow a degree of freedom in the practice of Islam and encourage a certain level of contact between Soviet Muslims and the rest of the Islamic world. For example, in the 1940s, Stalin tried to prevent Soviet Muslims from turning to Germany, which enjoyed a degree of sympathy among its Muslims by loosening some of the restrictions on Muslims' practice of their faith. The USSR also used Muslims as ambassadors to Arab states, especially under Khrushchev (Dawisha and D'encausse 1983, 166).

The fifth factor is Islam's role as an instrument of resistance against Russian/Soviet domination and Russification/Sovietization. Throughout the tsarist period in Central Asia and the Caucasus Islam was a main force behind the indigenous peoples' resistance to the advancing Russian armies and periodic revolts against the imperial administration. This pattern of resistance and Islam's role in it continued under the Soviet rule, albeit in a less overtly confrontational manner. Rather often secret practice of Islamic traditions, including those more cultural than religious, contributed to the preservation of the Central Asian and Caucasian Muslims' identity and traditions.[2]

The sixth factor is the failure of the USSR to deliver on its economic and political promises. The final factor is the paradoxes of Russia's nationalities policies that failed to engender a strong ethnic or civic nationalism in the Muslim-inhabited regions and hence further enhancing Islam's role as individual and collective identity marker.

Although Islam retained its hold on the peoples and societies of Central Asia and the Caucasus, the long Russian and Soviet rules and their anti-Islam policies had significantly adverse consequences for Central Asian and Caucasian Islam. The negative legacy of these policies and the consequences that have flown from them are responsible for some of the sociopolitical and religiocultural problems faced by these regions today, including problems posed by a degree of Islam's radicalization.

ISLAM IN CENTRAL ASIA AND THE CAUCASUS UNDER THE RUSSIAN AND SOVIET RULE

The Russian treatment of Muslims in Central Asia and in the Caucasus differed somewhat under the tsars. In the South Caucasus, or to be precise in what is now the Republic of Azerbaijan, Russia did not interfere with the local practice of Islam. The North Caucasus was not completely conquered until 1865, largely because of the resistance of such Muslim leaders as Shaykh (Imam) Mansur and Shaykh Shamil. During a period from 1785–1791, Shaykh Mansur Ushurma succeeded in uniting diverse North Caucasian groups through an elaborate network of Naqshbandi Sufi brotherhoods in resistance to the Russians. However, he was captured in 1793. After a lull of thirty years the Chechens resumed their fight against Russia, this time under the leadership of Shaykh Shamil who fought the Russians from 1825 to 1852. Shaykh Shamil's resistance, which after the Prophet's wars was named the Gazawat, has left a legacy that greatly contributed to later Chechen rebellions under the Soviets and to the post-Soviet events in Chechnya, Dagestan, and other parts of the North Caucasus.[3] In Central Asia, the extent and magnitude of anti-Islam policies partly depended on the character and inclination of Russian officials. In general, however, Islam suffered under the tsarist rule as the number of mosques and religious schools declined as did the quality of Islamic learning. However, the tsarist regime did not pursue an aggressive policy of religious proselytizing in Central Asia and the Caucasus.

Before victory over the tsar, the Bolsheviks tried to attract the empire's Muslims by promising them freedom to pursue their religion, as reflected in the famous appeal of Lenin and Stalin to the Muslims of the east. This *Appeal to All Laboring Muslims of Russia and the East* said: "Muslims of Russia, Tatars of the Volga and Crimea, Kyrgyz and parts of Siberia and Turkmen, Turks and Tatars of Trans-Caucasia, Chechen and mountain peoples of Caucasus, all of you whose mosques and prayer houses have been trampled upon by tsars and oppressors of Russia; *your beliefs and usages, your national and cultural institutions are forever free*" (cited in Pipes 1997, 155, emphasis added).

This appeal had certain success and rallied many Muslims to the Bolsheviks' cause. The so-called *Shari'ah* squadrons, the militia of

Zaki Validi Togan (1890–1970) in Bashkortostan, and the Chechen Red Army under the leadership of Aslanbek Shapirov, which served in the Red Army, and the fact that 70 percent of General Mikhail Frunze's Turkestan Red Army was made of Muslim soldiers reflects the success of Bolshevik propaganda (Salahetdinov 2001).

The Bolsheviks' other Muslim allies were the Muslim National Communists, whose leader was Mirsaid Sultan-Galiev (1880–1939), as well as some segments of the *Jadid* movement (Zenkovsky 1960, 189). All these Muslims joined the Bolsheviks because of their bad memories of tsarist conquest and hoped that the Bolsheviks would grant them more freedom.

The approach of Russia's Muslims toward the Bolsheviks reflects an old pattern of behavior on their part, namely that Russian Muslims always have sided with reformist elements in Russia. From 1905 to 1907, when hopes for political reforms in Russia had risen, Russia's Muslims joined the liberal group called the Kadets.[4]

However, not all of Russia's Muslims believed the Bolsheviks' propaganda. Moreover, the Bolsheviks' promise of freedom for Muslims had the paradoxical effect of reviving and intensifying Muslims' old aspirations for political freedom and independence. Thus, Muslims of the South Caucasus declared the formation of the Republic of Azerbaijan in 1918, and several autonomist movements were formed in Central Asia, such as the Alash Orda (the nation of Alash; Alash is the mythical ancestor of Kazakh people), which declared the autonomy of the Kazakh people in 1917 and the Ittifaq al Muslimin (the Union of Muslims), which declared the autonomy of the Muslims of Turkestan in November 1917 (Haghayeghi 1995, 17). Meanwhile, the Crimean Tatars elected a constituent assembly that adopted a constitution for the region, assumed legislative authority over the internal affairs of the Crimean Tatars, and appointed a military commander to oversee all Tatar military units in the Crimea and ministers for foreign affairs and war (Pipes 1997, 79–81). In the Volga-Ural regions Tatars and Bashkir formed the Idel-Ural Republic.

Because of the expressions of desire for independence on the part of Russian Muslims, in practice, the Bolshevik forces, notwithstanding their promises, treated Muslims more harshly than other minorities, especially in Central Asia. Thus the Tashkent Soviet formed by the local supporters of the Bolsheviks dismantled Muslim organizations, including mosques, and embarked on atheistic propaganda and profaned mosques. This behavior contributed to the outbreak of the Basmachi revolt in 1918, which continued with diminishing degrees of intensity until the mid-1930s (Broxup 1983, 57–83).

The Bolsheviks' attitude toward the Muslims hardened even further once they succeeded in defeating their opponents and consolidating their hold on power. Consequently, the new Soviet regime in a reversal of earlier policies proceeded to dismantle Muslim political organizations formed after the October Revolution.

Moreover, the USSR's nationality policies developed by Joseph Stalin were based on the principle of dividing the Muslims and other ethnic groups and leaving substantial ethnic and religious minorities in the newly formed republics. This policy was against Muslims' desire for greater consolidation of Muslim-inhabited areas into large political units. For example, in 1918, many of Russia's Muslims, especially those with pan-Turkist tendencies, had wanted to create three large Muslim political units (Hunter 2004, 27).

Russia's policy of Muslims' fragmentation along ethnic lines was complemented by its policy of cultural fragmentation by, among other things, developing dialects of a single language into full-blown separate languages. This policy of ethnic, cultural, and territorial fragmentation has been primarily responsible for the ethnic, sectarian, and border disputes and cultural competition that has plagued the Muslim-inhabited parts of the post-Soviet space.

THE USSR'S ANTIRELIGIOUS POLICIES: IMPACT ON ISLAM AND MUSLIMS OF CENTRAL ASIA AND THE CAUCASUS

The USSR's strategy against Islam, which began to be implemented in 1924, was based on the following principles:

1. The eradication of Muslim judicial and educational institutions;
2. The elimination of the clerical establishment's financial independence by dismantling the *waqf*; and
3. Anti-Islam propaganda.

Of course, all religions were anathema to the Bolsheviks and to the Communist ideology, but Islam was especially targeted because it was viewed as particularly reactionary and backward.[5] This view of Islam and Muslims predated the advent of the Bolsheviks to power and is the reason many of the Bolsheviks' tactics against Islam resemble those of the tsarist era.[6]

Another reason for the Soviet authorities harshness toward Islam was what they saw as Islam's all-embracing nature and its pivotal role in the Muslims' individual and collective identities. This aspect of Islam was seen as threatening to the Bolsheviks' project of building a new socialist society and a new Soviet Man (*sovestskii Chelovek* or *Homo sovieticus*). *Homo islamicus* had to be eradicated in order to make room for *Homo sovieticus*.

As a result of this policy the number of functioning mosques in Russia/Soviet Union had dropped from 26,000 during the tsarist times to 1,312 and the number of clergy from 45,000 to 8,000 (Hunter 2004, 28–9). These numbers were further reduced in the following decades. In 1979, there were only 300 registered mosques and the number of clergy had sharply declined (Hunter 2004, 34).

The Second World War affected Soviet Muslims' fate in a contradictory fashion. On the one hand, the defection of a large number of Muslim Soviet soldiers to Germany brought Stalin's wrath on them. On the other hand, it forced Stalin to make some concessions to Muslims such as creating the Muslim Spiritual Boards in order to regulate Muslims' religious affairs and allowing the resumption of instruction at the Mir Arab Madrassa in Bukhara.

The Soviet Unions' policies toward Islam and Muslims had several highly negative consequences for Muslim-inhabited regions of the Soviet empire including the following: the deterioration of Islamic learning and quality of Islamic clergy; the undermining of these regions' mostly *Hanafi* traditions and the growing influence of nonindigenous Islamic traditions, as people from Central Asia and the Caucasus went to other parts of the Islamic world to get religious education; and the erosion of the credibility and, hence, influence of the official clergy among the people because of their perception of them as mere government officials and part of the corrupt Soviet bureaucracy.[7] Since the 1970s, and increasingly in the 1980s, this phenomenon has led to the peoples' gravitation toward unofficial figures educated in the Arab World and often with radical tendencies.

Meanwhile, folk Islam, which is deeply mixed with local traditions, continued to flourish, aided by the fact that the paradoxical nature of Soviet nationalities policy failed to foster a strong sense of nationalism and statehood (Hunter 2004, 34). Moreover, in these regions, there had always been a close link between a sense of nationalism and Islam as reflected in the following comment by the antireligious Dagestani writer S. Muslimov writing in 1983: "It is well known that religious revivals are tightly linked to nationalistic trends. The nationalistic revivals often take on a religious appearance, whereas religious revivals are propagandized under the flag of defense of national traditions" (Muslimov 1983, 38–39).

THE IMPACT OF OUTSIDE DEVELOPMENTS ON SOVIET MUSLIMS: THE IRANIAN REVOLUTION AND THE SOVIET-AFGHAN WAR

Developments in the neighboring countries of the Soviet Union's Muslim-inhabited regions significantly impacted the evolution of Soviet Muslims. In particular, they led to their greater politicization. One such development was the Iranian revolution, but the most influential factor was the Soviet invasion of Afghanistan and the ensuing Soviet-Afghan war. Four consequences of the Afghan war were particularly significant in Islam's revival and its politicization in the USSR. First, the war introduced Central Asian members of the Soviet army to their fellow Muslims in Afghanistan. Some found fighting against other Muslims difficult, thus leading the Soviets to refrain from sending Central Asian soldiers to Afghanistan.

Second, the war galvanized both the West and the Muslim World against the Soviet Union and led to an all-out propaganda campaign against the USSR through a variety of radio programs aimed at Soviet Muslims from stations based in Muslim and Western countries. Even the Islamic Republic of Iran, despite its anti-Western ideology, in its broadcasts to the Soviet Union's Muslim-inhabited areas took a consistently anti-Communist line, and its leaders condemned Soviet policies toward Islam in Central Asia and the Caucasus (Bennigsen 1982). These broadcasts had an important impact on the perceptions of the Soviet Muslims, the extent of which can be judged by the intensity of Soviet responses. In 1980, the head of Azerbaijan's KGB general Zia Yusuf Zade denounced ". . . the harmful influence of imperialist propaganda on certain representatives of our [Azerbaijani] intelligentsia and youth" (Dzhabarov 1985).

Third, the war led to the establishment of direct contacts between Afghan Mujāhidīn and their Pakistani and Saudi supporters and the

Central Asian Muslims. Hundreds of illegal students in Central Asia and elsewhere in the USSR went to study in religious schools and train in the military camps set up by Pakistan's General Zia ul Haq with the financial assistance from Saudi Arabia and Western support. In these camps they learned about Islamic movements, their ideology, and their tactics. P. I. Dzhabarov characterized what was taught in these camps as "Western anti-Communist reactionary Islamic clericalism" and accused Pakistan's Jama`at-i Islami, Turkey's Society for Struggle against Communism, and the Muslim Brotherhood of being involved in these activities. Fourth, the Soviet Union's withdrawal from Afghanistan shattered the perception of its invincibility and enhanced Islam's image as an effective instrument of resistance and liberation.

ISLAM, NATIONALISM, AND TRANSNATIONALISM IN CENTRAL ASIA AND THE CAUCASUS ON THE EVE OF SOVIET COLLAPSE

The outpouring of nationalist and Islamic sentiments in Central Asia and the Caucasus during the period of Perestroika and Glasnost starkly exposed the failure of the Soviet Union's policy of creating a *Homo sovieticus* and eliminating religious and ethnonationalist feelings.

When independence was thrust upon Central Asian and South Caucasian republics a need emerged to find a new framework for social and political organization and a new basis of state legitimacy. In this context, Islam, nationalism, and transnationalism emerged as the main competitors to fill the ideological vacuum left by the Soviet demise as reflected in the names and agenda of various political parties that had emerged during Perestroika.

During the period of Perestroika a number of Islamically oriented political groups emerged in Central Asia and the Caucasus including the following: the Alash Party (named after Alash the mythical ancestor of the Kazakhs) in Kazakhstan, which also had pan-Turkist tendencies; the Edolat Party (Justice Party) in Uzbekistan; and the Islamic Rebirth Party, which was initially conceived as extending to all Muslim-inhabited regions of the USSR. The founding conference of the Islamic Rebirth Party was held in Astrakhan in June 1990 and its first leader was a native of Dagestan. However, the party soon splintered and its center of gravity shifted to Central Asia, especially to Tajikistan and Uzbekistan (Hunter 1996).

In Azerbaijan in the South Caucasus the following were the most significant of Islamically oriented political parties: the Party of Islam (Islam Partiyasi), a Shi`a party whose leader was Hadji Hadji Agha; the Muslim Brethren (Islam Ghardaslari); and Union of Young Muslims (Javan Islam Chilarin Birliki; Hunter 1994, 78–79). In the postindependence period most of these parties either disappeared or refashioned themselves under different names. Other Islam-based political groups and parties also emerged, most of which were forced underground.

THE CONSOLIDATION OF SECULAR AUTHORITARIANISM: ISLAM'S RADICALIZATION

The demise of the USSR did not result either in the democratization of Central Asia's politics or in the dismantling of the Soviet era bureaucracy and nomenclature, with few exceptions and for brief periods, such as the presidency of Abul Fazl Elcibey in Azerbaijan (1992–1993).

Consequently, the political trend in Central Asia and Azerbaijan has been toward the establishment of authoritarian rule under the so-called presidents for life and with a growing tendency toward dynastic presidencies. Notably, in Azerbaijan, Heidar Aliev's son, Ilham, assumed presidency after his father's death, and it is widely speculated that the daughters of Uzbekistan's Karimov and Kazakhstan's Nazarbaev have presidential ambitions.

The result of this development has been the closure of the democratic and parliamentary road for political engagement for independent political parties, including those that are Islamically oriented. Indeed, the latter have fared worse than others, as they have been banned.

The inability to pursue their goals through legal and legitimate channels has led these parties either to resort to violence—as was the case in Tajikistan with the IRP (Islamic Rebirth Party), which led to a long and highly destructive and debilitating civil war from 1992 to 1997[8]—or to transform into radical movements engaged in terrorist acts—as happened with the Edolat Party, which became subsumed under the Islamic Movement of Uzbekistan (IMU).

The Edolat Party and its leader Tahir Yoldash were particularly bitter against Islam Karimov, Uzbekistan's Soviet era leader who sought and won election to the presidency against the nationalist Muhammad Salih. Their bitterness was due to the fact that Karimov used them in his 1992 campaign against Salih by promising him and his supporters to establish an Islamic state. According to an article in Ferghana.ru, dated October 15, 2007, during a meeting on December 12, 1991 organized by Yoldash and his supporters in which demands were made that Uzbekistan be declared an Islamic state, Islam its official religion, and elections be postponed so that Muslims could field their own candidates, Karimov promised he would implement all their demands once elected president. Because of this promise the Namangan region voted for Karimov. One year later, all of Tahir Yoldash's supporters were behind bars and he himself had fled to Tajikistan, where he became involved in the civil war on the side of the Islamic opposition.[9] There is none.

Interestingly, during the first years of his presidency Karimov tried to use Islamic symbols to enhance his government's legitimacy. For instance, during his inauguration he swore on a Qur'an. He also performed the *Umra Hajj* pilgrimage during a visit to Saudi Arabia in 1992. However, he soon embarked on a policy of suppressing all Islamic groups, including nonpolitical groups, and bringing the entire Islamic establishment of the country under governmental control.

Pushed out of Uzbekistan by Karimov in 1996, Yoldash, together with another founder of the Edolat Party, Jumma Namangi, and the remnants of another Islamically oriented group, Islom Lashkeri, formed the IMU (Baran 2006, 25–27). IMU established close connections with the Taliban and Al-Qaeda, and between 1999 and 2001 it was responsible for a number of terrorist attacks in Uzbekistan and Kirghizstan.[10]

After the US invasion of Afghanistan the IMU moved to Pakistan, where it got into conflict with the Taliban. Reportedly, Jumma Namangani was killed as a result of US air strikes, but so far his death has not been confirmed.[11] In Tajikistan, the IRP is legal but powerless.

The radicalization of Central Asia's Islamic movements has also been abetted by the region's economic problems, notably unemployment, especially among the youth, and poverty. In fact, there appears to be a clear correlation between the economic situation and Islamic militancy. Thus the Ferghana valley, which comprises parts of Uzbekistan, Kirghizstan, and Tajikistan and is one of Central Asia's poorest regions, has most of the region's Islamists. It is also in this region that new movements such as the Hizb al-Tahrir have developed roots by attracting the followers of the region's indigenous, but now banned, Islamic groups as well as new recruits.[12]

In addition to economic problems, government repression, pressure on nonpolitical Muslims, and a general disregard for human rights enhance the appeal of more radical interpretation of Islam. The Andijan revolt in 2005 and the way the Uzbek government dealt with it best exemplify the combined result of economic problems and repression.[13]

Until the last few years Kazakhstan had denied the existence of any radical Islamic groups except in the country's southern parts, which are inhabited by ethnic Uzbek. However, recent evidence has emerged of the development of radical groups among ethnic Kazakhs, some of which reportedly have links with Al-Qaeda. One such organization, which reportedly was discovered and dismantled, was the Jamā'at of the Central Asian Mujahedin. Reportedly the group included four female members trained as suicide bombers. Another group is the "Takfirchilar, in other words Takfiris. They are also known as Hizb ul Takfir. This group reflects the influence of Salafi, the Takfiris of Pakistan, and Afghanistan (Azizian 2005). Among recent groups also with alleged links to Al-Qaeda is the Jaish ul Khalifa, which was involved in terrorist acts in 2012. In general Islamic radicalism has been spreading in Kazakhstan. For example, it is no longer limited to the southern part of the country, which borders Uzbekistan and has spread to the western parts of the country (see Jacob Zenn, "Salafists Challenge Kazakh Future," Asia Times, September 19, 2012).

In Azerbaijan, meanwhile, the interaction between Islam and politics has become more complex. The fact that the majority of the Azerbaijanis are Twelver Shi'as, coupled with the Republic's historical and cultural ties with Iran, which goes back to pre-Islamic times, and political differences between the Republic's leadership and Iran has meant that the government has had a more hostile attitude toward Shi`ism.

As part of its policy of countering Iran's influence, at one point during the second Chechen war (1999–2000),[14] the government of Heidar Aliev encouraged the spread of Salafi Sunni Islam in Azerbaijan. Other influences came through Turkey, especially the Nourjou (Followers of Said Nursi) and its offshoot, the Gullen movement (Cornell 2006). The result has been growing sectarian tensions in Azerbaijan, which according to one Azerbaijani professor has even affected universities where Shi`as and Salafi students do not talk to each other.[15]

However, as the number of Salafis grew in Azerbaijan, and in 2006 were estimated between 7,000 and 15,000, the government began to curb their activities (Cornell 2006). Thus the Abu Bakr mosque in Baku where the Salafis congregate was closed for a period in 2001. So far the Salafis have concentrated on religious prose-lytization and staying out of politics. According to some non-Salafi sources, two factors, namely the country's economic and political problems notably, high youth unemployment and corruption plus the availability of resources probably coming from the Persian Gulf region, help the Salafis to attract disadvantaged and disaffected youth (Cornell 2006).

The Abu Bakr mosque has also been accused of recruiting fighters for Iraq, Chechnya, and Afghanistan. In 2006, it was revealed that one of the Guantanamo prisoners was an ethnic Azeri by the name of Polad Safarov. Reportedly, he worked as translator for Bin Laden and was recruited through the Abu Bakr mosque. The mosques' Imam Gamet Suleimanov denied having ever met Safarov (Day.az 2005).

The Azerbaijani government has tried to promote the Gullen movement in the Sunni-inhabited regions of the north as a counterweight to the Salafis, but so far without much success. The Salafis have an extremist wing, which calls itself the Jeyshullah (Army of God). It has been engaged in terrorist acts, including against the followers of Hare Krishna, and was suspected of wanting to bomb the American embassy in Baku. The leaders of the group were imprisoned in 2000 (BBC 2005).

The Azerbaijani government's treatment of Shi`a activists has been much harsher. For example, unlike the Abu Bakr mosque, which was reopened and its imam remained free, the Shi`a Jummă mosque was closed in 2003 and its Imam Ilgar Ibrahimoghlu was tried and condemned to five years in prison. Part of this harsher treatment has to do with factors noted above and partly because Ibrahimoghlu became involved in politics, including during the 2003 presidential elections. His combining of religious discourse with that of human rights is also viewed as more threatening. In fact, the charge against him was that he had mixed religion and politics and thus had endangered the country's secular political system. Ibrahimoghlu has studied in Iran and in Poland where he became acquainted with Polish resistance during Soviet times. Earlier, he was compared to Muqtada Al Sadr of Iraq, but now he is a human rights activist and has created an organization called the Center for Protection of Religious Freedoms.

Another controversy erupted in 2009–2010 when the Azerbaijani government tried to demolish the Fatima Al Zahra Shi`a mosque. However, it had to back down in the face of strong Shi`a opposition. Key Iranian clerics, notably Ayatullah Safi Golpayegani, also intervened. He wrote a letter to the president of Azerbaijan admonishing him that he should protect the Shi`a faith and not undermine it.

Interestingly, the upshot of the government's anti-Shi`a policies has been a revival of Shi`ism and its influence has been referred to as the "Shi'a Renaissance" by the Azerbaijani professor Altoy Gayushov ("Islamic Revival in Azerbaijan").

The other Shi'a political group is the Islamic Party of Azerbaijan, not to be confused with the Party of Islam, which was formed during Perestroika. The party was formed in the mid-1990s. In 1995–1996 it suffered a crackdown reportedly because it wanted to acquire paramilitary forces (Rotar 2000). When riots broke out in 2003 in the village of Nardaran, which was the party's power base, its chairman Haci Ali Akram Aliev was arrested and the party's registration was revoked. The party has tried to register again and has staged protests but no avail. The IPA (Islamic Party of Azerbaijan) has leftist leanings as well and is part of a coalition of leftist parties. Neither the supporters of Ibrahimoghlu, nor the IPA have been accused of involvement in terrorist acts. Haci Ali Akram died in 2012.

In Azerbaijan, the question of Islamic veiling has also become very controversial, reflecting a growing secular-religious divide in the country. There have been a number of protests against banning the Hijab in Azerbaijan, which often also have political undertones.

ISLAM, POLITICS, AND CONFLICT IN THE NORTH CAUCASUS

The dynamics set in motion by Gorbachev's reforms and the competition, which ensued within the Soviet Union's top leadership between first Gorbachev and the hardliners led by Ligachev and later between Gorbachev and Yeltsin, also deeply affected developments within those Muslim-inhabited regions of the USSR, such as Tatarstan Bashkortostan and in the North Caucasus (Hunter 2004).

In both of these regions, Islam experienced a significant revival as did ethnic nationalism and pro-independence movements. The pro-independence movements were greatly encouraged by Yeltsin's statement to the Soviet minorities to get as much sovereignty as they could handle.

However, after the Soviet demise, Yeltsin resumed power and he set upon reining in the independence-seeking republics. In the case of Tatarstan, this goal was achieved through negotiations. However in Chechnya Moscow's efforts led to a bloody war, first from 1994 to 1996 and then from 1998 to 2000.

THE CHECHEN WAR AND THE POLITICIZATION AND RADICALIZATION OF ISLAM IN THE NORTH CAUCASUS

The Chechen conflict was the outcome of a complex set of factors including the following: power struggles and rivalries in the Kremlin; personal animosity between Boris Yeltsin and Dzhokar Dudaev, the Chechen leader and hence Yeltsin's unwillingness to reach a negotiated settlement with Chechnya as it had with Tatarstan; tribal rivalries in Chechnya; and regional and international competition over pipeline routes.

Initially, Islam played little or no role in the start of the Chechen war (Isayev 2007). For instance, Dudaev was not a particularly observant Muslim. Rather he was a product of the Soviet system and as a fighter pilot had participated in the carpet bombing of Afghanistan, a fact that Russia used to undermine his Islamic credentials once he discovered Islam as a useful instrument in his quest for power and Chechen independence (Praslov 1995, 5). Moreover, during his first year in office, he ruled out the establishment of an Islamic state in Chechnya. In an interview in August 1992 he told the *Literaturnaya Gazeta*, "Where any religion prevails either the

Spanish inquisition or Islamic fundamentalism [will] emerge" (Malashenko 1995, 46). For this reason, the 1992 constitution of the self-declared Chechen Republic stated that "religious organiza-tion are separate from state organs, administer their affairs autono-mously, and operate independently from state organs" (Chechen constitution, 35).

It was first the Russian intrigues and then the war that led to the flow of foreign fighters to Chechnya, including the so-called Afghan Arabs, namely the veterans of the Soviet-Afghan war, and figures such as the Saudi-born Samir Abdullah Al Suweilam, known as Emir Khattab, that finally led Dudaev and even more so leaders who came after him to resort to Islam both as an instrument of legitima-tion of power and as a way to foster opposition to Russia. Later Islam became a tool in the power struggles of various Chechen leaders who engaged in a race to prove which one was more Islamic.[16]

Consequently, in August 1994, the National Congress of the Chechen People gave Dudaev the authority to declare an Islamic uprising in the tradition of the Gazavat of Imam Shamil the legendary Chechen leader, and in September 1994, Dudaev declared Chechnya an Islamic state (Interfax News Agency 1994). He also created an Islamic Battalion to counter the activities of opposition forces supported by Moscow and indicted that he wanted to apply the *Shari'ah* (Dunlops 1998, 149).

After the Russian campaign began in full, the Chechen public's identification with Islam became stronger. When after Dudaev's assassination in April 1996 Zelimkhan Yanderbaev became Chechnya's acting president, he declared that he would "take the lead in a war, in a 'jihad' of the Chechen people in the name of Allah and in the name of the freedom of the Chechen people" (Hirst 1996). The end of the first round of the Russo-Chechen war in 1996 did not stop the increasing use of Islam for political purposes. Thus shortly after the signing of the Kasavyurt agreement in August 1996, Yanderbaev abolished secular courts, created a supreme *Shari'ah* court, and implemented a criminal code for Chechnya based on the *Shari'ah*, which included the death punishment for apostasy (Akaev 1999; Human Rights Watch 1997).

Maskadov, who became president in January 1997, went even further and renamed Chechnya the Islamic Republic of Ichkeria (Walker 1998). The only country to recognize it was Afghanistan under the Taliban.

Since the end of the intense period of the Chechen war in 2003 and the relative stabilization of the Republic under the presidency of Ramazan Kadyrov, the son of Chechnya's former Imam Ahkmed Kadyrov, the use of Islam as an instrument of political legitimation has continued.[17] In 2009, Kadyrov imposed strict Islamic law as part of its strategy of combating the influence of extremist Muslims and gaining legitimacy for his arbitrary rule. He has also resurrected local traditions, which have nothing to do with Islam, such as honor killing (Berry 2009).

Between the period of the end of the first Chechen war and the start of the second, militant Islamic groups with a very strict inter-pretation of Islam and with links to Afghanistan and Pakistan gained influence in Chechnya and in the neighboring Dagestan (Hunter 2004). In fact, it was their activities that provoked the second Chechen war.

CONTAGION EFFECT OF CHECHNYA: DAGESTAN

In view of the close ties between the peoples of Dagestan and Chechnya the contagion effect of Chechnya was first felt in Dagestan, where Arab missionaries and fighters who had come to Chechnya crossed over into Dagestan. This led to the emergence of a number of extremist groups, some of which engaged in terror attacks on Russian targets. For example in November 1996 in Kaspisk in Dagestan, a bomb destroyed a building housing Russian border guards. Then in April 1997, a bomb exploded in the railway station in Russia's Krasnodar Krai and two bombs in May 1997 in the railway station in Pyatigorsk in the Stavropol Krai.

The activities of the Islamists went beyond terrorist acts, and in summer 1998 had led to the creation of miniature Islamic states known as "autonomous *Shari'ah* territory" in the villages of Karamakhi, Shabanmakhi, and Kadar. In addition, Chechens who had always had always considered Dagestan as part of Chechnya and nurtured the hope of uniting Chechnya and Dagestan and possibly the rest of the North Caucasus within an Islamic state set out to prepare the groundwork for it. In August 1997, the first deputy prime minister of Chechnya, Movladi Ugodov, organized a meeting of more than thirty representatives of Muslims of the North Caucasus in order to found the Nation of Islam along the lines of earlier efforts dating back to the period immediately following the falloff of the tsarist regime to create a political entity made of all the so-called mountain peoples of the North Caucasus.

However, differences that emerged between those loyal to Dagestan's traditional Islam highly influenced by Sufism and the new followers of Salafi Islam resulting in fighting, division, and rivalries among Muslim leaders of Chechnya and between them and Dagestanis prevented the success of these plans.

In the summer of 1999, large-scale warfare erupted in the North Caucasus when several thousand Muslim militants together with volunteers from Central Asia, Arab countries, and others crossed into Dagestan with the stated objective of liberating Dagestan from Russian rule and establishing an Islamic state. The Chechen President

Aslan Maskhadov condemned this incursion, but Chechen commander Shamil Basaev and Khattab assumed the leadership of the invading forces. This attempt by Muslim militants to push Russia out of the North Caucasus was a main reason for the second Russian war. However, it must be added that some sources have claimed that plans for a second war on Chechnya were prepared by Russia by March 1999 well before the Dagestan incursions (Felshtinsky 2008, 105). Dagestan's extreme poverty, ethnic, tribal, and sectarian divisions, plus the region's massive corruption contributed to the success of extremist ideas and groups (International Crisis Group 2008).

The Chechen conflict also deeply affected the Republic of Ingushetia through the influx of Chechen refugees. At their peak the number of Chechen refugees in Ingushetia was 240,000. Influx of refugees also brought with it militants who flourished in Ingushetia, which had since the 1990s experienced a degree of Islamization (Kantysheva 2007). Some of these militants created military wings such as the Ingush Regiment, whose members were disarmed by Russian forces in 1999 (Jamestown Foundation 1999).

However, it was Ingushetia's extreme poverty, massive corruption, and harsh treatment of its people by its president, Murat Zyazikov, that led to the growth of radical Islamic cells known as *Jama`at*, which finally resulted in full-scale civil war in 2007. The Russian overreaction to activities of a group of Islamists imported from Chechnya, including a massive security operation in July 2007, contributed to the worsening of the crisis.

The assassination of a major opposition figure, Magomad Yevloyev, further intensified the conflict. Finally in October 2008, Dmitry Medvedev dismissed Zyazikov. The new president, Yunus Bek Yevkurov, is said to try to rule with a softer hand (Pan 2009). However, the fighting with Islamist groups continued in 2009, and reportedly between January and March 2009 led to fifty people, including twenty-seven rebels, eighteen policemen, and two civilians, being killed. On June 10, the deputy chief justice of the Ingush Supreme Court Aza Gazgireeve was killed, and on June 13 former Deputy Prime Minister Bashir Aushev was wounded (BBC 2009; AP 2009). Then in August 2009 the police department in Nazran was attacked. In general it is agreed that Ingushetia has replaced Chechnya as the main trouble spot in the North Caucasus (Eckel 2009).

The Chechen conflict and the general revival of Islam have also spread to Kabardino-Balkaria, Adygeya, and Karachaevo-Cherkessia (Matveeva 1999; East-West Institute 2001). The *Jama`at* movement has been particularly active in Kabardino-Balkaria. Some of them such as the Yarmuk Jama`at have been engaged in violent actions (McGregor, 2006). Russia's efforts to reign in these groups, including the closing of mosques in Kabardino-Balkaria, especially after the school siege and massacre in Beslan in the neighboring Republic of North Ossetia in 2004 (Borovnikov 2005), finally led to the so-called Nalchik uprising when in October 2005, 200 militants targeted security forces in the Republic. After that the government closed down many mosques and has, according to some sources, targeted not only armed militants but also observant Muslims charging them of subscribing to what it calls Wahhabism (Fagan 2008). However, these actions do not seem to have eradicated extremist groups, and in January 2008 it was reported that militants had killed the director of the region's antiorganized crime directorate Colonel Anatoly Kyarov (Radio Free Europe Radio/ Liberty 2009).

The causes of the growth of extremism and violence related to it, in addition to the contagion effect of the Chechen conflict, are strikingly similar to those in other North Caucasian republics, namely, poverty, unemployment, ethnic divisions, and rampant corruption. According to one report, "The economy of the entire North Caucasus is based on black market industries and theft from the Federal government." Moreover, "the local government elite [are] interested in self-enrichment and for ordinary people there is nothing" (Finn 2005). However, the desire for independence from Russia, especially in the absence of any economic benefits, should also be factored in as inspiration for violent acts.

The upsurge in Chechen-inspired violence against Russian targets in 2010, especially the devastating attack on the Moscow underground by the so-called Black Widows (women who have lost husbands or close relatives as a result of Chechen conflict) in March 2010, reflected the fragility of the country's Russian-imposed calm ("Russian Security Services Hunt 21-Strong 'Black Widow'cell," TIMESONLINE, March 30, 2010).

Violence in the North Caucasus continued unabated throughout 2012. In Dagestan sectarian differences, notably between the Salafis and the Sufis have even increased the risk of civil war (see "UPDATE1-Islamic Cleric Warns of Civil War In Russia's Dagestan" *Reuters*, August 29, 2012).

This same has been true of other North Caucus republics, notably Kabardino-Balkaria and Ingushetia (see "Russia Police Launch Deadly Raid in Kabardino-Balkaria," BBC News-Europe, September 20, 2012).

Observers expect more violence in the region as the 2014 winter Olympics, which will be hold in Sochi, is approaching. However, the event might encourage the development of other resorts in the region, which could tackle some of area's poverty and unemployment issues and possibly help reduce militancy and violence (see "Russia Boosts Ski Resort Security after Attacks," BBC News-Europe, February 21, 2011).

CONCLUSIONS

Given Islam's deep roots in Central Asia and the Caucasus, its central role as an identity marker both at individual and collective levels, and its traditional role as the basic ethical and legal framework for collective life in Central Asia and the Caucasus, its emergence and a degree of its politicization after the Soviet collapse were inevitable.

However, Islam's radicalization, which has occurred to varying degrees, was not inevitable and has directly resulted from the evolution of Central Asia's and the Caucasus's governments and polities in an authoritarian direction, economic degradation, corruption, and repression of even peaceful practice of Islam.

In addition, regional and international developments, most importantly the Afghan civil war and growth of extremist Islamist groups in Pakistan and Afghanistan, have further helped radicalize Islam in Central Asia and the Caucasus.

Moreover, Central Asia and the Caucasus is paying a price for the Russian/Soviet practice of undermining these regions' traditional and more moderate Islam, which has created an opportunity for more strict and/or radical interpretations of Islam and their proponents from the Arab World and South Asia to find their way into these regions. This, too, has given a radical tinge to the interaction of Islam and politics in Central Asia and the Caucasus.

NOTES

1. Some parts of Central Asia and the Caucasus did not come under Russian control until the 1860s. In the Caucasus the present-day republic of Azerbaijan was conquered by 1828 after Iran's defeat in the second round of the Russo-Iranian wars (1824–1822). The conquest of Chechnya, Dagestan, and the neighboring areas was not completed until the late 1860s. Some parts of Central Asia such as Turkmenistan came under Russian control also later in the nineteenth century.

2. Sufi brotherhoods were very important in Islam's preservation. See Bennigsen and Wimbush 1985 and Bennigsen and Broxup 1983.

3. For an account of the Chechen resistance to Russia's advance, see Broxup 1992.

4. For a brief summary of Muslim political activism under the tsars, see Hunter 2004, 16–22.

5. For a list of Islam's flaws, according to the Bolsheviks, see Hunter 2004, 29.

6. Alexander Pushkin's characterization of the Muslim holy book the Qur'an as "a collection of new lies and old stories" sums up the Russian view of Islam. Cited in Karam 1999, 31.

7. Since the time of Catherine the Great, Russia has tried to bring Muslim religious organizations under state control. See Hunter 2004, 9–10. For recent times, see Hunter 2004, 102–120.

8. The Tajik Civil war, however, had many complex reason behind it, including the unwillingness of the Communist era Khojandi Uzbek economic and political elite to share power plus Uzbek and Russian manipulation. See Gretsky 1995.

9. "Tahir Yoldash: US Fiasco Is Nearing. Look Us up in Washington" 2007.

10. Among attacks attributed to the IMU was the abduction of a Japanese geologist in 1999 in Kyrgyzstan and the 2002–2003 bombings in Bishkek and Osh.

11. "Notes on Jumma Namangani" 2001.

12. Reportedly in 2005 there were at least 2000 to 3000 HT members in Kyrgyzstan. See Azizian 2005 and Kasmali 2000.

13. For background to the Andijan events, see Raman 2005 and on the Akramia movement that was involved in the events, see Rotar 2005.

14. The year 200 marks the end of the active phase of full-scale warfare. The insurgency continued well into 2005 and is still alive, albeit in a diminished way.

15. Conversation with the Azeri professor visiting Georgetown University.

16. One such race was between Aslan Maskadov, who became Chechnya's president in January 1997, and Shamil `Basaev, who broke away from him.

17. It is hard to establish the exact date of the end of the Chechen war. However, the passing of a new constitution in April 2003 that granted Chechnya a significant degree of autonomy is a reasonable date. However, it must be added that insurgent groups are still active in the republic.

REFERENCES

Akaev, Vahid. 1999. Religious and Political Conflict in the Chechen Republic of Ichkeria. *In Political Islam and Conflicts in Russia and Central Asia*, ed. Lena Jonson and Murad Esenov. Luela, Sweden: Center for Social and Political Studies. Available at: http://www.ca-c.org/dataeng/m_akaev.shtml.

Avtorkhanov, Abdurakhman, and Marie Broxup, eds. 1992. *The North Caucasus Barrier: Russian Advance towards the Muslim World*. New York: St. Martin's Press.

Azizian, Rouben. 2005. Islamic Radicalism in Kazakhstan and Kyrgyzstan: Implications for the Global War on Terror. *CSRS discussion paper* 5, no. 56 (September 2005).

Baran, S. Zeyno, Fredrick Starr, and Svante E. Cornell. 2006. Islamic Radicalism in Central Asia and the Caucasus: Implication for the EU Silk Road Paper. Central Asia and Caucasus Institute. Available at: www.silroadstudies.org.

Bennigsen, Alexandre. 1982. Soviet Islam since the Invasion of Afghanistan. *Central Asian Survey* 1: 2.

Bennigsen, Alexandre, and Marie Broxup. 1983. *The Islamic Threat to the Soviet State.* New York: St. Martin's Press.

Bennigsen, Alexandre, and S. Enders Wimbush. 1985. *Mystics and Commissars: Sufism in the Soviet Union.* Berkeley: University of California Press.

Berry, Lynn. 2009. Chechen Leader Imposes Strict Islamic Code. *New York Times*, March 2.

Borovnikov, Vladimir. 2005. The Beslan Massacre. *ISIM Review* 15.

Broxup, Marie. 1983. The Basmachi. *Central Asian Survey* 2: 57–83.

Chechen Constitution, Article IV. 1992. In Paul Henze. 1995. *Islam in the North Caucasus: The Example of Chechnya.* Santa Monica, CA: RAND.

Cornell, Svante E. 2006. The Politicization of Islam in Azerbaijan. *Silk Road Paper.* Washington, D.C.; Central Asia—Caucasus Institute. Available at: www.silk-roadstudies.org.

Dawisha, Karen, and Helene Carrere D'Encausse. 1983. Islam in the Foreign Policy of the Soviet Union. In *Islam in Foreign Policy,* ed. Added Dawisha. Cambridge: Cambridge University Press.

Day.az. 2005. Interview with the chair of Azerbaijan's State committee for Religious Affairs, Rafiq Aliev. Available at: http://www.Day.az.

Dunlop, John. 1998. *Russia Confronts Chechnya: The Roots of a Separatist Conflict.* Cambridge: Cambridge University Press.

Dzhabarov, I. B. 1985. Religious Propaganda Aimed at Muslims in USSR: Ideological Subversion. *Soviet Uzbekistani.*

Eckel, Mike. 2009. Ingushetia Is Latest Kremlin Trouble Spot. *Associated Press,* October 4. Available at: http://www.sfgate.com/cgi-bin/article.cgi?f=c/a/2009/10/04/MNRG19TFIE.DTL&type=p.

Fagan, Geraldine. 2008. Russia: Detained and Tortured for Faith, Kabardino-Balkaria Muslims Claim. *The Muslim News,* August 18. Available at: http://www.muslimnews.co.uk/news/news.php?article=14722.

Felshtinsky, Yuri, and Vladimir Pribylovsky. 2008. *The Age of Assassins: The Rise and Rise of Vladimir Putin.* London: Gibson Square Books. Sergei Stepashin's interview with the Russian minister of interior.

Finn, Peter. 2005. Crackdown Provoked Shootout in Russia. *Washington Post,* October 15.

Gretsky, Sergei. 1995. Civil War in Tajikistan: Causes, Developments and Prospects for Peace. In *Central Asia: Conflict, Resolutions and Change,* ed. Roald Z. Sagdev and Susan Eisenhower. Washington, DC.

Haghayeghi, Mehrdad. 1995. *Islam and Politics in Central Asia*. New York: St. Martin's Press.

Hirst, David. 1996. Chechen Leader Pledges Holy War. *The Guardian*, April 16.

Hunter, Shireen T. 1994. *The Trans-Caucasus in Transition: Nation—Building and Conflict*. Washington, DC: Center for Strategic and International Studies.

Hunter, Shireen T. 1996. *Central Asia Since Independence*. Westport, CT: Praeger.

Hunter, Shireen T. 2004. *Islam in Russia: The Politics of Identity and Security*. Armonk, NY: M.E. Sharpe.

Isayev, Ruslan. 2007. The Role of Religion in the Chechen Conflict. *Prague Watchdog*, May 27. Available at: http://www.watchdogcz/?show=000000-000015-000006 -000017&lang=1.

Kantysheva, Saida. 2007. Islam in the Life of Ingush People Today. *Prague Watchdog*, December 20. Available at: http://www.watchdog.cz/?show=000000-000015 -000006-000026&lang=1.

Karam, Patrick. 1999. La Russie et l'Islam: entre alliance et rejet. *Les Cahier de l'Orient* 41.

Kasmali, Gulnara. 2000. Will Fighting Return To Batken, Kyrgyzstan This Spring. Central Asia—Caucasus Institute, *Analyst*, March 15. Available at: http://www .cacianalyst.org/?q=node/533.

Malashenko, Alexei. 1995. Does Islamic Fundamentalism Exist in Russia. In *Muslim Eurasia: Conflicting Legacies*, ed. Yaakov Roi. London: Frank Cass.

Matveeva, Anna. 1999. *The North Caucasus: Russia's Fragile Borderland*. London: Royal Institute of International Affairs.

McGregor, Andrew. The Movement in Kabardino-Balkaria. *Terrorism Monitor* 3: 7.

Muslimov, S. 1983. In Search of Persuasiveness—Some Pressing Problems of Atheistic Propaganda [in Russian]. *Sovetskiy Dagestan* 6: 38–39.

Pan, Phillip P. The Softer Hand. *Washington Post*, November 12.

Pipes, Richard. 1997. *The Formation of the Soviet Union: Communism and Nationalism, 1917–1923*. Cambridge, MA: Harvard University Press.

Praslov, Alexander. 1995. Contazvedka e Chechne [Counterintelligence in Chechnya]. *Argumenty i Fakty* 5.

Raman, B. 2005. The Andijan Uprising: The Background. South Asia Analysis Group, Paper no. 1380, May 14. Available at: http://www.southasiaanalysis .org/%5Cpaper1380.html.

Rotar, Igor. 2000. Islamic Fundamentalism in Azerbaijan: Myth or Reality. *Jamestown Prism* 6.

Rotar, Igor. 2005. Uzbekistan: What Is Known about Akramia and the Uprising. Oslo, Norway, *Forum 18 News Service*, June 16, 2005. Available at: http://www .forum18.org/Archive.php?article_id=586.

Salahetdinov, Muhammed. 2001. Unification under the State Roof. *Nezavisimaya Gazeta* 74.

Walker, Edward. 1998. Islam in Chechnya. *Contemporary Caucasus Newsletter*. University of California at Berkeley, Issue 9.

Zenkovsky, Serge A. 1960. *Pan-Turkism and Islam in Russia*. Cambridge, MA: Harvard University Press.

1994. Detailsof Mobilization Edict. Interfax News Agency's *Daily News Bulletin*. Moscow, August 11.

1997. *Civil and Political Rights in Post-War Chechnya*. Human Rights Watch.

1999. Muslim Extremists Suspected in Vladikavkaz Blast. *Jamestown Foundation Monitor* 5: 58 (March 24).

2001. Islamic Groups Active in Adygeya: East-West Institute. *Russian Regional Report* 6: 37.

2001. Notes on Jumma Namangani. November 19. Available at: http://www.spongobongo.com/em/em9873.htm.

2005. Azeri God's Army Cult Members to Stand Trial for Murder. *BBC Monitoring Central Asia*, July 25.

2007. Tahir Yoldash: US Fiasco Is Nearing. Look Us up in Washington. *Ferghna.ru*, October 15. Available at: http://enews.ferghana.ru/article.php?=id2167.

2008. Russia's Dagestan: Conflict Causes. *Europe Report*, 192, International Crisis Group, June 3.

2009. Attack on Russian Regional Leader. *BBC News*, June 12. Available at: http://news.bbc.co.uk/1/hi/world/europe/8112109.stm.

2009. Another Killing in Region Bordering Chechnya. *Associated Press (New York Times)*, June 10. Available at: http://www.nytimes.com/2009/06/14/world/Europe/14ingushetia.html?_=1&ref=world.

2009. Four Years after Nalchik, How Strong Is insurgency in Kabardino—Balkaria. *Radio Free Europe Radio/Liberty (RFE/RL)*, October 13. Available at: http://www.rferl.org/articleprintview/1850860.html.

Chapter 5

Islam and Politics in South Asia

IRFAN AHMAD

THE ARGUMENT

July 2010: The Bangladesh government led by Mrs. Sheikha Hasina
of the Awami League (AL), considered a "secular" party, ordered
libraries and mosques to remove from their shelves books written
by Abu al-A`la Mawdudi (1903–1979), founder of South Asia's
Jama`at-e Islami (hereafter Jamaat). Justifying the ban, a govern-
ment official remarked that Mawdudi's books promoted "militancy
and terrorism" (BBC 2010).

September 2007: The Conservative Party leaders from London's
Tower Hamlets took to the streets demanding that the Whitechapel
Idea Store not stock books written by Islamic authors. According to
BBC (2007) Phil Briscoe, the local councilor said that "although
Mein Kampf by...Hitler might be available in libraries for educational purposes, some books by Islamic thinkers were too offensive
to have a place in libraries." He further explained that "some of
the books have been written by convicted...terrorists and in those
cases those books are not suitable to be...in a public library." The
libraries of Tower Hamlets had become a hot topic in the media
after a think tank, the Centre for Social Cohesion, reported that they
stored books by authors like Mawdudi and Egypt's Sayyid.

Clearly, both in Bangladesh and the United Kingdom there were local factors behind the ban on books by authors like Mawdudi. However, at work were also supralocal factors in these two global sites. Behind the ban on Mawdudi's books, apparently more dangerous than *Mein Kampf*, is a larger premise: a liberal, geostrategic understanding of Islam. Central to this understanding is the notion that religion in general and Islam in particular is a storehouse of illiberalism, extremism, and intolerance. Qutb's borrowing from Mawdudi's (Shepard 2003) and Berman's (2003) christening in the *New York Times* of Qutb as "The philosopher of Islamic terror" further exemplifies such a framework. Integral to this framework is the reigning assumption that for Islam to become "moderate" and "secular" it must be liberalized and reformed. Holding that Muslims are outside of modernity, Rushdie (2005) advised them that "a new Reformation will bring your faith into the modern era."

Based on an analysis of the changing trajectory of Jama`at-e Islami in Bangladesh, India, and Pakistan, I critically examine Breman's and Rushdies's line of thought also manifest in dominant academic writings. Demonstrating the folly, even poverty, of such a framework, I aim to offer a nuanced (and possibly a fresh) understanding of Islamism[1] in south Asia. Central to my argument is that we begin to study the transformative moments in Islamism for it marks a shift from discourse to the profoundness of praxis. Here I am persuaded by Trouillot's (1995, 89) observation that the Haitian revolution "thought itself out politically and philosophically as it was taking place," in a context where "discourse always lagged behind practice." Critical to this is the process of transformation. Since it is a process, Islamism is not a frozen entity immutably locked into a dead end. In showing this dynamism, my aim is to destabilize the premise that while liberalism is open to self-examination, thinkers like Mawdudi and their followers are not. My contention is to the contrary. It seems that Muslims and Islamists such as Ghannoushi (1998) have reexamined many of their assumptions; it is liberals like the French secularist (see Bowen 2007), notably the philosopher Blandine Kriegel (Foucault's associate, advisor to Jacques Chirac, and the chair of the High Integration Council), and Indian academics like Zoya Hassan who are obstinate on not reexamining theirs. This obstinacy has only been accentuated with the ascendance of the post-9/11 paradigm I have called "securitization" of Islam (Ahmad 2009, 6). "Alarmed" at the recent initiative (2010) by Indian Jamaat to participate in democracy, Zoya Hassan described it as "unfortunate and uncalled for." The electoral participation of a "Muslim party [Jamaat]," she warned, "will trigger polarization" and derail "progress" and "growth" (*Times of India* 2010). Javed Anand, a fellow liberal and secularist, was more explicit: "They [Jamaat] want to weaken the political culture from within by first being part of it.... The Jamaat too will launch into its true mission once it gets a firm political foothold in India" (*Times of India* 2010, 6; see also Anand 2012). This paranoia resembles the West's where commentators justified the denial of Islamists' participation in democracy saying Islamists believed in "one man, one vote, one time" (Esposito 1994, 21).

I am also critical of the dominant post-9/11 framework, which often links south Asia's Jamaat with terrorism. Before 9/11, most writings on Jamaat referred to it as "antiprogressive," "antisecular," "conservative," "militant," "fundamentalist" (e.g., see Agwani 1986; Ahmed 1994; Bahadur 1977; Hassan 1997); post-9/11 these terms either stand mostly replaced or subsumed under "terrorism." In discussing radicalization in the Middle East, Juergensmeyer (2003, 84, 261n53) suggests how Mawdudi's thought contributed to terrorism. He, however, does not dwell on the complexity of Mawdudi's thoughts and transformation of his politics and how Jamaat in south

Asia underwent change. If Juergensmeyer's position is reflective of the post-9/11 *global discourse* on terrorism, Ganguly's (2006, 5) is the *Indian version* informed by the geopolitics of south Asia. Despite denial by Jamaat of its any ties with militant organizations and categorical condemnation of terrorism (Bangladesh Jama`at-e Islami 2012; Kabir 2006, 190ff.), Ganguly directly links the 2005 Bangladesh bomb blasts to Jamaat and its student wing, Islami Chhatra Shibir (ICS), arguing how Bangladesh, in cahoots with Pakistan's Inter Service Intelligence (ISI), is set to harm India through terror. Indeed there is a striking resonance between a position such as Ganguly's and *The Washington Post's*, which, in 2006, called Bangladesh "a new regional hub of terrorist operations that reach into India and Southeast Asia." To Karlekar (2005, 264), Bangladesh is on the path of Talibanization led by Jamaat; hence the title of his book: *Bangladesh: The Next Afghanistan?*[2]

Against this dominant post-9/11 framework of securitization of Islam, I argue that political Islam as represented by Jamaat in south Asia is neither monolithic nor static. My main contention is that Jamaat has significantly transformed itself in India, Bangladesh, and Pakistan and thereby become an important participant in politics of the respective nation-states. However, an understanding of Jamaat in south Asia will remain skewed as long as we continue to see it through the mere lenses of the nation-states because globalization entails transcending the (neo)relist premise of the nation-state as the ultimate unit of analysis.[3]

This essay is divided into three sections. In the first, I historically situate the formation of Jamaat and its ideology as formulated by Mawdudi in colonial India. In the second section I discuss Jamaat's monumental transformation in postcolonial India. Continuing this theme of transformation, I discuss how Jamaat also changed in Pakistan and Bangladesh. For reasons of space, my discussion of

Jamaat in three different countries will be purposively brief. I will conclude with some general observations on the modality and nature of Islamist politics in south Asia, especially on its ideological templates.

FORMATION AND IDEOLOGY OF JAMA`AT-E ISLAMI

The founder of Jama`at-e Islami, Mawdudi, did not have a fully fledge traditional Islamic education. Till the age of nine, he received his education in Urdu, Persian, Arabic, *fiqh*, law, and *hadith* through private tutors.[4] At eleven he went to a madrasa, but studied there only briefly. Largely self-taught, Mawdudi was well versed in the history and theology of Islam as well as modern social sciences, including Marxist literature. In his diagnosis of Muslims' decline, he held that Muslims lagged behind Europe because the latter produced philosophers such as Fichte, Hegel, Comte, Adam Smith, Malthus, Rousseau, Voltaire, Goethe, Herder, and so on. He admired the Turkish writer Halide Edip (a judgment he later revised), who visited India in the mid-1930s. His call to Muslims was to master modern sciences. Not only were his thoughts influenced by modern sciences, to some *ulema*, Mawdudi's appearance was also modern. Until 1936 he remained clean shaven. In 1938, when Manzoor Nomani, a Deoband theologian, first met Mawdudi in Delhi he was "jolted" to see an Islamic figure with too short a beard. He was also aghast at his "Western (*angrezi*) hair" (Ahmad 2009, 54). A year before he founded Jamaat, he wrote:

> In the age of *jāhiliyat* I have read a lot on ancient and modern philosophy, science, history, economics, politics, etc. I have digested a whole library. But when I read the Qur'an with open

eyes then I realized, by God, that whatever I had read was insignificant. Now I got the root of knowledge. Kant, Hegel, Fichte, Marx, and all other great philosophers of the world now appear to me as kids. (Ahmad 2009, 53)

Mawdudi initially supported the Indian National Congress (formed in 1885; hereafter the Congress) and published biographies of Mohandas Gandhi and Madanmohan Malaviya, a Hindu nationalist leader. He edited *Muslim*, the Urdu organ of the Jamiatul-Ulema-e-Hind, an organization of *ulema* (Islamic theologians) allied to the Congress. During the late 1930s, however, Mawdudi felt disillusioned with Congress's nationalism, which, he held, was far from secular as it favored Hindus against Muslims. The turning point in Mawdudi's career was the elections of 1937 and the subsequent formation of provincial ministries by the Congress. He equated the policy of the ministries (1937–1939) with heralding a "Hindu raj." He criticized the ministries for marginalizing Muslims and for gradually making them Hinduized. Another reason for his distrust of nationalism stemmed from the dismemberment of the Ottoman Empire by Western powers along nationalist lines.

After his turn to Islamism, Mawdudi began to interpret Islam unconventionally. He held that Allah sent his prophets to establish a state. Human history, he held, was the history of a contest between Islam and *jāhiliyat*, the period of ignorance before the Prophet Muhammad. For Mawdudi, *jāhiliyat* was a system with many forms. Politically, it expressed itself in human sovereignty. In 1941, Mawdudi founded Jamaat for the "establishment of an Islamic state (*hukumat-e-ilāhiya*)." Since the Muslim League, the party fighting for Pakistan, did not have as its goal the establishment of a *sharia*-based state, he described future Pakistan as "infidel state of Muslims." Secular democracy, to Mawdudi, was *haram* for it replaced divine sovereignty with human sovereignty. To Mawdudi, Muslims should boycott what he called *jāhiliyat, ṭāghūti niẓām*—an anti-Islamic polity.[5] The Jamaat's constitution obligated its members to boycott the following:

- Assemblies that legislate secular as opposed to sharia laws;
- An army that kills "in the path of non-God";
- Secular judiciary; also banks based on interest;
- Teaching or studying in colleges or universities, including Muslim ones, that serve *jāhiliyat*; Mawdudi called them "slaughterhouse[s]"; and
- Services and jobs in the antigodly system (Mawdudi 1942, 178–182).

Such a call to its members as the above, however, did not mean that Jamaat nursed no relations with non-Muslims. It sometimes invited non-Muslims to its open sessions. The Hindu leader Gandhi, for instance, took part in its regional meeting in Patna, the capital of Bihar, in April 1947 and appreciated Jamaat. Three months after this meeting, India was partitioned in August 1947. With Partition, Jamaat was divided into Jamaate-Islami Hind (India) and Jama'at-e Islami Pakistan. Mawdudi himself chose Pakistan. Jamaat was a tiny organization with a rather limited influence among educated people. In undivided India of 1947, its members numbered less than 1,000 (Ahmad 2009, 63).

THE TRANSFORMATION OF JAMA'AT-E ISLAMI ACROSS SOUTH ASIA

With this admittedly synoptic historical account of Jamaat's formation, in this section I describe important turning points in Jamaat's transformation across south Asia. Central to this descriptive analysis is my argument of how in each nation-state Jamaat gradually came to join the very mainstream (regarded as largely "un-Islamic") that its constitution of 1941 sought to replace with its own Islamic system (*niẓām*). I begin with Indian Jamaat. Next I will discuss the transformation of Jamaat in Pakistan and Bangladesh.

India

After India's Partition, Jamaat continued to stick to its earlier position. In 1951–1952, India held the first parliamentary elections in which non-Jamaat Muslims participated, but Jamaat did not. Abullais Islahi Nadwi, the first *amīr* (president) of Jamaat in independent India, justified the boycott of elections along Mawdudi's lines. "In whatever form you participate in elections," he wrote, "you are flouting the commandments and guidance of sharia" (Nadwi 1951, 63). However, before the third elections in 1962, a debate began in Jamaat's *markazī majlis-e-shura* (the central consultative council, hereafter *shura*). It centered on the (il)legitimacy of democracy and secularism. In July 1961, *shura* set up a committee to determine whether elections could be used for pursuing *iqāmat-e-dīn* (establishment of religion). The Qur'anic phrase *iqāmat-e-dīn* was the new objective Jamaat had inserted into its constitution after Partition to replace its earlier mission of *ḥukumat-e-ilāhiya*—a change also incorporated in the constitution of Pakistani (and Bangladeshi) Jamaat. The committee concluded that Jamaat could compete in elections to make the Indian constitution Islamic. The *shura* accepted the recommendation and went on to pass two separate resolutions that had no reference to *iqāmat-e-dīn* but to the legitimacy of participating in the elections, both as voters and candidates. It did not lift the ban on voting for the 1962 elections.

In 1967, however, *shura* approved some criteria under which members could vote. The most important criterion was that the candidate "must believe in the *kalima* [i.e., he must be a Muslim]" and regard legislation against Allah as *haram*.

Debate continued with many in *shura* favoring a lifting of the ban on voting. The issue, however, remained in limbo until emergency imposed by Mrs. Indira Gandhi in 1975. When the emergency was lifted and elections announced, Jamaat ended its ban, disregarding its earlier criteria (e.g., the candidate must be a Muslim), and participated actively. The foremost criterion now was that the candidate must favor the "restoration of democracy," because Mrs. Gandhi had banned most parties, including Jamaat. The debate further continued until 1985 when *shura* permanently lifted the ban against voting. Since 1985, participation in and defense of democracy and secularism by Jamaat only intensified.

Another significant development since 1985 took place in April 2011 when Jamaat backed the formation of a political platform aiming to contest elections, the Welfare Party of India (WPI). Mujtaba Farooque and Qasim Rasool Ilyas—well-known leaders of Jamaat—are president and secretary, respectively, of WPI. WPI will work "not only for Muslim causes," Farooque said, "but will try to deliver justice to…every section of India…" (Beyondheadlines 2011a). WPI's objectives (Beyondheadlines 2011b) are as follows:

- "Party will aim at the establishment of a welfare state. Party believes that sufficient nutritious food, decent clothing, proper shelter, essential healthcare, and elementary education are among the fundamental human rights…"
- "…women should get full growth and development opportunities with full protection to their femininity."

- "Party envisages a society where all cultures have full opportunities to thrive...in...India, all cultural entities should get fullest opportunities, resources, and powers to protect and promote their cultural values and identities."

Five of WPI's sixteen national leaders were non-Muslims—Christian and Hindu—as well as women (*Indian Express* 2011). How WPI will fare in elections is yet to be seen. However, what is less uncertain is that formation of WPI by Jamaat marked yet another watershed. So significant was it that some critics suggested if WPI's aim was "the establishment of a welfare state" there was no need for it for this objective was already enlisted in India's constitution and espoused by a plethora of parties. One such critic (Sayyid 2011) hoped that by forming WPI, Jamaat would not get derailed from its goal of *iqāmat-e-dīn* and that it would maintain a balance. Another critic (on other side of ideological divide) disapproved of WPI, saying that though its aims were noncommunitarian, one of its leaders spoke of establishing *niẓām-e-muṣṭafā*, Prophetic Order (TwoCircles.Net 2011).

How and why did Jamaat undergo such a monumental change? Clearly, democracy played a key role. This factor distinguished Indian Islamists from their counterparts in the Middle East, where neither nonauthoritarian secularism nor democracy is well established.[6] It was manifest in the Muslim public's disavowal of Jamaat, which also played itself out in the realm of democratic politics. Critical to this disavowal is what I call an "ideological dissonance" between Jamaat's agenda and political subjectivity of Muslim public. Before I might get misunderstood, let me clarify that I do not take democracy as external to Islam. Contra many Muslims (including the Deoband ulema), Mawdudi regarded, as a matter of contingency, *a specific form of democracy* as external to Islam (see Conclusion).

Democracy not only acted upon Jamaat externally but did so internally as well. The whole debate was conducted on the principle of majority votes. This democratic basis of decision making became so crucial that even the Islamic creed, the *kalima*, from which, according to Mawdudi, the voting ban had been derived, was put to vote, and clinched by a majority vote. The debate took place within two fora—*shura*, and *majlis-e-numāindegān*. While *shura* existed in Mawdudi's time, the *majlis* did not. However, the role of *shura* significantly changed in postcolonial India. Mawdudi, as the Jamaat's *amīr* had been the sole decision maker. The task of the *shura* whose members he himself nominated had been to advise the *amīr*. With Jamaat's democratization, *shura* members began to be elected, and the *amīr* had to accept decisions made democratically by *shura*. The formation of *majlis* was a new development. It is like the Jamaat Parliament elected directly by its members who, on occasions, are required to vote.

During its transformation, Jamaat indeed became more democratic than other political formations. None of the Indian parties ever practice democracy internally as the leaders in the party are *not elected*; they are *selected* or *nominated* along multiple ascriptive grids: family, caste, region, religion, and so on. In contrast, Jamaat practiced democracy internally but opposed democracy (elections) externally. Jamaat's initial opposition to democracy was *not intrinsic* but *contingent* as its subsequent transformation shows.

Pakistan

In line with his opposition to future Pakistan as an "infidel state of Muslims," until 1949 Mawdudi regarded it as a sign of *jāhiliyat*, because it based itself on popular sovereignty.[7] In 1948 the western Punjab government mandated its employees to pledge an oath to the state. Mawdudi forbade his party members to do so until the state became Islamic. In March 1949 Pakistan's Constituent Assembly passed the Objectives Resolution acknowledging God's sovereignty. Only then did Mawdudi (2003) no longer regard contesting elections or joining the Pakistani army as *haram* (Nasr 1994, 121–124, 246n40; Nasr 1996, 42; Niazi 1973, 106–13). Mawdudi justified many changes in his position by grounding them in the so-called Islamic orientation of the Pakistani state and its constitution.

Soon after Pakistan's formation Mawdudi was jailed because he had dubbed Pakistan's covert support (1948) to insurgents in Kashmir while upholding a ceasefire with India un-Islamic and reeking of "hypocrisy." The government accused Mawdudi and Jamaat of sedition. Released in 1950, Mawdudi activated his party, which, in 1951, took part in provincial elections but with little impact. This failure, *inter alia*, led to fights in Jamaat with many leaders leaving the party. The 1953–1954 anti-Ahmadi mobilization aimed at pressuring the government to declare Ahmadis as "non-Muslims" brought Mawdudi to prominence. Mawdudi himself did not play a role in that mobilization; he wrote a pamphlet on Ahmadis. However, with the crackdown on anti-Ahmadis activists a military tribunal charged Mawdudi with "sedition" and served him a death sentence (later annulled).

With the installation of military rule in 1958 by the Sandhurst-trained General Ayub Khan, the government became harsher toward Jamaat. Khan's developmentalist and modernizing regime (1958–1969) viewed figures like Mawdudi at best as nuisance. Jamaat's offices were closed, its publications curbed, and its leaders monitored. Mawdudi himself was jailed in 1964 and again in 1967. So opposed was he to the regime that Mawdudi backed a woman, Fatimah Jinnah, against Khan for the presidency of Pakistan. The result, however, went against Mawdudi's wish. Mawdudi's support to Fatimah Jinnah contradicted his earlier position according to which Islam did not allow a woman to lead the government. Yet, it is important to note that Mawdudi was perhaps the first South Asian thinker to open his party's membership to women on the basis of the Qur'an and *hadith*. Jamaat's constitution even urged women to "disobey the commands of their husbands and guardians if such commands were sins against Allah." In Pakistan, Jamaat women now contest elections. In India Jamaat's *shura* discussed in 1999 women's absence in leadership (in 2000, of 4,776 members, 303 were women). It proposed that Jamaat's president be empowered to nominate women to assume leadership roles (Ahmad 2008; Nasr 1996).

The outcome of Pakistan's national elections of 1970 was not favorable to Mawdudi either: only four of his party members won. In the war of 1971, Mawdudi's sympathy lay with the army as he did not support Bangladesh's independence. Following the breakup of Pakistan, Mawdudi battled against Zulfikar Ali Bhutto's (d. 1979) socialist populism, including his land reforms. As an alternative, Mawdudi intensified the movement for the installation of *niẓā m-e muṣṭafā*. So effective did the slogan of *niẓā m-e muṣṭafā* become that, after the 1977 military coup, General Zia-ul-Haq (d. 1988) made it the cornerstone of his regime. Mawdudi died in 1979; more than a million people participated in his funeral (Nasr 1996).

In Pakistan's national elections of 1988, 1990, 1993, Jamaat won seven, eight, and three seats, respectively (Nasr 1994, 208, 213; Gardezi 1994, 111). It boycotted the 1997 elections. Electorally, student wings of Jamaat on college campuses have performed better than the parent party. In Pakistan and Bangladesh, Jamaat's student wings exercise considerable influence and are known to have resorted to violence. Compared to mainstream parties, Jamaat activists, however, are often seen, even by their nemesis, as less corrupt and more dedicated to their cause. Seeking to transform itself into a

popular party, in the 1990 elections Pakistani Jamaat used the repertoire of mass mobilization: posters, billboards, sloganeering, mass
rallies, processions, film songs, and by some accounts, even dancing
to the tune of popular numbers. It also floated an allied organization, Pāsbān, whose membership was open to a broad range of
Muslims, including those who did not stick to *sharia*. The 1990
elections demonstrated that Jamaat was no longer the party for
the few pious Muslims averse to using the modern repertoire of politics. In early 1940s, claiming that Jamaat's structure and workings
were "exactly like those of the party Muhammad had established,"
Mawdudi had described processions, flags, sloganeering, resolutions, addresses, and so on as poison (Ahmad 2009, 72; Moten 2003).

Under Qazi Hussain Ahmed's leadership (1987–2009), Jamaat
underwent many changes. To broaden its reach, Jamaat began to
speak to lower strata hit hard by liberalization of economy. When
General Musharraf's military regime intensified privatization of
higher education, Jamaat opposed it. Ahmed invited even leftists
to jointly resist globalization. Contra Mawdudi, Ahmed attacked
feudalism and advocated the interests of the dispossessed. During
her post-9/11 fieldwork, Iqtidar (2011b) observed how under liberalization there was a shift in Jamaat from a preoccupation with the
state to the society/market. Led by Ahmed, Jamaat became a stri-
dent critic of West-led war on terror terming Pakistan's role therein
as a surrender of its sovereignty (Iqtidar 2011a, 57–58, 90–94;
Outlook 2002). Supporting the bill aimed at fusing the two posts
of president and army chief, in Pakistan's Senate, a pro-Musharraf
senator argued that Musharraf's bid for fusion was true to the teachings of the Qur'an and practices of caliphs. Along with other parties,
Jamaat decried that move with opposition shouting "no-no, shame-
shame" (BBC 2004). Among others, the basis of Jamaat's opposition to Musharraf's regime was its antidemocratic foundation. In

the 2002 elections, which took place in the shadow of the war on terror and the invasion of Afghanistan, Jamaat participated as a key partner of the coalition of six religion-based parties, Muttaheda Majlis-e-Amal (MMA). MMA scored notable victory forming government in two out of four provinces: the Northwest Frontier Province, which borders Afghanistan and Baluchistan. MMA won 62 of the 342 seats in the National Assembly (International Crisis Group 2003; Iqtidar 2011a, 164n8). Jamaat boycotted the 2008 elections, arguing that under the military regime they would be far from fair.

Like India's, the case of Pakistan's Jamaat shows that democratic processes make Islamists more democratic/moderate. Over the decades, Pakistani Jamaat's "commitment to the electoral politics" has only increased and it is by now an important participant in the mainstream politics. That some associated with Jamaat later turned cold toward democracy and advocated violence—consider Hafiz Mohammad Saeed, founder of Jamaat-ud-Dawa (Iqtidar 2011, 4–5)—does not mean the dilution of Jamaat's won commitment to democracy and mainstream politics. Individuals influenced by Jamaat adopted a variety of positions, including what some Westerners might call "moderate" and "liberal." An apt example is the group of scholars-activists led by Javed Ahmad Ghamidi, a former Jamaat member and a known intellectual of Pakistan (see Masud 2007; Amin 2010).

Bangladesh

Pakistan consisted of two territorially separate wings—West and East. In 1947, East Pakistan had just one Jamaat member.[8] The West Pakistan Jamaat sent Rafi Ahmad Indori to East Pakistan to build Jamaat; under his leadership a committee of four members was formed in 1948. In 1951, Abdu Rahim of Barisal was made East Pakistan's *amir*. By 1954, Jamaat had thirty-eight members (Rahim 2001, 237). Jamaat expanded when, in 1955, Ghulam Azam (b. 1922), a college lecturer with degrees in Islamic studies and political science, joined Jamaat. A student leader, Azam was twice elected as secretary of the prestigious Dhaka University Student Union (DUSU; 1947–1949). He was an early leader of the Bangla language movement. Against the imposition of Urdu, protests broke out in East Pakistan. As DUSU's secretary, Azam submitted a memorandum to Prime Minister Liaqat Khan demanding that Bangla should also be recognized as an official language.

While lecturing (1950–1955) at Carmichael College, Rangpur he joined Tablighi Jamaat and later Tamaddun Majlish. Azam then began reading Mawdudi's books. Fascinated with his "scientific approach to politics," Azam learned Urdu to read wider Islamic literature. He gained Jamaat's membership in jail; in 1952 and 1955 he was jailed for criticizing the government. To work for Jamaat, he resigned his lectureship position. In February 1956, Mawdudi took a forty-day trip to East Pakistan. In his speech in Dhaka, he advocated recognizing Bangla as an official language and criticized the biases East Pakistan faced under the federal government. Azam accompanied Mawdudi during his trip. In 1957, Azam was elected as secretary—a post he held until 1967 when he became Jamaat's *amir* (Husain and Siddiquee 2004, 386; Rahim 2001, 239; Bangladesh Jama`at-e Islami 2001). During Ayub Khan's rule (1958–1969), Jamaat in East Pakistan too faced the government's ire. In 1963, Azam was imprisoned. Under repression, Jamaat continued its services like establishing schools and clinics and giving funds to the poor. In 1969 Jamaat's membership had risen to 425; associates constituting 40,000. Of 425 members, 40 were full-time workers and most of its leaders had a modern, not madrasa, education (Banu 1994, 86).

Against Ayub Khan's regime, with the AL, National Awami Party, and others, Jamaat joined coalitions like the Combined Opposition Parties (1964–1965), the Pakistan Democratic Movement (1966–1968), and the Democratic Action Committee. However, to the intensified movement for linguistic-regional autonomy in East Pakistan Jamaat stressed that only a return to Islam would keep the country united. Meanwhile, Khan resigned in March 1969. Yahya Khan, a military general reputed for heavy drinking, assumed power and promised elections in 1970. In the 1970 elections, led by Sheikh Mujiburrahman, AL scored a clinching victory in provincial (East Pakistan) and national assemblies over Pakistan People's Party (PPP), and Jamaat which won just four seats. Democratically speaking, AL was destined to form a government at the federal level. However, neither Yahyah Khan nor PPP allowed it on the pretext that it would lead to Pakistan's breakup. Jamaat urged Yahya Khan not to discriminate against Mujiburrahman and allow him to form a government. As Khan rejected its demand, Jamaat accused the general of unadulterated biases against AL and undemocratic favor to PPP (Kabir 2006, 64–66; Nasr 1994, ch. 7).

With the undemocratic denial to AL to form a government, the protests in East Pakistan intensified. The Pakistani military intervened to crush Bengali nationalists, after which Jamaat stopped working as an intermediary between AL and Yahya Khan and sided with the latter. Ghulam Azam, as Jamaat *amīr*, supported the army against the "enemies of Islam" (Nasr 1994, 168–169). During the war ensuing between the army and Mukti Bahini (freedom fighter), the army killed more than 2.5 million people (Ahmad 2012c).[9] With India's military intervention against Pakistan, in 1971, Bangladesh was born. The new state adopted the four-pronged ideology of

Bengali nationalism, socialism, secularism, and democracy (Hashmi 2004, 45). In 1972, the state banned Jamaat (and other religion-based parties) thereby aggravating its credibility crisis. In 1973 Azam's citizenship was cancelled for his "collaboration" with Pakistan. In fact Azam's controversial citizenship became part of Jamaat's subsequent history. When Bangladesh was declared as a state, Azam was in Pakistan from where he went to the United Kingdom and returned to Bangladesh in 1978 holding his Pakistani passport. On return, he applied for citizenship, which was granted in 1994 (Moniruzzaman 2009, 90). Earlier, in 1991, Azam's citizenship had become a major issue after Jamaat elected him as its *amīr*. While the liberal-secular section formed a people's court and served him the death sentence for his alleged role in the 1971 war, AL and its allies unleashed violence against Jamaat (Banu 1994, 82; Moniruzzaman 2009, 90). In 2012, the Bangladesh government led by AL again imprisoned him (and others) after the International Crimes Tribunal (ICT) dismissed his bail plea (bdnews24.com 2012).

With the assassination of Bangladesh's founder, Mujiburrahman in 1975—he had turned authoritarian and installed one-party rule—there began the military rule of Ziaurrahman (1975–1981), who legalized parties like Jamaat, substituted secularism in the Preamble with "absolute trust and faith in the Almighty Allah," and, in 1978, formed Bangladesh Nationalist Party (BNP). In 1981, Ziaurrahman was killed. From 1982 to 1990, General Hussain Ershad ruled the country. Faced with a legitimacy crisis, in 1988 he made Islam the official religion (Riaz 2010, 47–49). Most "secularist" accounts depict Jamaat as a supporter of the army; rarely is it recognized that Jamaat opposed Ershad's military regime to institutionalize democratic processes. So hostile was Ershad to Jamaat that, in 1988, he vowed to "eliminate" Jamaat. After Ershad's open call for violence four Jamaat activists were killed (Ahmad,

Mumtaz 1991, 503). However, in 1990, Ershad's regime fell because, among other reasons, with en-block resignation of Jamaat's ten members from Parliament, the popular protests against the regime had heightened (Ahmad, Irfan 1991; Rahim 2001, 250).

After Ershad's fall, in the 1990 elections, Jamaat garnered 12 percent of the total votes and won eighteen seats (Parliament comprises 300 members) and backed the formation of BNP government led by Khaleda Zia, wife of Ziaurrahman. However, soon Jamaat sided with BNP's archrival, AL (Kabir 2006, 16–17). The ties between Jamaat and AL thus grew strong. In the 1996 elections Jamaat suffered a loss, winning only three seats. Sheikh Hasina of AL formed the government. After the elections, Jamaat, however, supported BNP. In October 2001 elections that took place in the shadow of war on terror, as a constituent of the alliance headed by BNP, Jamaat won seventeen seats and for the first time two of its members became ministers under Khaleda Zia's leadership. Contrary to the popular view that Jamaat promoted terrorism, the BNP-JI government banned four militant outfits and arrested and put on trial several of their leaders. In the subsequent elections, held in December 2008, Jamaat performed abysmally, as it won only two seats; AL scored a landslide victory to form the government. Jamaat's defeat notwithstanding, it received 3.16 million of the votes (Riaz 2010, 56, 61).

IN LIEU OF A CONCLUSION: SOME OBSERVATIONS

As the publications on Islam boomed after 9/11, the description of Islamic fundamentalism, even Islam, as innately violent, antisecular, antimodern, a nemesis of democracy, and Manichean/dualistic intensified (Antoun 2010; Appleby 2002; Benjamin and Simon 2002; Juergensmeyer 2003; Mazarr 2007; Philips 2006). Scholars presented different timelines of the "radical Islam." While some (e.g., Cook 2005, 209) traced the 9/11 attacks back to the early seventh century when the Prophet Muhammad began to receive revelations, others (e.g., Wiktorowicz 2005) traced their antecedents to the writings of the fourteenth-century theologian Ibn Taymiyah. Scholars also presented a list of figures fundamental to radical Islam; virtually all such lists included, among others, Hassan al-Banna, Qutb, Osama Bin Laden, and yes Mawdudi (Appleby 2002, 506 ff.; Hansen 2009, 16; Lincoln 2003, 16).

I disavow such a line of argumentation on two counts. First, it is a selective secularist account of fundamentalism (see Casanova 2009; Van der Veer 2008); in itself it is dualistic even as it sees dualism only in its other, the fundamentalists. Dualism is indeed important to modern politics as articulated by Schmitt (2006) in his notion of politics as drawing a boundary between foe and friend and also manifest in post-9/11 "liberal" politics that saw Muslims as good and bad, moderate and fundamentalist/terrorist (Mamdani 2002; Ali 2002). Manichean worldview is equally central to "New Atheism," itself precipitated, inter alia, by Muslims' presence in the West (Prothero 2010, 322ff). Thus in Bangladesh's secularist history of independence there are only two types of people—freedom fighters and collaborators. The "secular" Awami League that led the independence movement obviously regards itself as freedom fighter and considers Jamaat, sometimes many who disagree with AL, as collaborator. Second, theoretically it is unproductive to posit secular as obverse of fundamentalist; they are not neatly separate. The secular constitutes the religious (fundamentalist) in such a way that it is difficult to distinguish one from the other (Euben 1999). As Asad (2003, 2006) rightly observes, even as secularism is premised on the separation of religion from the state, it is the state that regulates and determines what is religious. From the perspective I maintain, the recurring citation of Mawdudi that he held a depersonalized and totalizing view of religion does not add much because such language is not exclusive to fundamentalists; secularists speak similarly. To the French secularists during the 1970s and later, "*True laïcité,* based on the scientific spirit and democracy, provides a complete critical knowledge of reality *and encompasses all aspects of human life and activity*" (Roy 2007, 107, italics mine).

An important secularist critique of Mawdudi has been his notion of "theodemocracy," often posited as antithetical to democracy. Theodemocracy, I suggest, is not the obverse of democracy. On the contrary, a certain type of democracy fashions theodemocracy. Let me explain this as most academics also hurriedly quote Mawdudi to prove fundamentalists' (also Muslims') intolerance to democracy. What they do not ask is why Mawdudi coined the term theodemocracy. Initially, Mawdudi championed democracy. It was the majoritarian democracy of the Congress, especially the anti-Muslim practice of the 1937 Congress ministries, which drove him to theodemocracy. In 1938, he wrote:

> The real issue is not if the political system... should proceed along the path of democracy because no sane person can disagree with the spirit of democracy... The spirit of democracy and this specific notion of democracy based on the principle of a single community should not be conflated.... It is assumed that because of a shared geography... we Hindus, Muslims, Untouchables, Sikhs, Christians are a single community and thus the grammar of democracy should be such that the state should be run by the wish of the majority community. Based

on this ideology, the constitution has been framed.... Such a situation has made Hindu nationalism and Indian nationalism coterminous. In contrast to Hindus, our condition is such that under this [democratic] system our community aspirations remain unfulfilled; rather they are...killed because we are in a minority (Ahmad 2011, 466).

This long quotation demonstrates that "fundamentalists" like Mawdudi have not been averse to democracy as such, but to a *specific kind of* democracy. It is this Islamic-modernist impulse that made Mawdudi recast his view. He came to hold that the state "should not be enforcer of the sharia but the implementer of the will of the people" (Nasr 2006, 107). Clearly, such a notion of democracy will not be the replica of Western democracy for the simple reason that democracy has no singular origin or form (Ahmad 2011; Esposito and Voll 1996). The trajectory of Jamaat in India, Bangladesh, and Pakistan I analyzed here shows the democratizing dynamic and impulse Jamaat is at once promoter and product of. Against the view that "Islamic fundamentalists" do not engage in "the quotidian political struggle" and valorize "self-sacrificing acts of true believers willing to risk everything to vanquish *jahiliyya* society once and for all" (Appleby 2002, 511), Mawdudi, his followers, and Jamaat across south Asia, as this essay demonstrates, are keenly engaged in the quotidian political struggle of and for democracy. Whether or not and to what degree Islamists such as Jamaat activists will continue to act as vital agents of democratization and change depends not only on their own sweat desire but, more importantly, also on the (re)alignments of forces in the global, regional, and national field in which Islamists are one among several actors and by no means the dominant ones.

NOTES

1. By Islamism I mean a distinct socio-political movement which regards Islam as a comprehensive system of life and foregrounds the pursuit of an Islamic state as its principal aim (Ahmad 2009: 4–8). Islamism, therefore, should not be squarely conflated with Islam as a discursive tradition (Asad 2009).
2. Hashmi's (2004, 62–66) and Kabir's (2006, 208–210) works are rare sober analyses of this issue. Against the sensationalist accounts, such as those of Datta (2007), Ganguly, and others who uncritically take journalistic sources and intelligence/police reports as "truth," Hashmi interrogates the accuracy of such sources to suggest how "terrorism" in Bangladesh might have been manufactured by forces such as the Awami League, among others, by planting stories in magazines such as *Far Eastern Economic Review* so as to position her party as a friend of the United States in the post-9/11 global scenario.
3. For more on this, see Ahmad (2010).
4. In transliterating non-English words, I largely follow the *Annual of Urdu Studies* guideline 2007, also available on the journal's website. However, I write "Jamaat" because Jamaat in India, Bangladesh, and Pakistan write it in English like this.
5. For a succinct account of Mawdudi's life and thought, see Ahmad (2012b); for a different and detailed account, see Nasr (1996) and Ahmad (2009).
6. On the absence of democracy in the Middle East, see Ahmad (2012a).
7. Many Pakistanis still hold that Jamaat opposed Pakistan's creation; see Rashid (2001).
8. Bangladesh's Jamaat has not received much attention in the English-medium academic literature. With the exception of chapter-/article-length works of Ahmad (1991), Ahmed (1994), Banu (1994), Rahim (2001), Husain and Siddiquee (2004), Huq (2008), and Shehabuddin (2008a, also see 2008b), Kabir's (2006) is perhaps the first comprehensive study of Jamaat.
9. According to the Bangladesh government, 15,000 Urdu-speaking Biharis were killed by Bengalis. Other accounts put the figure between 70,000 and 100,000; see Ahmad (2012c).

REFERENCES

Agwani, Mohammad Shafiq. 1986. *Islamic Fundamentalism in India*. Chandigarh: Twenty-First Century Indian Society.

Ahmad, Irfan. 1991. "Bangladesh aur Jamhūriat." *The Sadā-e-'ām*. Patna. Edit Page. January 30.

Ahmad, Irfan. 2008. "Cracks in the 'Mightiest Fortress': Jama'at-e Islami's Changing Discourse on Women." *Modern Asian Studies* 42(2&3): 549–575.

Ahmad, Irfan. 2009. *Islamism and Democracy in India: The Transformation of Jama`at-e Islami*. Princeton: Princeton University Press.

Ahmad, Irfan. 2010. "Is There an Ethics of Terrorism? Islam, Globalisation, Militancy." *South Asia* 33(3): 487–498.

Ahmad, Irfan. 2011. "Democracy and Islam." *Philosophy and Social Criticism* 37(4): 459–470.

Ahmad, Irfan. 2012a. "How the West De-democratised the Middle East." *Al-Jazeera*. March 30. http://www.aljazeera.com/indepth/opinion/2012/03/201232710543250236. Accessed May 21, 2013.

Ahmad, Irfan. 2012b. "Mawdudi, Abul Ala: 1903–1979." In G. Böwering et al., eds. *The Princeton Encyclopedia of Islamic Political Thought*, 112–115. Princeton: Princeton University Press.

Ahmad, Irfan. 2012c. "Modernity and Its Outcast: The Why and How of India's Partition." *South Asia*. 35(3): 477–494.

Ahmad, Mumtaz. 1991. "Islamic Fundamentalism in South Asia: The Jama`at-e Islami and Tablighi Jamaat of South Asia." In Martin Marty and Scott Appleby, eds., *Fundamentalisms Observed*, 457–530. Chicago: University of Chicago Press.

Ahmed, Rafiuddin. 1994. "Redefining Muslim Identity in South Asia: The Transformation of the Jamaat-I-Islami." In Martin Marty and Scott Appleby, eds. *Accounting for Fundamentalisms: The Dynamic Character of Movement*, 669–705. Chicago: University of Chicago Press.

Ali, Tariq. 2002. *The Clash of Fundamentalisms*. London: Verso.

Amin, Husnul. 2010. *From Islamism to Post-Islamism: A Study of a New Intellectual Discourse on Islam and Modernity in Pakistan*. Unpublished PhD Thesis. Erasmus University.

Anand, Javed. 2012. "Jamaat in Hindustan." http://www.viewpointonline.net/jamaat-in-india. Accessed October 4, 2012.

Antoun, Richard. 2010. "Fundamentalism." In Bryan Turner, ed., *The New Blackwell Companion to the Sociology of Religion*, 519–536. London: Wiley-Blackwell.

Appleby, Scott. 2002. "History in the Fundamentalist Imagination." *The Journal of American History* 89(2): 498–511.

Asad, Talal. 2003. *Formations of the Secular: Christianity, Islam, Modernity*. Stanford: Stanford University Press.

Asad, Talal. 2006. "Trying to Understand French Secularism." In Hent de Vries, ed., *Political Theologies*, 494–526. New York: Fordham University Press.

Asad, Talal. 2009. "The Idea of an Anthropology of Islam." *Qui Parle* 17(2): 1–30.

Bahadur, Kalim. 1977. *The Jama`at-e Islami of Pakistan*. Delhi: Chetna.

Bangladesh Jama`at-e Islami. 2001. "Prof. Ghulam Azam." http://www.Jama`at-e Islami.org/jib/Overview/azam.htm. Accessed May 25, 2001.

Bangladesh Jama`at-e Islami. 2012. "Policies: Introduction." http://www.Jama`at-e Islami.org/en/details.php?artid=MTQ4. Accessed April 11, 2012.

Banu, Razia Akter. 1994. "Jama`at-e Islami in Bangladesh." In Hussin Mutalib and Taj Hashmi, eds., *Islam, Muslims, and the Modern State*, 80–99. London: Macmillan.

Benjamin, Daniel, and Steve Simon. 2002. *The Age of Sacred Terror.* New York: Random House.

Berman, Paul. 2003. "The Philosopher of Islamic Terror." *The New York Times,* March 23.

Beyondheadlines. 2011a. "JIH Political Party: A Journey from 'Politics of Dependence to Politics of Self Reliance.'" http://beyondheadlines.in/2011/04/jih-political-party-a-journey-from-politics-of-dependence-to-politics-of-self-reliance. Accessed January 21, 2012.

Beyondheadlines. 2011b. "Concept Note of Jamaat 'supported' Welfare Party." http://beyondheadlines.in/2011/04/concept-not-of-jamaat%E2%80%99s-welfare-party. Accessed January 21, 2012.

Bowen, John R. 2007. *Why the French Don't Like Headscarves.* Princeton: Princeton University Press.

BBC. 2004. "Vardī aur Qur'an kī barābrī par hangāmā." http://www.bbc.co.uk/urdu/pakistan/story/2004/10/printable/041029_senate_row_rza.sAccessed July 11, 2004.

BBC. 2007. "Tories Complain about Radical Books." http://www.bbc.co.uk/london/content/articles/2007/09/18/towerhamlets_tory_protest_video_feature. Accessed November 9, 2010.

BBC. 2010. "Bangladesh Bans Books Written by Radical Islamic Author." http://www.bbc.co.uk/news/world-south-asia-10661454. Accessed November 9, 2010.

Bdnews24.com. 2012. "Ghulam Azam Lands in Jail." http://bdnews24.com/details.php?id=215760&cid=3. Accessed April 20, 2012.

Casanova, Jose. 2009. "The Religious Situation in Europe." In Hans Joas et al. eds., *Secularization and the World Religions,* 206–227. Liverpool: Liverpool University Press.

Cook, David. 2005. *Understanding Jihad.* Berkeley: University of California Press.

Datta, Sreeradha. 2007. "Islamic Militancy in Bangladesh." *South Asia.* 30(1): 145–170.

Euben, Roxanne L. 1999. *Enemy in the Mirror: Islamic Fundamentalism and the Limits of Modern Rationalism.* Princeton: Princeton University Press.

Esposito, John. 1994. "Political Islam: Beyond the Green Menace." *Current History* 93: 19–24.

Esposito, John L., and John O. Voll. 1996. *Islam and Democracy.* New York: Oxford University Press.

Ganguly, Sumit. 2006. *The Rise of Islamist Militancy in Bangladesh.* Washington, DC: United Institute of Peace. Special Report. 171.

Gardezi, Hassan. 1994. "Politics of Religion in Pakistan's Elections: An Assessment." *South Asia Bulletin* 14(1): 110–113.

Ghannouchi, Rashid. 1998. "Participation in a Non-Islamic Government." In Charles Kurzman. ed., *Liberal Islam: A Sourcebook,* 89–95. Oxford: Oxford University Press.

Hansen, Stig Jarle. 2009. "Asia and the Middle East: Borders at the Centre of Islam?" In Stig Jarle Hansen et al. eds., *The Borders of Islam,* 15–22. New Delhi: Foundation Books.

Harrison, Selig S. 2006. *The Washington Post.* "A New Hub for Terrorism?" http://www.washingtonpost.com/wp-dyn/content/article/2006/08/01/AR2006080101118. Accessed April 11, 2012.

Hashmi, Taj. 2004. "Islamic Resurgence in Bangladesh." In Satu Limaye at el., eds., *Religious Radicalism and Security in South Asia.* 35–72. Honolulu: Asia Pacific Centre for Security Studies.

Hassan, Mushirul. 1997. *The Legacy of a Divided Nation: Indian Muslims since Independence.* London: Hurst.

Husain, Ishtiaq, and Noore Siddiquee. 2004. "Islam in Bangladesh Politics: The Role of Ghulam Azam of Jama`at-e Islami." *Inter-Asia Cultural Studies* 5(3): 384–399.

Huq, Maimuna. 2008. "Reading the Qur'an in Bangladesh: The Politics of 'Belief' among Islamist Women." *Modern Asian Studies* 42(2&3): 457–488.

The Indian Express. 2011. "Jamaat Launches Party, Christian Priest Is Vice-President." http://www.indianexpress.com/news/jamaat-launches-party-christian-priest-is-vicepresident/778016. Accessed April 22, 2011.

International Crisis Group. 2003. *Pakistan: The Mullahs and the Military.* Brussels: ICG, Asia Report, 49.

Iqtidar, Humeira. 2011a. *Secularizing Islamists? Jama`at-e Islami and Jamaat-ud-Dawa in Urban Pakistan.* Chicago: Chicago University Press.

Iqtidar, Humeira. 2011b. "Secularism beyond the State: The 'State' and the 'Market' in Islamist Imagination." *Modern Asian Studies* 45(3): 535–564.

Juergensmeyer, Mark. 2003. *Terror in the Mind of God: The Global Rise of Religious Violence.* 3rd ed. Berkeley: University of California Press.

Kabir, Bhuian Md Monoar. 2006. *Politics and Development of Jama`at-e Islami Bangladesh.* Delhi: South Asian Publishers.

Karlekar, Hiranmay. 2005. *Bangladesh: The Next Afghanistan?* New Delhi: Sage.

Lincoln, Bruce. 2003. *Holy Terrors: Thinking about Religion after September 11.* Chicago: Chicago University Press.

Mamdani, Mahmood. 2002. "Good Muslim, Bad Muslim: A Political Perspective on Culture and Terrorism." *American Anthropologist* 104(3): 766–775.

Mawdudi, Abul Ala. 1942. *Musalmān aur maujūda seyasī kashmakash.* Vol. 3. Pathankot: Daftar risāla Tarjumānul Qur'an.

Mawdudi, Abul Ala. 2003. *Taḥrīk-e-Islamī kā āinda lāha-e-'amal.* Lahore: Islamic Publications.

Mazarr, Michael J. 2007. *Unmodern Men in the Modern World: Radical Islam, Terrorism and the War on Modernity.* Cambridge: Cambridge University Press.

Masud, Muhammad Khalid. 2007. "Rethinking Sharia: Javed Ahmad Ghamidi on Hudūd." *Die Welt des Islams* 47(3–4): 356–375.

Moniruzzaman, M. 2009. "Party Politics and Political Violence in Bangladesh: Issues, Manifestation and Consequences." *South Asian Survey* 16(1): 81–99.

Moten, Abdul Rashid. 2003. "Maududi and the Transformation of Jama`at-e Islami in Pakistan." *The Muslim World* 93(July–October): 391–413.

Nadwi, Abul Lais Islahi. 1951. *Masala-e-intikhābāt aur musalmānān-e-hind*. Vol. 1. Rampur: maktaba Jama`at-e Islami hind.

Nasr, Syed Vali Reza. 1994. *The Vanguard of Islamic Revolution: The Jama`at-e Islami of Pakistan*. Berkeley: University of California Press.

Nasr, Syed Vali Reza. 1996. *Maududi and the Making of Islamic Revivalism*. New York: Oxford University Press.

Nasr, Syed Vali Reza. 2006. "Maududi and the Jama`at-e Islami." In Ali Rehnema, ed., *Pioneers of Islamic Revival*, 98–124. Updated edition. London: Zed Books.

Niazi, Kausar. 1973. *Jam`āt-e-islamī avāmī 'adālat meñ*. Lahore: qaumi kutubkhana.

Outlook. 2002. " 'We Will Continue to Oppose the One-Man Dictatorship': Qazi Hussain Ahmed." http://www.outlookindia.com/article.aspx?217713. Accessed November 3, 2002.

Philips, Melanie. 2006. *Londonistan: How Britain Is Creating a Terror State Within*. London: Gibson Square.

Prothero, Stephen. 2010. *God Is Not One*. New York: Harper One.

Rahim, Enayetur. 2001. "Bengali Muslims and Islamic Fundamentalism: The Jama`at-e Islami in Bangladesh." In Rafiduddin Ahmed, ed., *Understanding the Bengal Muslims*, 236–261. Delhi: Oxford University Press.

Rashid, Amber. 2001. "Opinion: Questions for the Jamaat." *The News International*. London. February 8. p. 10.

Riaz, Ali. 2010. "The Politics of Islamization in Bangladesh." In Ali Riaz, ed., *Religion and Politics in South Asia*, 45–70. London: Routledge.

Roy, Oliver. 2007. *Secularism Confronts Islam*. Translated by George Holoch. New York: Columbia University Press.

Rushdie, Salman. 2005. "Muslims Unite! A New Reformation Will Bring Your Faith into the Modern Era." http://www.timesonline.co.uk/article/0,,1072-1729998,00.html. Accessed on 8/19/2005.

Sayyid, Qasim. 2011. "Taḥrīk-e-Islamī fikrī dorāhe per." *Rashtriyā sahārā*. Delhi. April 21. Edit Page.

Schmitt, Carl. 2006. *The Concept of the Political*. Translated with an Introduction by George Schwab. Chicago: University of Chicago Press.

Shehabuddin, Elora. 2008a. *Reshaping the Holy: Democracy, Development and Muslim Women in Bangladesh*. New York: Columbia University Press.

Shehabuddin, Elora. 2008b. "Jamaat-i-Islami in Bangladesh: Women, Democracy and the Transformation of Islamist Politics." *Modern Asian Studies* 42(2&3): 577–603.

Shepard, William E. 2003. "Sayyid Qutb's Doctrine of jihad." *International Journal of Middle East Studies* 35: 521–545.

Trouillot, Michel-Rolph. 1995. *Silencing the Past: Power and Production of History*. Boston: Beacon Press.

TwoCircles.Net. 2011. "Why Jamaat-backed Welfare Party Received Cold Response?" http://twocircles.net/2011apr21/why_jamaatbacked_welfare_party_received_cold_response. Accessed April 22, 2011.

Van der Veer, Peter. 2008. "The Religious Origins of Democracy." In Gabriel Motzkin et al., eds., *Religion and Democracy in Contemporary Europe*, 75–81. London: Alliance.

Wajihuddin, Mohammed. 2010. *The Times of India*. "It Will Only Trigger Further Polarisation." Delhi, August 24. p. 6.

Wiktorowicz, Quintan. 2005. "A Genealogy of Radical Islam." *Studies in Conflict and Terrorism* 28(2): 75–97.

Chapter 6

Islam and Politics in Southeast Asia

FRED R. VON DER MEHDEN

INTRODUCTION

The complex interaction between Islam and politics in Southeast Asia needs to be interpreted within the historic and cultural milieu of the heterogeneous societies of the region. This interplay takes place within two different environments. Indonesia, Malaysia, and Brunei Darussalam are majority Muslim states. Indonesia's Muslims comprise 86 percent of the population, and Malaysia is a multireligious, multiethnic country with 60 percent Muslims.[1] The second environment is composed of Muslim minorities primarily in southern Thailand, the southern Philippines, the Arakan in Burma-Myanmar, and Singapore. With the exception of Singapore, significant numbers of these minorities have sought autonomy or separation. There are also Muslim minorities who have generally worked with the majority political systems and have been more integrated into the dominant society. These include Thai Muslims outside the more separatist southern provinces and Burmese Muslims in areas other than the Arakan prior to the establishment of military rule in 1962. Singapore's Muslims have the right to participate fully in the political system and have religious courts with limited jurisdiction. All of them are 10 percent or less of their respective national populations, with the exception of Singapore, with 13 percent. This study analyzes both cases of Muslim majority states and where Muslims are in the minority. However, prior to a more detailed analysis of politics and Islam in the individual Muslim societies, it is useful to address the wide range of common, although not universal, factors that have tended to frame Islam and politics in the Muslim world of Southeast Asia.

1. Throughout the region there has been a strong co-identity of Islam and ethnicity. Muslims in most of these societies define themselves in religious-ethnic terms. In preindependence Indonesia, nationalists emphasized the divide between Dutch Christians and Indonesian Muslims. Numerous studies have found that many Muslim communities in Indonesia have difficulty in distinguishing between their Islamic and ethnic identities. In Malaysia the co-identity of Malay and Muslim has dominated politics since before independence. The vast majority of Malays are also Muslims and most Muslims are Malays, blurring understanding of causality. Both the dominant party in the country's multiethnic and multireligious ruling coalition and its chief Islamic rival must be seen as both Malay and Islamic parties. This interaction of ethnicity and Islam is most obvious in Muslim minority states where these minorities differentiate themselves from the majority society by both religion and ethnicity. This co-identity of religion and ethnicity further separates these Muslim communities from the dominant societies.

2. Unlike the Middle East, there traditionally has been a high level of syncretism among Muslims in Southeast Asia. This reflects the influence of animism and other pre-Islamic beliefs and cultures. This is not unique to Islam but is also to be

found in Christian and Buddhist societies. A significant number of Muslims in the region, particularly in Indonesia, have traditionally reflected this pre-Islamic and particularly Hindu foundation. Differing views on the acceptance of "non-Islamic" elements often have divided Indonesian society and politics. Twentieth-century political parties reflected these differing interpretations while several of Indonesia's presidents have supported the more syncretic belief patterns. In Southeast Asia, Hindu influences have also played an important role in molding the institutions and activities of traditional rulers.

3. Radical interpretations of Islam have not succeeded in gaining significant electoral support in Muslim-dominated states. In Indonesia, radical parties have had almost no representation in the elected national parliaments of 1956 or after the return to democracy in 1999. In Malaysia, the ruling Muslim party has rejected radical interpretations and has attempted to eliminate "deviant" Islam. Its Muslim rival promotes a more conservative agenda and supports a stricter implementation of the *sharī`ah*, but both accept political pluralism. In Thailand, Singapore, and the Philippines, where Muslim minorities have elected members of the national legislature, they have tended to be moderate.

4. Although electorally weak, radical Islamic groups have been involved in violent activities in the name of Islam in every Muslim majority and minority country. Muslim separatist movements have clashed with authorities, including the Moros in the Philippines, Malay-Muslims in southern Thailand, and the Arakanese in Burma. At first, many of these groups did not espouse radical Islamic ideology, but recent years have seen an increasing influence of Salafi and radical foreign

religious and political interpretations. Domestically, both Indonesia and Malaysia have faced a number of violent Muslim groups, particularly in the past decade. There has also been the rise of cross-national radical Islamic organizations with ties to the Middle East, most notably Jeemah Islamiyh, which has been active throughout Southeast Asia. The strength of international and domestic groups has weakened over the past few years but is still capable of isolated acts of violence.

5. Southeast Asian Islam has been deeply influenced by Islamic ideology and state action from outside the region. At the intellectual and religious level, Modernist interpretations of Islam came to the region at the turn of the twentieth century. After World War II, a range of Islamist writers from the Middle East and South Asia have been translated into indigenous languages and have become part of the religious and political dialogue. Radical interpretations of Islam and Salafi-Wahabbi ideas from Saudi Arabia have been influential among disaffected Muslims in the region. Muslims in Southeast Asia also have been affected by events such as the Iranian Revolution, the Israeli-Arab conflict, and the Afghan and Iraq wars.

Muslim governments in the Middle East have also attempted to influence Muslims in the region. Funds have been given for Islamic education and other social activities, particularly from Saudi Arabia. International groups, such as the Organization of the Islamic Conference, have passed resolutions regarding problems of Muslim minorities in the region, and individual states have provided training and funds to minority separatists, especially in the Philippines.

6. The Islamic resurgence has influenced both the public face and actions of Muslims in Southeast Asia. There have been

changes in dress and a greater observance of Islamic rituals such as prayer and fasting. The region has also experienced an increase in Islamic publications and organizations. Muslim youth have displayed a growing interest in their religion and its relationship to political action, and there has been a significant growth in Islamic educational institutions at all levels. At the local and national levels political leaders have employed more Islamic symbols and language. Internationally, Muslims in Southeast Asia have become more aware of and involved in the wider Islamic world.

ISLAM AND POLITICS IN MUSLIM MAJORITY STATES

Majority status does not coincide with religious or political unity and Muslims in Malaysia and Indonesia have been politically fragmented and have not displayed a common Islamic agenda. This section analyzes the interaction of Islam and politics in the two largest Muslim majority states in the region, Indonesia and Malaysia. Three areas will be considered: the role of national leadership, the role of Islamic political parties, and religious issues in the political arena.

The role of national leadership

There have been significant differences between Indonesia and Malaysia in terms of the role of government leadership and Islamic-oriented parties in determining national religious policies. In Indonesia the relationship of Islam to politics has varied since the end of World War II and the achievement of independence. Yet, in spite of having the highest percentage of Muslims of any country in

the region, a broad-based Islamic agenda has never been implemented. When the initial debate took place in 1945 over the role of
Islam and the state, Muslim organizations were unable to successfully achieve their goals of a state based upon the *sharī'ah* and
the requirement that the president of the republic be a Muslim. The
only reference to religion was that "the Indonesia state is founded
on belief in God." Both President Sukarno (1945–1967) and
President Suharto (1967–1999) based their rhetoric upon a more
secular and syncretic ideology called the *pancasila* (five principles).
Over time, Muslim organizations have differed in their willingness
to accept the *pancasila*, although many Muslims have been discom-
forted by its interpretation of belief in God as also recognizing the
legitimacy of religions other than Islam.

Both Sukarno and Suharto sought to restrict the influence of
political Islam. After democratic election in 1955 when Islamic
parties received more than 40 percent of the vote, the influence of
Islam at the national level was short lived. Sukarno declared "guided
democracy" in 1959, emasculating the parliamentary system, and
sought to establish his power base upon secular parties. Although in
his last years Suharto attempted to appear more pious, he saw the
role of Islam to be a more private matter and not part of the political
dialogue. This view of "Islam yes, but Islamic politics no" was also
fostered by some within the Indonesian intellectual community.
Islamic activists, severely limited in their national political activities,
turned to the mosques and madrasahs as the centers of their
opposition to the Suharto regime.

The return of democracy in 1999 brought a vigorous movement
toward political pluralism. While the retention of the *pancasila* was
not at issue, the new democratic system brought the reentrance
of Islam into Indonesian politics. However, Islamic politics were
highly fragmented and the series of presidents after the fall of

Suharto displayed ambivalence toward a political role for Islam. None of the four presidents that followed attempted to formulate a comprehensive Islamic agenda, although there was support for limited Islamic policies. An obvious exception to Indonesia's more secular-minded presidents was Abdur Rahman Wahib. His father was a well-known `ulama' and Wahid had been head of the mass organization Nahdlatul Ulama. A political and religious pluralist, his presidency failed from combination of weak parliamentary support, governmental style, unpopular policies, and personal illness. All of Indonesia's presidents have found it necessary to deal with violent Islamic groups, but at no time since independence has Islam played a dominant role in Indonesian national politics.

The Malaysian constitution states that Islam is the official religion of the country, and the Malay Sultans have traditionally been the protectors and authority in Islamic matters. However, in the first decades after independence in 1957, Malaysian national governments generally maintained secular policies and emphasized the need to reinforce Malay rights rather than promoting an Islamic agenda. They still attempted to portray themselves as protectors of Islam and as illustrated by the statement in 1959 of then deputy prime minister and later prime minister and "Father of Development," Abdul Tun Razak, that "we have done all we could within our power to maintain the Islamic religion" (*Straits Times*, March 24, 1959). Their administrations did see a proliferation of state-built mosques and the beginnings of the Islamization of the bureaucracy, and at the state level *sharī'ah* laws were reinforced and penalties for noncompliance were increased.

This pattern changed significantly after Mohammad Mahathir became prime minister in 1981. He initially followed his predecessors in accentuating the need to develop Malay economic and social standards. However, prior to the 1982 national elections, he began to develop an Islamic agenda, exemplified by his recruitment of Anwar Ibrahim, leader of the main student *dakwah* movement, ABIM (Islamic Youth League of Malaysia). For the next two decades, until his retirement in 2003, Mahathir sustained a policy of Islamization of Malaysia. His efforts led to the formation of Islamic banking, the establishment of the International Islamic University of Malaysia, the expansion of federal authority in religious affairs that were previously the domain of the states, the formation the Department of Islamic Development in Malaysia to promote the faith and confront un-Islamic activities, attacks upon "deviant Islam," requiring an examination "religious knowledge" for Muslim students, and greater attention to supporting international Islamic policies. This became a concerted effort to bureaucratize the religious establishment and to define the limits and goals of Muslims in Malaysia.

Mahathir's successors have maintained the same Islamic framework but have attempted to give their own emphases. Thus, Prime Minister Abdullah Badawi, who followed Mahathir, promoted "Islam *hadhari*" (civilizational Islam), which tried to meld development and Islam, much like many before him. He also described Islam *hadhari* as supporting a "tolerant, inclusive, moderate, and modern" Islam.

The role of political parties

There have been significant differences in the role of Islamic political parties in Indonesia and Malaysia. In Indonesia, from independence until Sukarno launched "guided democracy," Islamic parties did play an important part in governing in national and provincial governments. Islamic political strength was in evidence in the only free elections held during the Sukarno-Suharto era in 1955. However, the elections also showed the continuance of prewar divisions between more traditional and more Modernist oriented political parties. The two major Muslim parties each obtained approximately 20 percent of the vote for the national parliament. However, there was limited effort within parliament to assert an Islamic agenda. This was largely due to a fragmented parliament that made promulgating controversial legislation difficult, a lack of unity within Muslim parties on a common Islamic agenda and Sukarno's more secular position backed by communist and nationalist parties. These factors hindered the promotion of any significant Islamic political or religious aspirations. Under President Suharto's "new order" political parties were severely limited in their ability to affect policy. All organizations, including religious parties, were required to support the *pancasila*. Islamic political parties were forced to join the PPP (United Development Party), which was prohibited from running on an expressly religious platform. Islamic political power was also weakened by the withdrawal from politics of many Muslims, including the Nahdlatul Ulama, who became frustrated with the limitations put on Islamic political action.

The return of democracy after Suharto's fall from power in 1998 again underscored divisions within the Islamic political community and continued their inability to establish an electoral majority. In spite of 87 percent of Indonesians being Muslim, this has not translated into electoral support. National elections for parliament (People's Representative Assembly or Dewan Perwakilan Rakyat) showed a continuing but declining minority role of Islamic parties, dropping from 38 percent in 1999 to 32 percent in 2004 to 24 percent in 2009. Lack of electoral support arose from a multitude of local and national issues, but significant blame can be put upon Islamic political parties for their lack of agreement on an Islamic agenda and other issues, the personality orientation of Muslim party leadership, and, more recently, charges of corruption.

In stark contrast to Indonesia, Muslims in Malaysia have played the dominant role in determining national and Islamic policies. The Malay-Muslim United Malay National Organization (UMNO) has been the principal party in the multiethnic ruling Barisan Nasional (National Front). Since independence every prime minister, deputy prime minister, and home minister has been a member of UMNO. The dilemma for the party leadership has been how to maintain the multiethnic and multireligious coalition and at the same time appeal to the Malay-Muslim aspirations of its constituents. Malay and Islamic politics have been defined by UMNO and its chief rival the Malay-Muslim Party, Partai Islam (PAS). Historically, UMNO and PAS have each declared themselves to be the best protector of Malay and Muslim interests. However there have also been religious policy differences both within UMNO and between the two parties. PAS and more conservative local UMNO representatives have supported a more aggressive Islamic agenda and questioned decisions made to meet the needs of non-Muslims in the coalition. Both parties have employed religious appeals and have developed political backing from local Islamic leaders.

Indonesia and Malaysia show significantly different political contexts. Attitudes toward Islam between the political leaders in the two countries were markedly different until the return to democracy in Indonesia. Indonesian presidents until the end of the twentieth century reflected secular tendencies and suspicion of political Islam. No president has promoted an extensive Islamic agenda, although there has been support for more limited proposals. In contrast, Malaysian prime ministers prior to Mahathir did not press an Islamic agenda, but recognized their Malay-Muslim constituency and were prepared to buttress their needs. While Sukarno and Suharto supported development as a secular goal, in Malaysia development was interpreted as a means of improving the conditions among Malay-Muslims and allowing them to compete with non-Muslims. There has never been a national leader in Indonesia who implemented an Islamic agenda similar to the policies of Mahathir.

The role of Islamic parties in Malaysia has also been fundamentally different from Indonesia. Islamic parties were marginalized under Sukarno and Suharto and have remained a fragmented minority in this century. In Malaysia, religious policies have been framed by the UMNO-PAS rivalry and internal divisions within these parties.

Islamic political issues

There have been three major interacting long-term points of contention among the plethora of religious issues that have become part of the political dialogue of Indonesia and Malaysia: the establishment of an Islamic state, the role of the *sharīʿah*, and religious and political pluralism. On all of these issues public opinion has not always been reflected in public policy. Polls have shown agreement to issues in the abstract, but a lack of consensus on details. Thus, the idea of an Islamic state and implementation of the *sharīʿah* are widely supported by Muslims in Indonesia and Malaysia, but there is not agreement on their meaning.

In Indonesia, there have been significant differences regarding the establishment of an Islamic state between parties and leaders at the national level and the views of nongovernmental Islamist elements. The establishment of an Islamic state has been rejected by all of Indonesia's presidents, the leaders of the country's major Muslim political parties, and the two mass Muslim organizations Nahdlatul Ulama and the Muhammadiyah. Individual members of these organizations have championed an Islamic state in various guises. Polls have shown that, while there has been a general consensus on public support for an increased role of Islam in the state, there has not been demand for a system similar to Iran.

The most forceful proponents for an Islamic state based upon the *sharīʿah* have been from traditional Muslim leaders and more radical Islamic organizations. The most prominent of Islamic *ʿulama'* groups has been the Majelis Ulama Indonesia (MUI), which has long called for the establishment of an Islamic state and expansion of the role of the *sharīʿah* at the state level. Since independence, various radical Islamic groups have demanded an Islamic state. In the 1940s and 1950s, Dar ul Islam fought the government and rejected the country's secular state. Its ideas remain influential among Islamists. In the 1970s and 1980s a small group, Kommando Jihad, had a similar agenda. It has variously been interpreted as an outgrowth of Dar ul Islam and a product of Indonesian state intelligence. In recent years a number of violent and nonviolent groups have proclaimed the necessity of an Islamic state. These have included *Laskar Jihad*, now disbanded, which carried out attacks against Christians in East Indonesia; Jemaah Islamiyah, which seeks a regionwide Islamic state; and the Majelis Mujahidin Indonesia (MMI), an umbrella organization connected to Jemaah Islamiyah.

Malaysia's constitution states that Islam is the official religion, but the issue of the establishment or existence of an Islamic state has only recently become a major matter of contention. In the first decades after independence, the leadership of the major Malay-Muslim Party, UMNO, rejected the idea of an Islamic state, although more conservative party members have supported it. UMNO's major rival, PAS, has backed the formation of an Islamic state since its formation in 1951, although it has often muted its position to attract non-Muslims. Prime Minister Mahathir initially rejected the idea, in part due to the multireligious composition of his coalition. However, he later asserted that Malaysia is an Islamic state in that it has met all the necessary religious criteria. This has been defined as a political, not constitutional interpretation and it is asserted that this does not mean the diminishment of the rights of non-Muslims. However, non-Muslims remain skeptical and PAS views it as politically motivated. Mahathir's successor, Abdullah Badawi, stated in 2007 that Malaysia was neither secular nor theocratic, but a parliamentary democracy. Prior to becoming prime minister, Badawi's successor, Tun Razak Najib, increased tensions by defining Malaysia as an Islamic state and not a secular one. However, as prime minister, he has proclaimed Islam in Malaysia to be moderate and modern. While it remains a contentious issue, the vast majority of Malaysian Muslims support an Islamic state, although not like Iran.

The second issue relates to the implementation of the *sharīʿah*. The Muslim public has shown wide agreement on the importance of the *sharīʿah* in both Indonesia and Malaysia. However, there have been differences on details including what should be the role of the state, what parts of *sharīʿah* should be promulgated, and what the effect of its implementation would be on non-Muslims.

The Indonesian public has not been as supportive of the expansion of the *sharīʿah* as the Malaysians. However, local and provincial governments have been the most active official entities reinforcing elements of Islamic law. There have been regulations regarding the observance of Ramadan, dress, liquor, tithing, and other religious practices by Muslims. However, they have often not been complied with or enforced and the national government has rarely interfered with these local rules. At the national level there has been a reluctance to expand the official role of the *sharīʿah*. However, in order to end its conflict with the strongly Islamic province of Aceh it allowed the implementation of *sharīʿah* law, courts, and punishments in the province. This and other efforts to expand the role of the *sharīʿah* and "morality legislation" have pitted more conservative Muslims against those with more liberal interpretations.

In Malaysia issues regarding the sharī'ah have had political relevance involving differences between PAS and the national government. PAS has asserted that the full sharī'ah should be enforced, not just in private matters, and was necessary to the establishment of an Islamic state. The promotion of its interpretation of the expansion of the sharī'ah has also been part of the PAS effort to prove itself more Islamic than UMNO. PAS has attempted to enact hudud laws and punishments in states under its control and has passed legislation against liquor, gambling, and other "non-Islamic" practices. Non-Islamic groups fear that hudud laws would be expanded to cover them, although PAS has stated that only Muslims would be affected. Hudud legislation was rejected by the UMNO-led national government as unconstitutional. However, given popular and support for expanding the role of the sharī'ah positive statements by Islamic leaders, and the views of some of its own members, UMNO has been publicly ambiguous about expanding sharī'ah law.

The third interlocking issue has been religious pluralism. Both the Malaysian and Indonesian governments and all major political parties support freedom of religion. However, this must be viewed against legal restrictions and conservative and radical rejections of religious and political pluralism. In Malaysia, limitations on religious pluralism have usually come from state religious courts and the federal government rather than from religious activists. Non-Muslims are forbidden to proselytize Muslims and apostasy has been effectively blocked by state religious courts. Other religions cannot advertise services or follow other practices that could lead to the conversion of Muslims. The importation of Christian books that use Islamic interpretations of words and Malay translations of the Bible and other Christian literature that might influence

Muslims have been targeted. Accusations have been made against local authorities for making difficult the building of non-Muslim places of worship there. In Indonesia, limitations on religious pluralism have come from activists and local religious courts and secular authorities, with limited input from the national government. Thus, conversion is legal, but there have been numerous attacks upon Christians by local groups and Islamic courts have opposed conversion, although without the legal authority found in Malaysia.

Both Indonesia and Malaysia have sought to contain "deviant Islam," although the latter has been more active. This allows the government to define the meaning of Islam and is employed to maintain religious purity, for national security and to contain the political opposition. Thus, UMNO leadership defined as deviant the efforts of PAS to implement *hudud* laws. Government and Islamic organizations in Malaysia have named scores of groups guilty of deviancy including Shi`as. The government has closed many of these alleged deviant groups and members have been punished by fines and imprisonment. In Indonesia local authorities also have fined and imprisoned members of "deviant" groups, frequently on charges of blasphemy or defamation of Islam. However, the national government has been more flexible than its Malaysian counterpart. Thus, the Ahmadiyah is banned in Malaysia, but allowed to exist in Indonesia with restrictions, in spite of political and religious pressure.

A significant difference between the two countries is that Malaysian controls on religious pluralism have centered upon institutionalized local and national laws, although there have been isolated violent incidents in both countries. In Indonesia, there has been far more attacks from nongovernmental activists and conservative religious groups. In the latter, there have been numerous occasions of mob violence against Christian institutions, organizations considered to be un-Islamic such as the Ahmadiyah, and shops and individuals allegedly guilty of breaking Islamic law or practicing immoral behavior. Major conservative religious groups have also criticized religious pluralism. The `ulama'-based MUI has issued fatwas against the Ahmadiyah, secularism, and religious pluralism, although these fatwas do not have the force of law.

MUSLIM MINORITY COMMUNITIES

The political role played by Islamic minorities can be divided into three patterns: (1) where the minority is completely excluded from power (Myanmar-Burma); (2) where there is a significant separatist or autonomy movements, although the community now has a greater right to participate in national and local government (Muslims in southern Philippines and southern Thailand); and (3) in Muslim communities rejecting separation or autonomy and prepared to participate in the political system (Thai Muslims outside the Muslim-Malays in the far south and Muslims in Singapore). However, there are important common factors among these minority groups including co-identity of religion and ethnicity, economic and social inequality, perceived government repression, and new religious currents.

Ethnicity and religion

Every minority group in the region reflects the co-identity of religion and ethnicity different from the dominant society. This combination can reinforce a sense of alienation and foster political tensions. No Muslim minority in Southeast Asia has been so consistently excluded from national government involvement as in

Burma-Myanmar, although Muslims from central Burma did hold political leadership during Burma's democratic era. Muslims in Burma are largely the descendants of immigrants from South Asia and can be divided between the more integrated group that settled into core areas of Burma and those from the Arakan in southwest Burma. The former's origins, religion, and economic power have fostered anti-Muslim antagonism since colonial times. They have been considered *kala* (foreigner) by many Burmese. The Muslim Arakanese originally came into the area in the nineteenth and early twentieth centuries when Burma was still a province of India. Their Bengali background and differences in language and religion have made them distinct from the Burmese Buddhist majority. The desire of some Arakanese for autonomy, separation, or even annexation to Bangladesh has further reinforced official views that they are not loyal. The military regime has defined them as noncitizens because their decedents did not live in Burma before 1824 when colonial power was initially established and has implemented policies limiting their economic development, housing, travel, and education opportunities.

Thailand and the Philippines provide examples of Muslims who generally differ from the majority in their ethnicity, but have gained increasing political power and religious autonomy in the past several decades. Muslims in Thailand can be divided into two groups. Thai Muslims speak Thai and have generally been integrated politically and socially, but remain loyal to their faith. They are multiethnic and include Malays, immigrants, and Thai converts. The second and largest Muslim group is composed of Malay-speaking Muslims who have attempted to maintain their religious and ethnic identity, leading to significant support for autonomy or separation. The difference between the two communities can be explained in large part by history and geography. The majority of Thai Muslims have been part of the traditional boundaries of the kingdom in close proximity with the Buddhist state and society. The most southern provinces, where the Malay-speaking Muslims reside, only became part of the kingdom in 1906. Until the latter half of the twentieth century they were isolated from the rest of the country by poor roads and communications with Malaysia easier to reach than Bangkok. Within this context, they have retained their Malay-Muslim heritage and rejected the political role and religious and social cosmology of the dominant Buddhist state and society.

The Muslims in the southern Philippines, called the *bangsa moro*, are not an ethnic group in the traditional sense, but are composed of some ten ethnic groups that view themselves as a common social and religious culture endangered by an encroaching Christian society, government, and economic power.

Economic and social inequality

Reinforcing this ethnoreligious identity have been the perception and reality of economic inequality. In the case of southern Thailand, it was largely neglected by Thai authorities until the 1960s. An absence of a reliable road network meant that the economy languished. Even after significant government development programs were implemented, more than one third of Malay-Muslims in the southernmost provinces lived under the poverty level and had comparatively low levels of education, although a significant percentage of Buddhists in the area are also poor. Unlike the Philippines, the area has not experienced the large immigration of outsiders.

In the southern Philippines two Muslim provinces ranked seventy-third and seventy-sixth in development out of the republic's seventy-seven provinces. Where, in the past, agricultural land had belonged to the local Muslim population majority ownership became increasingly held by Christian immigrants and large corporations, often with the backing of the national government. Manila under the Spanish, American, and independent republic have sought to encourage the immigration of the Christian population from high-density areas to the south. In recent decades, large agribusiness interests in the area displayed considerable influence in national politics. The *bangsa moro* are now only 20 percent or less of the population in the southern island of Mindanao and issues of land have fired separatist movements and reinforced their ethnoreligious identity.

Perceived government repression

Two major criticisms of government actions have related to assimilation policies and what are perceived to be questionable efforts to contain separatist movements. Thai policy until the last decades of the past century was to assimilate non-Buddhists into the Thai nation. This has led to efforts to press for acceptance of the Thai language, Buddhism, and loyalty to the king. The provincial and district bureaucracy in the south was composed almost entirely of Thais, usually with limited knowledge of the population. Malay-Muslims have seen this assimilation policy as an attack on their religion and customs. They do not want to be integrated into the Thai state, which is intimately entwined in Buddhist cosmology. Malay-Muslims have interpreted police and military action against separatist organizations as an effort to enforce Thai hegemony and weaken aspirations to maintain their own culture.

From the beginning of the Spanish colonial era through the American and Filipino administration, efforts have been made to assimilate the southern Muslims into the nation. The Spanish reasoning was religious and political; it wanted to convert the entire archipelago to Catholicism and to weaken Islamic power by force and dilute it by bringing Christians into the area. The American and Filipino governments sought to alleviate population pressure, particularly in Luzon and the Visayas, and fostered movement to the south.

This continuing discontent has led to the formation of separatist organizations in both countries and armed conflict remains a serious problem. However, in both cases there have been divisions between groups based upon strategic goals, methods of opposition, and ideology. Differences have centered upon disagreement over what form of autonomy or separation is acceptable, the role of Islam, and willingness to participate in armed conflict. This is best illustrated by separatist organizations in the southern Philippines. Three groups have vied for leadership of the movement. The first major separatist group was the nationalist Moro National Liberation Front (MNLF), a primarily secular group that no longer engages in armed conflict and has worked with the government with the goal of achieving semiautonomy. The largest organization is the Moro Islamic Liberation Front (MILF), which broke from the MNLF. It presents a more Islamic-oriented program and has long called for complete separation and independence. It has more recently shown a willingness to discuss major political and religious autonomy. Finally, the small Abu Sayyaf Group is a faction-ridden, violent group, involved in mass killings, bombing, and kidnapping. It has articulated uncompromising demands for separation, radical Islamic ideals, and Salafi-Wahabbi influences and has demanded the expulsion of all Christians from parts of the southern provinces. Many observers have described it as a criminal organization.

Southern Thailand also displays a factionalized separatist movement, although there is general agreement on the need to protect Islam and the Malay people. Over time groups have ceased to exist, become fragmented, or changed their focus. Differences have existed over tactics, interpretations of Islamic doctrine, and willingness to work with the Thai government. Today almost all favor the necessity of violence as means to confront what is seen as Thai government repression. As a result of this violence and Thai domestic politics, Bangkok has also changed policies over time from forced assimilation to defining the separatist movement, as a criminal plot that could only be defeated by military means, to conciliation.

The governments of Thailand and the Philippines have recognized the religious and development issues facing their Muslim minorities and there have been political and economic reforms and concessions toward greater religious autonomy. However, government policies have not been consistent and separatist groups demand more autonomy, or independence in some cases, and continue to employ violent tactics.

CONCLUSION

While this essay has presented many similarities in the forces behind the interaction between Islam and politics in Southeast Asia, this is an evolving process with significant differences at the national and local levels. It needs to be underscored that we are dealing within both national and subnational contexts and within differing political environments. Islam plays a significant social and political role throughout the region, but there are important variations both between and within Muslim majority and minority communities. This relationship is further complicated by the interrelationship between religion and ethnicity and the impact of other secular factors. There also exist variations between rhetoric and practice. Thus, there is popular support for an increased role for Islam in the public sector, but little consensus as to how it is to be implemented.

NOTES

1. Brunei is a small sultanate in which the sultan is both the ruler and the prime minister, and there are no parties or competitive elections. Brunei is not considered in this analysis. The Cham Muslims of Cambodia, with 1–2 percent of the population, are also not included.

REFERENCES

Abuza, Zachary. 2003. *Militant Islam in Southeast Asia: Crucible of Terror*. Boulder: Lynne Riener.

Barton, Greg. 2004. *Indonesia's Struggle: Jemaah Islamiyah and the Soul of Islam*. Sydney: University of New South Wales Press.

Chalk, P. 2001. Separatism in Southeast Asia: The Islamic Factor in Southern Thailand, Mindanao and Aceh. *Studies in Conflict and Terrorism* 24: 241–269.

Che Man, W. K. 1990. *Muslim Separatism: The Moros of Southern Philippines and the Malays of Southern Thailand*. New York: Oxford University Press.

Feith, H. 2007. *The Decline in Constitutional Democracy in Indonesia*. Singapore: Equinox Press.

Hefner, Robert. 2000. *Civil Islam: Muslims and Democratization in Indonesia*. Princeton, NJ: Princeton University Press.

Liow, Joseph. 2009. *Piety and Politics: Islamism in Contemporary Malaysia*. New York: Oxford University Press.

McKennan, Thomas. 1998. *Muslim Rebels and Rulers: Everyday Politics and Armed Separatism in the Southern Philippines*. Berkeley: University of California Press.

Means, Gordon. 2009. *Political Islam in Southeast Asia*. Boulder: Lynne Riener.

Milne, R. S., and Mauzy, Diane. 1999. *Malaysian Politics under Mahathir*. London: Routledge.

Nasr, Vali. 2001. *Islamic Leviathan: Islam and the Making of State Power*. New York: Oxford University Press.

Schwarz, Adam. 2002. *A Nation in Waiting: Indonesia's Search for Stability*. Leonards, Australia: Allen & Unwin.

Sidel, John. 2006. *Riots, Pogroms, Jihad: Religious Violence in Indonesia*. Ithaca: Cornell University Press.

Yegar, Moshe. 2002. *Between Integration and Secession: The Muslim Communities in Southern Thailand, Southern Philippines and Western Burma/Myanmar*. Lanham, MD: Lexington Books.

Chapter 7

Islam and Politics in North Africa

AZZEDINE LAYACHI

Since the seventh century, when the Maghreb (North Africa west of Egypt) was Islamized by the invading Muslim forces coming from the east, Islam has played a direct and profound role in the social and political dynamics of the region. Except for the colonial period, during the past thirteen centuries, Islam has served many functions, including an identity base, a unifying factor in the face of internal conflict and external challenges, an instrument of political legitimation for the ruling authorities, and an inspiration for revolutionary fervor among the masses. Writing in 1964, Carl Brown acknowledged that "it still remains true that Islam remains one of the important indices for understanding developments in North Africa" (Brown 1964, 63). This observation continues to be valid today. It was well confirmed by the fact that, following the popular upheavals of 2011 in the Middle East and North Africa region, religious parties took the leadership reins in Tunisia, Egypt, and Morocco.

This essay examines the political dimension of Islam in the Maghreb region (Algeria, Libya, Morocco, and Tunisia) with a focus on the postindependence era; this is done by tackling several issues, including the role of Islam in national identity and its relationship to the nation-state; the reformist and the revolutionary tendencies inspired by Islam in the region; the interaction between the state and Islam; and the various manifestations of Islam in national political dynamics. These issues are tackled along five chronological sequences: (1) Islam in the nationalist struggle for independence, (2) the postindependence "nationalization" of religion, (3) the rise of grassroots Islam, (4) post-Islamism and the ascendency of Sufism following a bitter confrontation between the state and radical Islamism,[1] and (5) the rise to power of moderate Islamism through the ballot box in the wake of what was termed the "Arab Spring."

Political Islam has stimulated plenty of scholarly writing and journalistic accounts in the past three decades due its ascendency as a phenomenon that seemed to undermine domestic and international orders. In the countries where it appeared as a relatively new, but potent, force to be reckoned with, and in a region where it seemed to threaten the interests of regional as well as extraregional states, political Islam commended attention and stimulated concern and reaction. The way it manifested itself and the manner in which it was understood and dealt with were going to have a direct impact on its own evolution and even transformation. This has been the case of most of the predominantly Muslim countries and regions— Asia and the subregions of the Middle East and North Africa.

In the Maghreb region, political Islam manifested itself in a variety of ways and was tackled differently by state policies and actions. Regardless of the particular convolutions that the interactions between the state and political Islam went through—some violent and others not—in the end, two types of situations have developed across the key states of the region: in Algeria and Morocco, Political Islam has entered mainstream politics through what have been termed by many analysts as a moderation of Islamism or "post-Islamism," on one hand, and successful state co-optation strategies, on the other. In Tunisia and Libya, the initial utterances of grassroots political movements animated by a religious ideology were crushed by the state early enough to avoid a protracted confrontation. This reaction left room for neither the moderation of Islamism nor its co-optation by the state. However, the overthrow in 2011of Zine al-`Abidin Ben `Ali and Muammar al-Qaddafi, the autocratic leaders of Tunisia and Libya, allowed political Islam to openly return to the political scene and legally and freely compete for election.

In the first two cases, the moderation-integration of grassroots political Islam coincided with a general, albeit limited, opening of the political system, while in the second two cases, the exclusion and repression of all expressions of political Islam coincided with a closing of all venues of political opposition to all forces, be they religious or secular. This might partly explain why political Islam came back with a vengeance after the overthrow of the authoritarian leaders. In Libya, it instantly became a major force in the early post-Qaddafi era, and in Tunisia, it became the main political force in the institutions of transition from the Ben Ali era.

The way political Islam appeared in the postcolonial Maghrebi states, how it manifested itself in recent decades, and how it and its relationship with the state evolved have all been affected by several factors, including,

1. the role and place of Islam in the national liberation movement
2. the relationship that developed between religion and the state in the first decades of independence from colonialism (French in Algeria, Morocco, and Tunisia, and Italian in Libya)
3. the place and role of religious militancy in each country
4. the nature and outcome of the confrontation between the state and grassroots political Islam
5. the extent of doctrinal and political adaptation of both the state and grassroots political Islam to changing domestic and international conditions

These factors are explored below according to the chronological sequencing indicated above.

ISLAM AND NATIONALISM IN THE MAGHREB

In their struggle against French colonialism, Algerian, Moroccan, and Tunisian nationalisms based their calls for resistance to the colonizer and for the establishment of independent nation-states for their respective societies both on secular tenets of nationalism and on Islam. The secular elements included the usual tenets such as the homeland (*watan*), the common history, and its associated myths, the unique culture, and the unifying language. To these elements, which served to distinguish the colonized from the colonizer, was added Islam as a key religious and cultural factor of unity among the indigenous populations as well as a powerful instrument of distinction from the religion and culture of the colonizer.

French colonialism in all three countries stimulated thus nationalist movements, which "activated 'political' Islam as they sought roots in Islamic as well as national identities. Political Islam in turn shaped the nationalist movements against the French presence" in the three Maghrebi countries (Henry 2007, 87).

In Algeria, for example, the words of Shaykh Abdelhamid Ben Badis (1889–1940), a founder of the Association of 'Ulama' (Muslim scholars), which became a nationalist creed, were "Algeria is my country, Arabic is my language and Islam is my religion." Even though Ben Badis's work through the Association of 'Ulama' focused more on religious, cultural, and linguistic revival or affirmation and did not per se call for independence, his motto was successfully used by the secular nationalists, starting with Messali Hadj (1898–1974), whose nationalist association Etoile Nord-Africaine

(North African Star) called for the full independence of Algeria. "The *Etoile* rejected assimilation and demanded Algeria's self-determination. Messali's brand of nationalism took over all the major symbols and values of the 'glorious' Arab-Islamic past: 'The Muslim Algerian people have a glorious historic past, a religion and a language totally different from those of France....'" (Stora 1991, 74).

A similar evolution was experienced in Morocco and Tunisia, where the nationalist movements began with an accommodating attitude toward the colonizer but with an affirmation of the unique indigenous identity. However, the harsh and unaccommodating colonial rule pushed these movements toward an uncompromising demand for independence, which was undergirded by both a strong Islamic identity as well as secular nationalist values.

The way the French rulers handled both the nationalist movements and the religious orders of the colonized societies was going to affect the postindependence relationship between state and religion. In Algeria, which was a settlement colony annexed to France, the French rulers destroyed much of the religious structures, institutions, and schools, while preserving them in Morocco and Tunisia—possibly as a result of lessons learned in Algeria and also as a strategy aimed to weaken the secular nationalists in Tunisia and the monarch in Morocco. In Libya, the Sanusi religious order was also not much affected by the relatively brief Italian colonization. In spite of the fact that the Italians closed its lodges, arrested its shaykhs, and confiscated its *habous* land (i.e., those belonging to the mosque) because it actively resisted colonialism, the Sanusiya survived and established a monarchy at independence in 1951.

The religious tendencies in the Maghreb included conservative and modernist Salafi currents,[2] which permeated the nationalist movements, as well as Sufi orders and their respective *zawiyate* (shrines or schools). In Morocco, ʿAllal al-Fasi, a Salafist, founded the nationalist Istiqlal party and led its struggle against colonialism. In the Maghreb, particularly in Algeria, Morocco, and Tunisia, Salafism "corresponded to the patriotic expectations of the peoples who rejected colonial domination" (Addi 2009, 341). Again, in the Moroccan case, "The energy of religious fervor was rationalized, disciplined, mobilized to support the sultan in the struggle for independence" (Addi 2009, 339). The same can be said about the support extended to the secular nationalist movements in Algeria and Tunisia, which were led respectively by the National Liberation Front and the Neo-Destour Party. However, beyond the national unity it incited, Salafism, which inspired the ideological foundation of Islamism, was going to adopt a radical and even revolutionary attitude in the postcolonial Maghreb as it questioned the political, economic, and moral orders of the newly independent states. As will be discussed later, the Salafi tendency took both a peaceful track of Da`awa and protest and a track of violent action for redemption and revolution.

POSTINDEPENDENCE "OFFICIAL ISLAM" AND ITS LIMITS

In the first decade of independence, a common pattern in the relationship between Islam and the state developed in Algeria, Morocco, Tunisia, and Libya. That pattern was the active attempt by the state (and the monarchy in the case of Morocco) to control religion and religious forces by a variety of means. It was probably understood from the start that the reformist fervor of the Salafiya could prove to be a challenge in the early stages of building a secular and modern state. That process began in 1956 in Morocco and Tunisia and in 1962 in Algeria. In Libya it began in 1951 and was, paradoxically, started by the leader of the Sanusi order, who had just accidentally turned king—the process continued after the overthrow of the Sanusi monarchy by Mu`ammar al-Qaddafi in 1969.

The reformist tendencies that had existed during the colonial era but were muted by the need to close ranks in the struggle against a common occupier, oppressor, and non-Muslim enemy resurfaced after independence, as all political and religious tendencies wanted to affect the determination of the developmental path the state was about to in engage in. After the initial independence euphoria and sometimes confusion, as was the case in Algeria, the leaders of the newly independent states moved to not only reign in the Salafi reformist tendencies but also to establish a hegemonic control over the religious sphere through the oversight of the mosques and Friday sermons, the co-optation of the `ulama', the repression of the radical challengers, and the development of an official religious discourse that became the expression of what is termed "official Islam." This process is examined below in the four countries' cases.

Libya: Taming Islamism with Islamic reforms and repression

In Libya, where the Sanusi religious order itself inherited the command over the country, there was a somewhat reverse process whereby, "upon ascending to power, King Idris attempted to secularize the political system, rein in radical traditionalism, and bring about change. In the process, he relegated the Sanusiya order—and with it, religion—to a secondary position" (El-Kikhia 1997, 28). When he came to power in 1969, Qaddafi did not want to take on the religious establishment for fear of loss of popular support, avoiding, thereby, the mistake of his predecessor. However, once his power consolidated, he progressively established control over the religious sphere by openly taking on the traditional `ulama' and by "creating his own type of Islam which he viewed as more progressive and in line with the spirit of the nationalist era" (El-Kikhia 1997, 41). The Libyan leader wanted thus to start with a clean slate in which nationalism and a particular version of Islam were combined to form the ideological core of the Revolution. In his article "Qadhafi's Libya and the Prospect of Islamic Succession," Ray Takeyh indicated,

> During the first few years of the revolution, the regime went beyond rhetorical gestures and initiated substantive Islamic reforms. Qadhafi often spoke in mosques and consulted the clerics regarding public-policy initiatives. The `Ulama' were given prominent positions in the legal and educational spheres and oversaw the National Guidance Council, designed to reform Libya's legal system along Islamic lines. (Takeyh 2000, pp. 155–156)

In this process, al-Qaddafi pushed for a pan-Arabism and a socialist revolution that were "Islamed." He also introduced some Shari`ah law and made alcohol and prostitution illegal (Joffe 1995, 146). In other words, he skillfully pushed aside the old Sanusiyya order and used his relatively liberal version of Islam to build his legitimacy and to implement his socialist vision for Libya.

However, in the 1970s, and in spite of these efforts, al-Qaddafi was unable to prevent political Islam from rising. He faced challenges from the Libyan Muslim Brotherhood (Ikhwan), which he managed to dismantle easily, especially since they were not allowed to form charitable organizations, professional guilds, and student associations as they had done in Egypt. However, in the following two decades, two radical Islamist groups tried to organize a rebellion against his regime. They were the Harakat al-Jihad (the Jihad Movement, in the early 1980s) and the al-Jama`a al-Libiya al-Islamiya al-Muqatila

(Libyan Islamic Fighting Group [LIFG], in the mid-1990s). They too failed in their attempt to destabilize the regime.

The irony was that al-Qaddafi was finally overthrown by a popular rebellion that was not led by the Islamists. In fact, the 2011 popular upheaval was essentially secular without any specific agenda beyond overthrowing the existing regime. Several Islamists groups of different tendencies did finally form and join the rebellion, but when they tried to claim leadership (through the ballot box) after al-Qaddafi was killed, they failed.

Algeria: The socialist revolution challenged

After independence in 1962, the governing elite in Algeria understood well the potential political power of Islam, but they did not want the political order to be based on it or heavily inspired by it. They intended to build a secular system without dismissing the importance of Islam in national life and identity. In 1964, one of the key ideological and political documents of the National Liberation Front (FLN), the Algiers Charter, reinforced the socialist and secular orientation of Algeria. Even though the state was not set to impose its dominance over the religious sphere, it became clear later that the governing leadership would have to exercise some control over religion so as not to allow it to emerge as a political force that could be potentially destabilizing. In order to limit the dissension of the religious factions, the regime attempted to reassure it by declaring that Algeria's socialism would have the "color" of Islam (i.e., "Islamic socialism"), by introducing mandatory religious courses in public schools and by making Friday the weekly day of rest instead of Sunday (Frégosi 1995, 104). There developed also an "official Islam," which monopolized control over the places of worship and public religious discourse in the country.

In much of the 1960s and 1970s, the conservative religious elite, which would later inspire the Islamist movement, expressed at that time a merely moral reaction to the strong leftist tendency that permeated the bulk of the national leadership elite. The religious dissenters accused the government of drawing inspiration not from the Islamic faith but rather from foreign theories and models (e.g., historical materialism of the Marxists and European socialism). Religious conservatism permeated the Association of Algerian Muslim 'Ulama' and was articulated by important religious figures such as Abdelatif Soltani, Bachir Ibrahimi, Ahmed Sahnoun, Mesbah Houidek, and Omar Larbaoui. In 1963, Hachemi Tidjani, general secretary of the Algiers Faculté, created al-Qiyam al-Islamiya (the Islamic Values), an association for the defense of Islamic ideals and culture. Before it was banned,[3] this association had attracted several people who would later become instrumental in transforming this movement for cultural and moral regeneration into a political one. Among the most prominent was Abbasi Madani, who later became leader of the Islamic Salvation Front (FIS).

During the rule of President Houari Boumediene, who had come to power through a military coup in June 1965, the conservative religious elite continued to demand an increase in the overt role of religion in both society and government. It also continued to criticize attempts to link socialism with Islam (Burgat 1988, 45) and denounced the negative moral impact of modernization, which included such things as alcohol distribution, coed education, and women's adoption of Western dress codes. The limited—mainly verbal—opposition of this period became more politically assertive within a few years.

As a response to this mounting religious challenge, the state increased its control over the religious sphere while remaining steadfast on the socialist course. The regime began to repress its religious opponents while at the same time making use of religion in support of both regime and socialism. The use and consolidation of official Islam aimed at lending legitimacy to a regime that had come to power by force. This official Islam manifested itself in a tight supervision of the mosques and of all religious education and institutions, the creation of centers of Islamic learning, and in symbolic acts and events, such as televising weekly the president's attendance of the Friday prayer in the mosque.

In a change of strategy, the religious elite, especially the conservative `ulama', sought a compromise with the regime and decided to lend support to Boumediene with the hope that such support would help them temper the socialist orientation by way of controlling at least the spheres of culture and education. Due to his need for legitimacy and for support for the socialist revolution, Boumediene responded to the demands and allowed the ministries of culture and information, education, and religious education and affairs to be headed by members of the religious elite, such as Ahmed Taleb Ibrahimi and Mouloud Kassim. By accepting this compromise, Boumediene had hoped to use the religious elite to relay his revolutionary messages and to mobilize popular support behind them. To placate the religious elite, the regime also pushed for a formal and symbolic connection between Islam and the state, without necessarily undermining the inherently secular nature of the system of government and its policies. As a result, the 1976 constitution and national charter (political, economic, ideological, and cultural blueprint) merely reiterated the institutional importance of Islam but without giving it a central role. While declaring Islam to be the religion of the state, the charter confirmed the unshakable commitment to socialism when it stated, "The Muslim people will realize little by little that it is by reinforcing the struggle against imperialism and by committing themselves resolutely in the path of socialism, that they will best respond to the imperatives of their faith, and make action coincide with the principles."[4]

Unsatisfied by these formal concessions and seeking more tangible deeds from the government, the religious conservatives demanded more measures to help deal with the challenges to the faith by rapid modernization and increasing exposure to outside influences. However, the association al-Qiyam al-Islamiya, which expressed these demands, was suspended by the government in 1966 after it sent a letter to Egyptian President Gamal Abdel Nasser to protest against the execution of the Islamist ideologue Sayyid Qutb. Four years later, it was officially banned after its discourse turned more political. Its members, however, increased their *Da'wa* activities and their open opposition to socialism. Unable to attack the regime's social policies, which enjoyed wide support among the masses, they courted people opposed to socialism, such as big merchants and big landowners who stood to lose from state policies. Unable to quiet them, even after an initial crackdown, the government made yet another set of concessions to them, including dismantlement of vineyards, adoption of Arabic as the sole language of education,[5] promotion of religious education in schools, banning of alcohol in some cities, closing all restaurants during the month of Ramadan, prohibition of raising pigs, substitution of Friday instead of Sunday as the weekly day of rest, and reintroduction in 1973 of the recourse to Islamic laws as a secondary source available to civil court judges, and enactment later (in 1984) of a conservative family law code (Frégosi 1995, 106).

Toward the end of the 1970s, Boumediene seemed to have succeeded in establishing a delicate balance between the needs of advancing the socialist project with the help of the left and winning the acquiescence of the religious elite. However, this worked as long as the state was able to respond to the basic needs of society. Once the distributive function of the state started failing by the end of the 1970s and early 1980s, that balance collapsed and the religious sentiment started changing into a powerful political movement seeking a radical change, even by way of violence. This change was also affected by important external factors such as the Iranian Revolution.

The mounting economic crisis that affected negatively the state's distributive function was caused by external constraints due mainly to a high dependency on income from hydrocarbons only, and internal factors such as the failing development strategy itself, an inefficient bureaucracy, rising inflation, growing income inequalities, weak agricultural performance, and urban migration. These economic difficulties helped the development of a militant form of political Islam that proved later to be very violent and highly destabilizing.

At that point, the Islamist claims were no longer limited to the cultural and social spheres; the religious opposition attacked also, and directly, the nature of the political system and its policies, as well as a panoply of phenomena, including corruption, nepotism, injustice, pronounced socioeconomic inequality, and authoritarianism.

As indicated above, important concessions were made by the government to the Islamists, but Islam was not allowed to affect the fundamental structure or policies of the regime. Religion was used only as an instrumental "official Islam" for political purposes. Political freedom was severely curtailed under the banners of socialism, nationalism, unity, and conformity for the sake of the good of the whole society and there were no legal venues for the venting of dissenting opinions. As will be discussed later, this political strategy failed to inhibit the birth and development of a highly politicized grassroots Islam, which was going to constitute a serious challenge to the state and society by the end of the 1980.

Morocco: Salafiya and the "Commander of the Faithful"

The unity fomented by the struggle for independence between the monarchy, the religious leaders, and the secular nationalists came under stress right after independence. The monarch, Mohamed V, who, like his predecessors, claimed religious legitimacy was aware of the potential challenge of reformist Salafiya, which was partly embedded in the nationalist party Istiqlal, the left, represented by the National Union of Popular Forces (UNFP) party, and the military. The king worked then on weakening the Istiqlal party, which was mostly popular in the urban centers, and neutralizing the religious leaders through manipulation and control over the religious sphere (Zeghal 2005, 55). After Mohamed V died in 1961, his son, Hassan II, continued on the same course using political manipulation, control, and the co-optation of the leaders of the nationalist and *salafiya* tendencies, which, by the same token, he would play against the left, which he feared the most in the 1960s and 1970s.

While some religious leaders questioned the religious authority and autocratic methods of the monarch, there was no visible core group behind them capable of mobilizing the masses for political action until the 1980s, when political Islam gained momentum at a time when both the military (after the failed coup attempts of 1971 and 1972) and the left were totally neutralized by the king.

Morocco's Islamist movement was the last to enter the political arena en masse in North Africa. This was due to several reasons, including a tight control of the religious sphere and its symbols by a monarch who claimed to be *amir almu'minin* (Commander of the Faithful, based on a claim of *shorfa* lineage, that is, a descendent of Prophet Mohamed), and the use by King Hassan II of a wide-scale repression of all opposition, both religious and secular, during his reign from 1961 to 1999.

Besides repressing the groups that could not be controlled, King Hassan also tried to monopolize the religious sphere by establishing a whole system of expression of "official Islam" through the promotion of nonpolitical religious organizations, such as *Da'wa* associations—which he also used against the secular left— and the reactivation and control of the Council of `Ulama'. The monarch also promoted traditional religious structures and measures inspired by religion such as the enactment of a conservative Code of Personal Status (*Mudawana*), the creation of Qur'anic schools, and the imposition of prayer in school.

Contrary to his expectations, however, a rising Islamist movement took advantage of this invigorated religious life and developed as a moral, political, and social force. It included several organizations, but the most popular one was that of the al-`Adl wa al- Ihsan of the late Abdeslam Yassin, the schoolteacher who directly challenged the monarch in an open letter in 1974. Yassin's organization increased its appeal by way of social and charitable actions, by taking up the demands and grievances of students, and by denouncing the corrupt elements among the governing elite.

> By assisting the sick, the widowed and the unemployed, they have gained followers in the shanty towns in Tangier, Rabat and Casablanca. Their charities run blood banks and help people organize funerals. [On Aid al-Adha,] they offer lamb or mutton to the poor. [They also] have been steadily reaching into the educational system, enlisting high school teachers and university students [and have recruited urban professionals]. (Simons 1998)

By the time of King Hassan's death, `Adl wa al-Ihsan was a full-fledged Islamist movement that rejected the monarchical order and the legitimacy of the king. However, it was a movement that rejected the use of violence but also resisted being co-opted. Its shunned participation in a political system whose rules are already set in favor of the existing ruling system.

Tunisia: Modernization, demise of the left and the rise of Political Islam

In Tunisia, where the 2011 upheavals in the Arab world began, Islam played an important role in the struggle for Tunisia's independence just as in the rest of the Maghreb. The traditional Qur'anic schools established in the early 1900s helped the nationalist cause, but their role and place in the postindependence political and cultural dynamics was purposefully curtailed by the state, which was placed on a Western-style modernization trajectory. The nonthreatening elements of Tunisia's Salafi tendency were used in the context of nation and state building by Tunisia's first president, Habib Bourguiba.

According to Elbaki Hermassi, after independence, three ideological tendencies informally competed for deciding the course of the new state: the religious, the revolutionary Marxist, and the modern liberal tendencies (Hermassi 1972). It was the last tendency that ended up controlling the country, headed by President Bourguiba, who engaged Tunisia in a Western-style modernization process.

President Bourguiba followed a two-track policy, which, on one hand tried to contain the religious current while advancing social policies deemed clashing with prevailing religious interpretations, and on the other hand used religion as instrument of legitimacy and control, just as was done elsewhere in the Maghreb and other parts of the Arab world. After having promulgated in 1957 a personal status code containing the most liberal laws on gender equality in the region, he tried to preempt the resistance of the conservative religious current in the country. Among the various actions undertaken to limit the role of the traditional religious current—which seemed quite passive at that time—and to prevent it from becoming an obstacle to Bourguiba's modernization plan for Tunisia, the Zaytouna Mosque-University, a traditional center of Islamic learning and scholarship, was denied autonomy by its integration into the University of Tunis in 1960. Bourguiba also tried to institute an "official Islam" by way of rhetoric and action. He created a "Directorate of Religious Affairs," which would later become the Ministry of Religious Affairs, to help direct religious norms and actions from above. The state took control of public *habus* land and of the financial management of mosques and religious schools. The *Shari`ah* courts were abolished and replaced by a single-state judicial system (Perkins 1986, 111). Moreover, Bourguiba proclaimed himself *mufti* (one who issues *fetwas* and interprets Islam) and regularly praised the Islamic heritage of his people. However, his forceful modernization policies irked the then almost dormant religious reformist current in Tunisia, especially when he called on people not to fast during Ramadan because it hurt productivity and, according to him, breaking the fast was permitted in Islam during Jihad, that is, the Jihad for development. A faction of this religious current became politicized by the 1970s in response to the state's control of the religious sphere, to what was perceived as Bourguiba's Westernization of Tunisia, and to the rise of the left.

In the end, Bourguiba was not able to contain the incipient political Islam. On the contrary, when he was faced with an increasingly bold challenge from the left, he allowed the Islamist movement to come out in public and he indirectly supported its open activism, hoping that it would counterbalance the left. In the 1960s, the leftist group Afaq (Perspectives or Horizon) clashed several times with the government and the conflict culminated in the prohibition of the Communist Party in 1963. In the late 1970s, the clash was with the main labor union, the General Union of Tunisian Workers (UGTT) over economic and social policies. After violent clashes in the late 1970s, the labor movement was also tamed, which left the political arena wide open for the Islamist tendency to make headways as a popular movement seeking radical change in Tunisia.

Just as in Algeria, the Tunisian religious movement, which was initially concerned with cultural, social, and religious issues, inched its way into the political arena, expressing opposition to the left and later to the increasingly authoritarian state under Bourguiba. Also, just as in Algeria and Morocco, the regime used the religious current to face off the leftist challenge, and there too, the strategy backfired. By the early 1980s, "[the] Tunisian single-party regime... [which] had successfully mobilized Islam for the purposes of nation-building went furthest in reforms that upend the religious establishment" (Henry 2007, 87).

By the time Bourguiba was overthrown in 1987 by his interior minister, Zine al-`Abidin Ben `Ali, the Islamist movement was at its highest level of political mobilization under the leadership of Rashid Ghannushi, who had founded in 1979 the Movement of the Islamic Tendency (Mouvement de la Tendance Islamique [MIT]), later renamed al-Nahdah (Renaissance) party. As will be discussed later, the religious movement, which was essentially reformist and seeking change by peaceful means, stimulated a wide repression of all political opposition and ended up being eliminated by the mid-1990s. However, after President Ben Ali was overthrown in February 2011, al-Nahdah was quickly legalized as a political party and it became the most powerful contender in the political arena.

GRASSROOTS ISLAM CONFRONTS THE STATE

By the mid-1980s, all four Maghrebi countries were facing an Islamist challenge of varying degree and form. The causes of the rise of the Islamist movement as a challenge to the Maghrebi states were various and complex. Including and beyond the factors discussed above, it is important to mention the following internal factors and conditions:

1. worsening socioeconomic conditions for a vast number of people, especially in Algeria, Morocco, and Tunisia
2. the marked decline of the secular opposition due to repression and manipulation—the most challenging opposition figures were jailed, pushed into foreign exile, or eliminated
3. weak or absent ideological sign posts in the midst of a search of identity markers in a context of a waning nationalist and socialist ideologies and a perceived encroachment of Western culture and behaviors
4. weak or controlled independent civic and professional associations and student organizations and unions
5. weak representative institutions (the legislature in Morocco, Algeria, and Tunisia had no power of its own)
6. lack of independence of the judiciary branch, which often sided with government claims against dissidents
7. strict control of the media by the state

A consequential ideological and institutional vacuum was easily filled by religious slogans and networks that offered a radically different social and political project. With the combination of calls for democratization and religious revival, the Islamists pushed for the widening of the arena of political participation by making more people involved. Members of the governing elites inadvertently played a facilitating role by manipulating religious groups and symbols hoping that that would dampen the religious opposition and increase their own legitimacy. They often used the Islamist sentiment against the secular left and vice versa. That was the case of Presidents Boumediene and Bendjedid in Algeria and Bourguiba Tunisia and King Hassan of Morocco. The next sections will tackle the confrontation that took place between each Maghrebi state and the Islamists and will highlight the state reaction patterns and how they affected the outcome.

Algeria

Massive youth riots in October 1988, which were harshly repressed, brought about a fast-paced series of events with a profound impact on Algeria's political landscape. The following year, sweeping political reforms ended the one-party rule of the FLN and allowed the birth of opposition parties, independent associations, and printing presses. Among the most active new political formations was the al-Jabha al-Islamiya li al-Inqadh (Islamic Front of Salvation, or FIS), which wished to establish an Islamic republic governed by *Shari`ah*. In June 1990, the FIS made a strong showing in Algeria's first free municipal elections, which emboldened it to demand early presidential elections and electoral reform, and prompted it to organize acts of civil disobedience, and to call for a general strike and mutiny of the armed forces. In June 1991, the military cracked down on Islamist sit-ins, arrested thousands of Islamists, including the two leaders of the FIS, and imposed a regime of martial law. In December 1991, in the first balloting of the first multiparty parliamentary elections the FIS won overwhelmingly. However, on January 1992, right before the second balloting (run-offs) took place, the army intervened and cancelled the electoral process. It also forced President Chadli Bendjedid—who was appointed president after Boumediene died in late 1978—to resign and replaced him with a collective ruling body named the High State Council. In response, the FIS militants and other Islamist groups went underground and escalated violent attacks against the state. The government declared a state of emergency, banned the FIS, and a large-scale crackdown against the Islamists ensued.

From that time and until the late 1990s, the armed conflict between the military and the various Islamist groups claimed the lives of around 200,000 people. New armed organizations sprang up, including the al-Jama`at al-Islamiya al-Musallaha (Armed Islamic Groups [GIA]). This group became notorious for a brutality directed against state security services, civilians, journalists, intellectuals, and foreigners. However, its own indiscriminate violence, infiltration by Algeria's secret services, and state counterinsurgency actions, led to its demise. It eventually disappeared and was replaced by a new group known as the al-Jama`a al-Salafiya li-al-Da`wa wa al-Qital (Salafist Group for Preaching and Combat [GSPC]), which, in turn, assimilated itself in 2006 into the al-Qa`ida network and took the name of al-Qa`ida in the Land of the Islamic Maghreb. Since then, this group has mounted some spectacular violent attacks in the country against both state and foreign interests, including an attack against US oil workers and a United Nations building. It is today the most important radical Islamist group that is still active in Algeria and in the whole region of North Africa and the Sahel region (Chad, Mali, Niger, and Mauritania).

In the midst of the terrible violence of the 1990s, important political developments allowed a nonviolent political Islam to enter the political arena as a set of legal and legitimate political parties, starting with the first multiparty presidential election in 1995 and multiparty parliamentary elections in 1997. However, after an initial respectable result at the polls, Islamist parties—mainly, Harakat Mujtama` al-Silm (Movement of Society for Peace [MSP])—started declining.

The Islamist rebellion failed to achieve its objectives and its crude violence has negatively affected the standing of the religious movement among the population. In the 2002 parliamentary elections, there was a decline in support for the Islamist parties, which was due partly to the general irrelevance of opposition parties and to internal conflicts within the MSP, a moderate Islamist party (formerly known as Hamas) and within Harakat al-Nahda al-Islamiya (Movement for Islamic Renaissance [MRI], also known as Ennahda), also a moderate party. The MSP lost thirty-one of its sixty-nine seats and Ennahda kept only one of its thirty-four seats. However, a new party—a breakaway from the latter—Harakat al-Islah al-Watani (Movement for National Reform [MRN], known as Islah) obtained forty-three seats. Overall, the number of seats controlled by the Islamists declined from 103 to 82.

In the November 2005 partial local elections in 143 local municipalities, the Islamists obtained seven seats only, and in the May 17, 2007 parliamentary elections, the number of seats they controlled went down from 82 to 60; the pro-government FLN and the National Democratic Rally (RND)[6] parties had also lost forty-nine of the combined 246 they held—due to FLN losses—but they remained the two dominant formations. Between 2002 and 2007, the process had come full circle with the FLN—which has the highest number of seats—back in control and supportive of President Bouteflika. In the 2012 parliamentary elections, the Islamist lost more seats in spite of the "Green Alliance" they formed and the regional context of that time—Tunisia was already governed by al-Nahda, Morocco's dominant party was the Islamist Party of

Justice and Development (PJD), which obtained a majority of seats in the 2011 elections and took over the office the prime minister, and in Egypt, the Muslim Brothers became the most powerful political formation in the post-Mubarak transition institutions.

The 2012 Algerian parliamentary elections were preceded by a high hope of the Islamist formations making up the Green Alliance (MSP, Islah, and Ennahda) that they would follow in the footsteps of their fellow Islamist parties in Egypt, Tunisia, and Morocco. However, the ruling regime had managed to not only dodge the "Arab Spring" altogether, but it also pushed the Islamist parties into an almost irrelevant status. Together, the pro-government FLN and RND parties won 276 seats (out of 462), while the Green Alliance received forty-nine seats only. The newly created Islamist party, the Front for Justice and Development (also known as Adala/FJD) won only 7 seats. These results constituted a major setback for the Islamist parties, but, most importantly, the whole electoral process was received by the majority of people with unprecedented indifference (the real voter participation rate was probably 20 percent to 30 percent, the lowest ever). The government managed to dodge the winds of revolt in the region by lifting a nineteen-year-old state of emergency, promising political reforms, and pumping huge amounts of money into social and economic sectors, including infrastructure works, salary increases across the board, support for microcredit programs, and paid internships for the youth. The government has managed to buy off social discontent for now thanks to substantial windfall gains from hydrocarbon exports, but the strategy may not work forever. In this context, all opposition parties proved to be entirely irrelevant and powerless, including the Islamist ones.

In spite of the setback they experienced over the years since they were legalized, the religious parties continued to take advantage of their political inclusion to affect state policies and actions. The aim of political Islam may be that, once fully entrenched in the political institutions and processes, its militants will then work on implementing their vision for Algeria. As will be discussed later, these parties that have penetrated the state's fortress may have entered what some have called the "post-Islamist" era and, instead of struggling to bring down the secular state, they embarked on a two-track strategy: Islamizing society from below while, at the same time, trying to Islamize public institutions and policies from the top. They may have succeeded in the first track but have not fared well in the second.

Morocco

In Morocco, the monarchy managed to strike a delicate balance between the secular left and the religious forces by way of a constantly shifting game of repression and tolerance of one at a time, or both at once. Numerous Islamist organizations (more than twenty) were established, many of which with the approval of the state. However, most of them remain focused on charitable works in poor neighborhoods and recruit in schools and workplaces. By the late 1990s, some of them began gradually entering the political sphere, armed with a societal and political project that was very different from that of the traditional, secular opposition.

In the last two years of his life, King Hassan II enacted important institutional changes, allowed the opposition to form a government, and permitted, for the first time, a token Islamist representation in parliament, although not through a party of their own.[7] In 1998, the first openly Islamist PJD was admitted as a legal formation.

These changes came as a result of several factors, including strong domestic and international pressures for political liberalization, fears instilled by the violent Islamist rebellion in Algeria, and the need to co-opt the leftist opposition in preparation for the succession of Hassan's son to the throne. Such opposition may have become a serious problem to an inexperienced king if it remained on the outside. King Hassan's last-minute strategy of relative political inclusion worked. It neutralized the left by allowing it to lead the government and made it, thus, share the blame for people's economic hardship. However, one the most important challenges that the new king, Mohamed VI, had to worry about after taking over was the Islamist movement.

The Islamists sought to establish a faith-based social, economic, political, and cultural order but were divided on how to accomplish that. In the 2000s, the two main contenders to Islamist leadership have been the PJD and the unrecognized movement of al-`Adl wa al-Ihsan. Both reject political violence as a means. The first one is inspired by the Muslim Brotherhood and Wahhabi Salafism, recognizes the legitimacy of the monarch and his title of Commander of the Faithful, and accepts to work within the existing system in pursuit of change. The second one, whose leader combines both Sufism and Salafism, refuses to participate in the political process as long as the political order remains dominated by a king whose religious legitimacy is questioned. In spite of not being a legal party, al-`Adl wa al-Ihsan remains the most popular Islamist movement in Morocco. It attracts the sympathy of young and disaffected urban dwellers and has supporters among the poor, school and university students, and educated urban professionals in major cities.

In a stark contrast to his father, the new, young, and popular monarch began his rule with a competition with the Islamists in their traditional works of charity and fight against poverty and injustice—he became known as "the king of the poor." This partly explains why the Islamists (other than al-`Adl wa al-Ihsan) have, in recent years, sought to adapt to the changed circumstances. The discourse of groups like the PJD started focusing less on social, economic, and religious issues and more on the political institutions and processes they seek to change. However, not being able to make a dent in this area, they seem to have resigned themselves to working within the existing rules and to limiting their ambition to placing themselves in the existing system in way that can allow them to have some impact on public policy. In 2011 they succeeded in fulfilling that ambition by winning the most seats in parliament (107 out of 395) in the elections of November 25, which followed a constitutional reform a few months earlier that changed some of the institutional rules without undermining the preeminence of the monarch. In the end, the monarchy, under the new king, remains in control and in charge of the political institutions and their agendas. It managed to upstage the Islamists in their natural field of social works while at the same time relaxing somewhat the general political environment. Mohamed VI also made use of the divisive tactic of his father by agreeing to the legalization of two new Islamist parties, the Renaissance and Virtue Party (PRV), a breakaway movement from the PJD, and the Civilized Alternative Party.

Within the last decade, the Moroccan Islamists increased their pressure for change. They took advantage of the social and economic crisis and of the weakness of the leftist opposition and have tried to lead social protests. The bulk of the Islamist movement has used peaceful means to advance its goals, but a small number of violent radical groups have emerged and some of them have even conducted violent actions in recent years. These violent factions are often referred to as *jihadi Salafism*, which dates back to the early 1990s when an attack in Marrakesh hotel killed two Spanish tourists. These factions include organizations such as *al-Takfir wa al-Hijra* (Excommunication and Migration), Jamâ`at al-Sirat al-Mustaqîm (the

Group of the True Path), al-'Jamâ'a al-Salafiya (the Salafi Group), and Ahl al-Sunna wa al-'Jamâ'a (People of the Sunna and of the Community).

On May 14, 2003, 45 people were killed and around 100 were injured by five suicide bomb attacks in Casablanca. The perpetrators were all Moroccans, and many of them were from the slums of Casablanca. The event constituted a real shock to the country and it was immediately feared that the tolerated Islamist parties and movements would be repressed and banned as a reprisal for the attack. However, even though in the aftermath of the attack thousands of Islamists were rounded up for questioning and many were jailed, tried, and given prison or death sentences, the PJD and other Islamist parties and organizations were not banned, but their public image was tarnished by the violence even though they were not directly responsible for it or condoned it.

Another effect of the May 2003 attack was the adoption of a new antiterrorism law that substantially curtails the freedom of expression and gives the state more power to pursue and persecute suspected radicals. This situation made Aboubakr Jamai, editor in chief of the Moroccan newsweekly *Le Journal Hebdomadaire,* to observe that "...the Moroccan government seems to have made the decision to restrict liberty in the name of security, perhaps in imitation of the United States after the September 11 attacks.... But these moves are a mistake. To fight terrorism, Morocco needs more democracy, not less" (Jamai 2003).

Years after this shocking event, the legal Islamist tendency (PJD) and the tolerated one (al'Adl wa al-Ihsan) remained highly vibrant and active, each according to its own strategy, means, and limitations. However, both thrive in a highly restrictive political environment. The PJD has accepted the preeminence of the monarchy and seemed to limit its action to issues of social justice and development as well as some institutional reform, without questioning, though, the supremacy of the king's political and religious authority, even after taking over parliament and the office of the prime minister. As for al-'Adl wa al-Ihsan, it stands firm on not partaking in a system whose rules are set by the monarch and in the interest of the monarchy, but its social action and its political message remain very attractive for a large portion of the urban population that is increasingly disillusioned by the political establishment and by the powerlessness of representative institutions. This disillusionment is one of the reasons many have in the 1990s and 2000s rediscovered an alternative path, Sufism. In fact, Sufism has become so popular by the end of the first decade of the twenty-first century, that it is praised and espoused by all, including the monarch himself, the leader of al-'Adl wa al-Ihsan, and even the PJD leader, Benkirane, whose early political schooling was in Sufism. The significance of this development in Morocco, as well as in Algeria, is discussed below.

Tunisia

In a context of serious economic difficulties and unabating social unrest, interior minister Zine al-'Abidin Ben 'Ali overthrew President Bourguiba in November 1987. Seeking to swiftly reduce tensions and reconcile the government with most opposition groups, the new leader released hundreds of political prisoners, courted the exiled opposition, and promised political liberalization. The relative political liberalization that ensued allowed the Islamists to quickly turn into a visible and powerful political force after almost a decade of open challenge to President Bourguiba's rule. The Destourian Socialist Party was renamed the Democratic Constitutional Rally (RCD), and other political parties were recognized, except for the Islamist ones.

In the first free parliamentary elections of April 1989, the RCD won most seats in parliament and the Islamists, competing as independents, obtained 13 percent of all votes (even 30 percent in parts of the capital's outskirts). Realizing that the Islamists had become the second political force in country (the secular left had obtained only 3 percent of the vote), President Ben Ali tried to dampen their effect by making some concessions to them and by emphasizing his own religious background. However, after Algeria recognized in the same year several religious parties, Tunisia's Islamists increased their demand for a legal status. The ensuing tension culminated in an attack in May 1991 on the RCD office in Tunis, which killed one person. The state's reaction was swift and an all-out war against the Islamists began. Hundreds of Islamist militants were arrested and many fled the country.

From then on, except for a few tolerated small groups, all open political opposition was repressed and maintained under tight control. Fearing a contagion from the bloody war that was happening in neighboring Algeria in the 1990s, many people in Tunisia seemed to prefer this state of affairs rather than see an all-out Islamist rebellion take hold of their country. The RCD and the security services tightened their grip on the state and society as Tunisia regained stability and engaged in a comprehensive—and most successful in the region—structural adjustment program sponsored by the International Monetary Fund and the World Bank.

Because of tight security controls, an underground Islamist movement was not able to develop as happened in Algeria after the repression of 1992. However, there were a few violent acts attributed either to a homegrown neo-Salafi movement or to al-Qa`ida, such as the bomb attack in April 2002 against a synagogue in Djerba, which killed nineteen people and two shoot-outs between Islamist forces and the police in December 2006 and

January 2007. It was suspected also that these actions may have been tied to Algeria's GSPC, which changed into al-Qa`ida in the Islamic Maghreb in 2006.

"POST-ISLAMISM" AND THE RESURGENCE OF SUFISM AND POLITICAL ISLAM

The preceding discussion on the rise and evolution of political Islam showed that both exclusion and inclusion have been pursued by different Maghrebi states. Exclusion was favored in Libya and Tunisia, while the inclusion of an accommodating Islamism happened in Algeria and Morocco. This might partly explain why the winds of the "Arab Spring" had moderate effects in Morocco and Algeria while in Tunisia and Libya they resulted in the overthrow of the incumbent regimes.

In Libya, the al-Sanusiya movement, which had inherited the newly independent state, found itself in the awkward position of pushing for a secular outlook for the state. As a result, it ended up antagonizing not only its own ranks and file and constituency but also the truly secular forces in the country. After the Sanusi monarch was overthrown in 1969, no other religious movement was allowed to organize and mobilize people for social and political action. In Tunisia, once the postindependence Islamist movement started making political claims and challenging the ruling elite, it was plainly stopped in its tracks, repressed, and outlawed. For these two countries, the Islamist opposition that manifested itself before 2011 was either in exile or deep underground. In both cases, this opposition was weak and constrained by domestic and international security conditions. It was, however, fully unleashed by popular upheavals of 2011. Once the political system opened up, the Islamist formations were by far the best organized in the new Tunisian political land-scape and acquired a substantial presence in Libya's new polit-ical scene.

In Algeria and Morocco, after an initial rejection of grassroots political Islam, the two states opted for a strategy of accommoda-tion and inclusion of the least threatening movements, with the hope that such a move would inhibit and even end the radical and violent urges of Islamism. In the particular case of Algeria, political Islam seems to have been tamed for now by strong state repression of its radical fringe and a successful strategy that induced and co-opted its moderate wing (MSP, Nahda, and Islah) to participate in electoral politics. It is safe to say that this policy succeeded in ending the mass rebellion led by the Islamists and in controlling political Islam by incorporating in the political process its nonviolent and less threatening expressions.

Beyond this divergence in the strategic responses of the four states, political Islam in North Africa exhibited the shared patterns discussed above. For one, Salafism, the ancestor of today's Islamism, was widely present in the national liberation struggle, and played a key role in it. That Salafism had two strands: one modern reformist and another conservative. Another commonality was that after independence, the Salafi current attempted to push for reforms while criticizing the postindependence state elite for its secularism and its embrace of Western values. A third common pattern was the fact that, up to the 1970s, most religious currents limited their focus to the religious, cultural, and social spheres. Their shift to political concerns thereafter occurred as a result of domestic factors (eco-nomic crisis, state manipulation and repression of opposition forces, injustice, rising Western cultural influence, and the hegemony of secular elites) and international events, mainly the successful over-throw of Iran's authoritarian monarchy by a popular movement led by a religious figure, Ayatollah Khomeini. Another common feature was that, almost immediately after independence, the state leaders used Islam in their own favor and in the plans they had for their respective societies.

By the late 1990s, an important change happened in several countries of the region in the relationship between political Islam on one hand and the state and society on the other. At the same time, a transformation also happened in the Islamist movement itself after its failed confrontation with the states. These changes have been noted by academics and practitioners who saw them both as a plain defeat and an end of uncompromising militant Islamism and as a tactical adaptation to new domestic and international realities.

Several scholars and practitioners of politics have wondered in the past two decades about the future of political Islam and about the best strategy to deal with it, especially its violent expression. Three alternatives seem to have been explored and practiced in North Africa as well as the Middle East:

1. the total exclusion of Islamism from the political arena, as happened in Tunisia, Libya, and Syria
2. neither inclusion nor exclusion of the Islamists, but tolerating their activities as long as they do not forcefully challenge the existing system, as in the case of Egypt's Muslim Brothers
3. the inclusion of nonviolent "moderate" Islamists who agree to work within the existing systems of governance, as has happened in Algeria and Morocco, Jordan, and the special case of Lebanon

As discussed above, in the North African experience three different state responses to Islamism were tried with varying results.

In the cases of Algeria and Morocco there was a gradual shift from the first or second alternatives to the third one. In the cases of Libya and Tunisia, the first alternative was the only one pursued until the incumbent regimes were overthrown in 2011. After that, Political Islam became either central in Tunisia or only part of the governing institutions in Libya. The end result of this shift has been that political Islam is now part and parcel of the political landscape of these four countries. Two questions are prompted by this evolution: (a) how did this shift occur, and (b) how did it affect political Islam itself and the overall political dynamics in the these countries?

Post-Islamism in the Maghreb

In the debate of the last decade over the evolution of grassroots political Islam and of the states' response to it, the buzzword in academic parlance became "post-Islamism." This notion generated a lot of writing and acquired several meanings. In a 2005 article titled "What Is Post-Islamism," sociologist Asef Bayat averred,

> The particular way in which [post-Islamism] has been employed seems to have caused more confusion than clarity. For some (e.g., Gilles Kepel), post-Islamism describes the departure of Islamists from the *jihadi* and *Safafi* doctrines, while for others (such as Olivier Roy) it is perceived in terms of the "privatization" of Islamization (as opposed to Islamization of the state), where emphasis is placed on changes in how and where Islamization is carried out, rather than its content. Often used descriptively, post-Islamism has been presented and primarily perceived—including in my own work on Iran—as an empirical rather than an analytical category, representing a "particular era," or an "historical end." (Bayat 2005, 5)

It can be said that two meanings of post-Islamism have stood out so far, each being both empirical/descriptive and analytical. They are:

1. Prior to the "Arab Spring," post-Islamism referred to a political environment without the rebellious and challenging grassroots political Islam and to a return (or almost) to the pre-Islamism political order. Proponents of this definition pointed to what happened after militant Islamism ceased to exist as a significant sociopolitical phenomenon following its defeat in the confrontation with the state in the 1970s to 1990s period.

2. Post-Islamism is the tactical and discursive adaptation of grassroots political Islam whereby Islamism seeks accommodation with the existing political system, which it no longer wants to destroy. Proponents of this definition explain that this transformation happened after Islamism failed to achieve its key aims (overthrowing the existing regimes and establishing an Islamic state ruled by *Shari' ah* laws) and could not win in the frontal confrontation with both state and society.

Before the events of 2011, the first definition seemed to apply to the cases of Libya and Tunisia, where grassroots political Islam was almost entirely eradicated. However, in the wake of the "Arab Spring" an almost sudden and powerful resurgence of political Islam pointed to an almost totally new and unexpected direction: political Islam, which was in a dormant mode during the autocratic rules of Ben Ali and al-Qaddafi, is now at the forefront in Tunisia, Morocco, and Libya, but with less revolutionary fervor than in the previous decades.

Before and after the 2011 events, the second definition seemed to reflect more the situation in Algeria and Morocco. In these cases, and without a revolutionary mass rebellion similar to those of

Libya and Tunisia, the state accommodated a "domesticated" brand of Islamism, while Islamism itself (or at least a big part of it) changed into an accommodating force that is willing to play by the existing rules.

In the final analysis, post-Islamism may include elements of the two definitions, but the second one appears to have acquired more credence as reflected in relevant scholarly writings such as those of Gilles Keppel, Oliver Roy, and Asef Bayat. For Bayat, post-Islamism is a conscious effort of "transcending Islamism in social, political, and intellectual domains... it represents an endeavor to fuse religiosity and rights, faith and freedom, Islam and liberty. It is an attempt to turn the underlying principles of Islamism on its head by emphasizing rights instead of duties, plurality in place of a singular authoritative voice, historicity rather than fixed scriptures, and the future instead of the past" (Bayat 2005, 5).

In the Maghreb, these post-Islamist trends and characteristics are apparent in the Justice and Development Party (Morocco), the Movement of Society of Peace and Islah (Algeria), al-Nahda (Tunisia), and the Justice and Construction Party (Libya). The PJD, al-Nahda, MSP, and Islah accepted to work with and within the existing political system, are not calling for the establishment of an Islamic state, and seem to leave their religious agenda and endeavors out of, and independently from, the political sphere. Al-Nahda was not even allowed to exist during the rule of Ben Ali in Tunisia, but when the political system opened up in 2011, it wanted a full change of regime. Since it dominates today Tunisia's transition institutions, it is working hard to fully dismantle the old regime and to establish a new one that it promises will adhere to the fundamentals of liberal democracy.

According to what Oliver Roy called the secularization of the public space in which religious actions develop (Roy 1999b, 13), after the totalitarian and dogmatic attitude was abandoned, the religious movements of Tunisia, Algeria, and Morocco have learned to live with limited religious-political ambitions and among a multitude of contenders for leadership in *Da'wa* actions and religious rituals. As for Libya, the Muslim Brotherhood's party, the Justice and Construction Party, seems for now to exhibit the same post-Islamist characteristics. However, the situation in Libya at the time of this writing was still unclear and murky, which did not allow for a firm determination of the nature of all Islamist forces in place.

In Morocco, post-Islamism may be seen in the fact that the PJD does not question the religious authority of the monarch and does not condemn Sufism as traditional Salafism used to do. In Algeria, Morocco, as well as Tunisia, in this "post-Islamist era," the Islamist parties have come to accept the "individualization of religious practices or their exercise inside closed communal spaces (brotherhoods)" (Roy 1999a). This has manifested itself in the resurgence of Sufist orders in which membership is on an individual basis rather than group solidarity or shared ideology. Beyond the resurgence of the Sufi brotherhood, many other developments seem to have taken away from the Islamists the monopoly over religiosity and social action. There has been a multiplication of independent *Da'wa* groups and of religious festivities often led by independent preachers. This may partly explain why, when political Islam seemed in relative decline before 2011, there was a growing "Islamization" of society.

The Sufi resurgence and the integration of Political Islam

As already stated above, Sufism has an old presence in the Maghreb. The main North African Sufi orders were born between the sixteenth and early twentieth centuries. Each is distinguished by a specific doctrine, organization (*Zawiya*), and rituals. In most cases, they stayed out of the political sphere and focused on spirituality and worship rituals. However, in some periods, circumstances have made them play a political role.

There are today many Sufi orders, such as the Boutchichiya, Tijaniya, Qadiriya, `Isawiya, Jazuliya, Shadhiliya, Darqawiya, Taybiya, Rahmaniya, `Alawiya, and Sanussiya. Each order gave birth to several *zawaya* (schools) and many were linked by an ancestral spiritual leaders and/or saint.

Sufism has been the object of severe attacks by traditional Salafists, neo-Salafists, and grassroots Islamism. The reasons for these attacks are numerous, including the worshiping of saints and shrines, and passivity in the face of societal and political problems rather than reformist activism. During the colonial era in Algeria, Morocco, and Tunisia, "Islamic reformism spearheaded a consistent, and in each case amazingly successful, campaign against the Sufi brotherhoods. It was essentially a two-pronged attack: the brotherhoods were accused of introducing blameworthy innovations (*bid`a*) into Islam, and also of co-operating with the imperial power" (Brown 1964, 60).

In Morocco, "Salafi reformism coexisted with Sufi religious orders...under the overall supervision of the Alawi dynasty, which had played on both traditions since its emergence from maraboutic origins in 1666" (Henry 2007, 88). In 2002, King Mohamed VI appointed a young Sufi scholar (Ahmed Taoufiq from the Boutchichiya order) as Minister of Islamic Affairs and Habous. This move seemed to reflect both the acknowledgment of Sufism as a national heritage and the will to move official Islam away from doctrinal stiffness and toward some moderation (Pruzan-Jørgensen 2010). Also, in the case of Morocco, Salafi reformism did not entirely reject some aspects of Sufism and many Salafi leaders had some schooling in one Zawiya or another. The monarchy itself is said to have been established on a Sufi foundation. Sultan Sulayman (1760–1822) was a disciple of the Nasiriya *tariqa* (spiritual way) and welcomed the Tijaniya *tariqa* when it moved from Algeria to Fes in 1789 (Zeghal 2005, 43). A few years ago, King Mohammed VI celebrated the *Mawlid al-Nabawi* (birthday of Prophet Muhammad) in the shrine of Sidi al-Hadi Ben `Aissa in Meknes.

Today, Sufi orders know a vibrant life in Morocco partly encouraged by the monarchy as a way to combat political Islam and extremism, and also because some leaders of Salafi movements have themselves been more than keen to Sufism, including Abdesalam Yassin, the spiritual leader of `Adl wa al-Ihsan, which symbolizes the intertwining of political and social activism with spirituality, ethics, mysticism, and spiritual guidance. It is important to note, though, that spirituality and mysticism have been part of Yassin's discourse and practice since 1970s.

> By connecting mystical elements to Islamism, Abd al-Salam Yasin could aspire to transcend [the] hegemonic Salafi epistemology and reach out for the Sufi sensibilities of Moroccan masses.... While the re-appropriation of mystical elements certainly corresponded to his personal religious beliefs, it also allowed him to lay the foundations for a more comprehensive, uniting, and mobilizing approach to Islamism in Morocco. (Lauziere 2005, 244)

In Algeria, Sufism has also had a long history and similar characteristics. It was opposed by the Salafists and neo-Salafists and grassroots Islamism for the same reasons noted above. Also, the secular nationalists despised it for its pro-colonial attitude. Sufism experienced a deep decline after Algeria's independence from France as the governments' efforts to establish an "official Islam" had to cater to the reformist Salafist trend that dominated the Council of 'Ulama'. As a result, the activities of Sufi orders diminished drastically, up until the 1980s when their resurgence started after the state leadership began facing the challenge of radical Salafism.

Nowadays, Sufism is thriving again in Algeria not only because of the state's change of heart toward it, but also because many people have been attracted to it lately in search of guidance and identity in times of turmoil and uncertainty—especially after the dark decade of the 1990s. As the government's approach changed, it became common for the president himself to visit a Sufi shrine and its spiritual leader, especially in times of crisis or during an electoral campaign. In 1991, the National Association of the Zawyas was created with the blessing of the state and in 2005, state radio and television stations were created just for Sufism with the hope that they would help move people away from radical Islamism and toward a religious practice that focuses on contemplation—rather than violence—*dhikr* (invocation), social action, and the betterment of oneself and society by peaceful means.

> To give the Sufi "zaouias" a more central role in society, they are encouraged to arrange marriages, help take care of orphans, teach the Quran and distribute charitable donations. Followers of Sufism focus on the rituals of "Dhikr" or "Hadra"—"invocation" or "remembrance"—which feature sermons, reciting the Quran, praising the Prophet Mohammed, requests for intercession and rhythmic invocations of Allah. (Al Arabiya 2009)

Furthermore, Sufism has been presented as the expression of Algerian identity because it was an indigenous religious tradition, as opposed to the Islamism inspired by the Middle East, that is, Wahhabism and neo-Salafism.

In Libya, the dominant Sufi order is that of Sanusiya, sanusi, which goes back to the 1840s. Exceptionally for a Sufi order in the region, this one inherited the rule over Libya from the colonizer, but that did not last, as discussed above. The Sanusiya, sanusi's activities were drastically curtailed by al-Qaddafi, who put forth his own version of Salafism. However, the order survived and was a source of opposition, albeit very restrained by the regime. In the wake of the fall of the regime of al-Qaddafi, Sufism, and more particularly Sufi shrines and mosques, became the target of destructive attacks by what were believed to be hardline Salafists who believe that the popular practice of visits to shrines and mosques with graves of saints to be un-Islamic. "One of Libya's highest-profile cultural clashes since the toppling of Colonel Qaddafi has been between followers of the mystical Sufi tradition and ultraconservative Salafis, who have formed a number of armed brigades. They reject as idolatrous many Sufi religious rituals" (Reuter 2012). In August 2012, several Sufi places were either vandalized or destroyed by armed groups.[8]

In Tunisia, Sufism has also a very long history. The Shadhiliya order, which gave birth to many other orders, was established in Tunis by Sidi Abu al-Hassan al-Shaddili. After his death in 1258, the Shadhiliya, which stressed the intellectual basis of Sufism, flourished in North Africa, from Egypt to Morocco.

Another important order in Tunisia is the Madaniya order,[9] whose founder, Muhammad ibn Khalifa al-Madani, is said to have been the disciple of Ahmad al-Alawi, the spiritual leader of the Darqawi order in Algeria, itself an offshoot of the Shadhiliya order. He created a Zawiya in 1920 in the Tunisian town of Ksibet al-Mediouni. Because of his support for colonial France and opposition to the neo-Destour party and to its political agenda, President Bourguiba imposed restrictions on his activities and caused his self-imposed seclusion and downfall.

The Sufi orders in Tunisia experienced the same fate as those in Algeria after independence, that is, their activities were drastically curtailed and their lands and buildings turned into state property. Many Sufis are said to have migrated out of the country after that. Although the Sufi community is small in Tunisia today, its mystic tradition still permeates social and religious life, but that remains mostly limited to belief in spirits and visits to saint shrines and tombs for healing and guidance. Unlike the rulers of Algeria and Morocco, the Tunisian government has not felt the need to revitalize Sufism as a means to redirect the Islamist sentiment mostly because radical Islamism was crushed in the early 1990s.

As the above discussion indicates, Sufism is indeed gaining popularity in Algeria and Morocco, but not necessarily as a substitute for the political Islam these two countries have known in the past three decades. Rather, Sufism seems to serve as a complement, just as it has been reflected in the doctrine and actions of Abdeslam Yassin. However, the recent increase in the number of people attracted to it could also be an indication of dissatisfaction with both violent and nonviolent political Islam. The massive move away from violent political Islam—especially in Algeria—was caused by its failure to attain its aims, its horrible consequences on society and state repression. The relative disillusionment with nonviolent political Islam may have been caused also by its inability to deliver on its promises, even after Islamist parties joined parliaments and governments. Beyond these possible reasons, the attraction toward Sufism is also often personal whereby people find in it solace, guidance, and spiritual support in dealing with changing and challenging social and economic conditions.

One of the major consequences on the popular upheavals in the region against autocratic rulers was the rise to power of Islamist groups wherever none was previously allowed to reach that point or even to exist. This pertains to the cases of Tunisia, Egypt, and Libya.

In the Maghreb region, the most stunning rise to power was that of the previously banned al-Nahda party. Even though the Islamist tendency had nothing to do with the popular upheaval that began in December 2010 in the city of Sidi Bouzid, where a fruit stand vendor immolated himself, it, however, enjoyed fully the benefits of liberation from authoritarianism. Right after the fall of Ben Ali, Rachid Ghanouchi, the exiled leader of al-Nahda, led his newly legalized party to victory in the first free parliamentary elections. The party won 40 percent of the transition parliament seats and agreed to lead a coalition government that included seculars (the liberal Congress for the Republic and the left-of-center Ettakatol Party). Even though the party promised to live up to the democratic promises of the "Jasmine Revolution," many Tunisians fear that under an Islamist government, there will be a reversal in liberty and secular laws. Some of these fears were not necessarily inspired by al-Nahda itself but by a small but very active and vocal Salafist and international Islamist party, Hizb al-Tahrir (the Liberation Party), which was not allowed to become legal and partake in the elections due to its radical platform. Hizb al-Tahrir is an ultraconservative Islamist movement that advocates, among many other things, the establishment of the *khilafa* (caliphate).

In Libya, after the fall of al-Qaddafi—and even during the rebellion—Islamist groups of all kinds proliferated to a great extent. They range today from those espousing a pseudoliberal attitude to armed ultraconservative radicals. In the first free parliamentary elections on July 7, 2012, the Justice and Construction Party (Hizb al-A`dala wa al-Bina), which was created a few months earlier, won only 17 of 200 contested seats. Another Islamist group, the National Front Party (Hizb al-Jabha al-Wataniya), successor to the

National Front for the Salvation of Libya that was a resistance movement against al-Gaddafi, won 3 seats only. The biggest winner in this election was the National Forces Alliance.[10] This pro-liberal democracy formation was led by Mahmoud Jibril, a US-educated political scientist. While Libya is in the slow and convoluted process of creating adequate governing institutions, real power seems to reside in the streets, in the hands of armed groups, many of them of Islamist leaning. The latter seem, for now, more powerful than the transition officials and parliament members. It is feared that it is they who may determine the course Libya will follow in the coming years. Due to the historical circumstances of Libya before 2011, it was not possible then for nonviolent, pro-democracy Islamist parties to form and even maintain a latent life while the autocrat leader was in power. Therefore, if political Islam in Libya is to reach the post-Islamist stage, it may have to first go through the pains of building credibility, constituency, and power.

In the Moroccan case, where a movement of protest started in February 2011 calling for political and economic reforms, the Islamist party PJD, which managed to win the most seats in parliament, may owe its victory to four factors:

1. the very distinct nature of the PJD in contrast with the traditional secular opposition, especially, in the discursive area, organization, and leadership by example
2. the general dissatisfaction with the secular, leftist, opposition, which had its chance at running the government under the watchful eye of the king and failed to deliver on much of the promises it made when it was in the opposition
3. the social and economic conditions from which a great number of Moroccan suffer
4. the tailwinds of the "Arab Spring"

If the PJD is conceived as the illustration per se of the transformation of political Islam in Morocco from a radical, antiestablishment, and antimonarchical opposition to a regular political force that accepts to work from within the existing system, then the transition to post-Islamism can be said to have been accomplished. However, if the PJD is considered as only one element of the Islamist tendency in Morocco, then one has to account for the resistance of the remaining Islamist forces to following the same path the party of Benkirane followed.

CONCLUSION

Political Islam in North Africa, just as in the Middle East, came about as a response to internal and external conditions, challenges, and uncertainties. As shown in this essay, its expression was varied and so was its impact. In Libya and Tunisia, the independent expression of political Islam was repressed until the autocratic rule of Ben Ali and al-Qaddafi finally ended in 2011. After that, political Islam reclaimed its central place in the political landscape of the two countries—in Tunisia through the ballot box and in Libya through the control of the means of violence in a country that still lacks a powerful central authority. Before 2011, it was in Morocco and Algeria that political Islam found its freest expression, albeit within the constraints of the two systems. In these two countries, political Islam entered mainstream politics and may never retreat from it, unless another era of troubles would call for the eradication of all political expressions of religion, something that does not seem likely in the near or far future. The popular postulate that sees Islam as *din wa dawla* (religion and state) still serves as the backbone of the drive of political Islam for not only a perennial presence in the Maghrebi political systems but also for the realization of its self-prescribed comprehensive changes using a variety of means, be they reformed Islamism, that is, "post-Islamism," Sufism, or both.

The problem with the integration of political Islam in Morocco and Algeria today is that it may remain limited to a co-optation aiming to weaken the power of nonviolent religious parties and movements and to lessen the appeal of the violent groups. Since the Islamists have become in the past three decades very popular relays of social, economic, and political grievances, their integration in a system they no longer oppose, may create the ideological and representational vacuum that existed in the late 1970s and 1980s due to the decline of the secular left. This tendency is already visible in Algeria and Morocco, where there is an increasing loss of interest in the Islamist parties in parliament. These parties have become too embroiled in politics at the top at the expense of the interests of the constituencies. They have, in a way, become neutralized by a system with powerless representative institutions and by their own need to conform in order to remain relatively relevant in political systems where power to affect major public policy issues lie elsewhere. The 2011 constitutional amendments introduced by the Moroccan monarchy and approved by popular referendum did not change much in the institutional balance of power but gave some leeway to the PJD to affect public policy. In fact, its own political legitimacy—and that of Morocco's nonviolent political Islam in general—rests on delivering on key promises.

The street riots that developed spontaneously throughout Algeria and Tunisia in January 2011 reflected, in the first case, the failure of political Islam to take on the grievances of society, and, in the second case, the failure of systems that inhibited for too long both religious and secular voices of dissent. In an era of "post-Islamism" and resurgent Sufism, the question now is whether the Islamist parties that have made it to the top offices of political authority (Tunisia and Morocco) will succeed in living up to the high expectations placed in them, for if they, too, fail, as happened in Egypt in 2013, one wonders about who is going to take on those grievances and push, in a sustained way, for a meaningful and peaceful change in the Maghreb.

NOTES

1. Islamism refers here to militant mobilization for political change, using Islam as both inspiration and instrument. The Islamists generally belong to the *Salafiya* tendency. While the bulk of the Islamists are nonviolent, some have been extremists who do not hesitate to use violence to reach their main aim, the establishment of an Islamist state. Radical Islamists have also been referred to as neo-Salafists to distinguish them from the dominant, nonviolent, strand of Salafism.

2. Salafism is generally understood as a Muslim current that calls for the strict reading of the scripture (Qur'an), following the model of *al-salaf al-salih* (righteous or pious ancestors), and the return to pristine Islam. One of the targets of its call for the return to the path of the righteous ancestors was Sufism due to its veneration of saints and indulgence in sacred rituals.

3. For more information on this, see Mohammed Harbi, *L'Islamisme dans tous ses états* (Algiers: Rahma Editions, 1991), 133.

4. *National Charter* (Algiers: Popular Printing Press of the Army, 1976), 22.

5. The Arabization of the school curriculum was instrumental in the development of the Islamist movement later. Because of a lack of enough Algerian teachers to staff the schools, the government resorted to Middle Eastern teachers—mainly Egyptians—many of whom were linked to the Muslim Brothers. Furthermore, the Arabization process attracted many Algerian Islamists who used the schools to deliver their message and exert a strong influence on students.

6. The National Democratic Rally (RND) was created in 1995 to support incumbent president Liamine Zeroual in his bid for another term. It is headed by Prime Minister Ahmed Ouyahia.

7. Nine Islamists were elected to parliament in 1997 as members of a legal party, the Constitutional and Democratic Popular Movement (MPCD). In 1998, the MPCD changed its name to Party of Justice and Development (PJD) and thus became the first officially recognized Islamist party. The PJD managed in the 2007

parliamentary elections to garner a respectable place in parliament, outperform-
ing the tradition leftist opposition represented by the Union of Socialist Forces
(USFP). It became thus the second party in parliament, right behind Istiqlal.
In 2011, it became the first.

8. It was reported that the destruction affected the Islamic Center of Sheik Abdus
Salam al-Asmar in Zlitan, the mosque of Sidi Sha'ab in Tripoli, and the shrine of
Sidi Ahmed Zaroug in Misurata. Similar attacks against Sufi shrines took place
in the same month in Mali. The perpetrators were armed Islamist groups that
were said to have benefitted from large smuggling of weapons from Libya during
and after the popular rebellion.

9. For more on the Madaniyya *tariqa*, see its official website at http://www.
madaniyya.com.

10. The NFA is made up of 58 political organizations, 236 NGOs, and close to
300 independents.

REFERENCES

Addi, Lahouari, 2009. "Islam Re-Observed: Sanctity, Salafism and Islamism." *Journal
of North African Studies* 12, nos. 3/4: 331–345.
Al Arabiya News Channel, 2009. "Algeria Fights Insurgency with Sufism." July 8.
Available at: http://www.alarabiya.net/articles/2009/07/08/78165.html.
Accessed June 7, 2010
Asef Bayat, 2005. "What-Is-Post-Islamism?" *ISIM Review*, 16, Autumn. Available at:
http://www.nuansa.nl/uploads/ee/3c/ee3c13c38afebf47c6a68ed360afed5f/
What-is-post-islamism.pdf. Accessed April 2, 2010.
Brown, Leon Carl, 1964. "The Islamic Reformist Movement in North Africa." *The
Journal of Modern African Studies* 2, no. 1: 55–63.
Burgat, François, 1988. "L'Algérie: de la laicité islamique à l'islamisme." *Maghreb/
Machrek* 121.
El-Kikhia, Mansour O., 1997. *Libya's Qaddafi: The Politics of Contradiction.* Gainesville,
FL: University Press of Florida.
Frégosi, François, 1995. "Les rapports entre l'Islam et l'état en Algérie et en Tunisie:
de leur revalorisation à leur contestation." *Annuaire de l'Afrique du Nord*
34: 103–123.
Henry, Clement M., 2007. "The Dialectics of Political Islam in North Africa." *Middle
East Policy*, XIV (winter): 4.
Hermassi, Elbaki, 1972. *Leadership and National Development in North Africa: A
Comparative Study.* Berkeley: University of California Press.
Jamai, Aboubakr, 2003. "Morocco's Choice: Openness or Terror." *New York Times*,
Op. Ed., May 31. Available at: www.nytimes.com. Accessed June 5, 2003.

Joffe, George, 1995. "Qadhafi's Islam in Local Historical Perspective," in Dirk Vande-walle, ed., *Qadhafi's Libya 1969 to 1994*. New York: St Martin's Press, 139–156.

Lauziere , Henry, 2005. "Post-Islamism and the Religious Discourse of Abd al-Salam Yasin." *International Journal of Middle East Studies* 32 (May): 2.

Pruzan-Jørgensen, Julie E., 2010. "The Islamist Movement in Morocco: Main Actors and Regime Responses." *Diis Report* 2010: 5. Copenhagen: Danish Institute for International Studies.

Reuter, "Libyan Islamists Raze Sufi Sites in Bold Attacks." *New York Times*, August 25, 2012. Available at: www.nytimes.com. Accessed August 25, 2012.

Roy, Olivier, 1999a. "Pourquoi le 'post-islamisme'?" *Revue du Monde Musulman et de la Méditerranée*, nos. 85–86: 9–10. Available at: http://www.persee.fr/web/revues/home/prescript/article/remmm_0997-1327_1999_num_85_1_2633. Accessed December 29, 2010.

Olivier Roy, 1999b. "Le post-islamisme." *Revue du monde musulman et de la Méditerranée*, nos. 85–86: 11–30. Available at: http://www.persee.fr/web/revues/home/prescript/article/remmm_0997-1327_1999_num_85_1_2634. Accessed December 29, 2010.

Simons, Marlise, 1998. "Morocco Finds Fundamentalism Benign but Scary." *New York Times*, April 9.

Stora, Benjamin, 1991. *La gangrène et l'oubli, la mémoire de la guerre d'Algérie*. Paris: La Découverte.

Takeyh, Ray, 2000. "Qadhafi's Libya and the Prospect of Islamic Succession." *Middle East Policy*, vol. VII, no. 2. Available at: http://www.cfr.org/world/qadhafis -libya-prospect-islamic-succession/p7437. Accessed March 7, 2006.

Zeghal, Malika, 2005. *Les Islamistes marocain: le defi à la monarchie*. Paris: La Decouverte.

BIBLIOGRAPHY

Allani, Alaya, 2009. "The Islamists in Tunisia between Confrontation and Participation: 1980–2008." *Journal of North African Studies* 14, no. 2: 257–272.

Brown, Jack, "Algeria's Midwinter Uproar." *Middle East Research and Information Project* (MERIP), January 20, 2011. Available at: http://www.merip.org/mero/mero012011. Accessed February 10, 2011.

Burgat, Francois, 1997. *The Islamic Movement in North Africa*. Center for Middle Eastern Studies, Austin: University of Texas Press.

Green, Arnold H., 1976. "Political Attitudes and Activities of the Ulama in the Liberal Age: Tunisia as an Exceptional." *International Journal of Middle East Studies* 7, no. 2: 209–241.

Kepel, Gilles, 2000. *Jihad: expansion et déclin de l'islamisme*. Paris: Gallimard.

Kirkpatrick, David D., 2012. "Libya Officials Seem Helpless as Sufi Shrines Are Vandalized." *New York Times,* August 28.

Lowe, Christian, and Lamine Chikhi, 2012. "Algeria Ruling Party Snubs Arab Spring to Win Election." *Reuters,* May 11.

Heisler, Ryan, 2009. "The Secrets and History of the Madaniyya Sufi of Ksibet al-Mediouni, Tunisia." *ISP Collection.* Paper 655. Available at: http://digitalcollections.sit.edu/isp_collection/655. Accessed January 5, 2011.

Khemissi, Hamidi, Ricardo René Larémont, and Taybi Taj Eddine, 2012. "Sufism, Salafism and State Policy towards Religion in Algeria: A Survey of Algerian Youth." *The Journal of North African Studies* 17, no. 3: 553.

Layachi, Azzedine, 2011. "Meanwhile in the Maghreb: Have Algeria and Morocco Avoided North Africa's Unrest?" *Foreign Affairs,* March 31. Available at: www.foreignaffairs.com. Accessed July 30, 2012.

Layachi, Azzedine, 2011. "Algeria's Rebellion by Installments." *Middle East Research and Information Project* (MERIP), March 12. Available at: http://www.merip.org/mero/mero031211. Accessed July 30, 2012

Lee, Robert D., 2008. "Tunisian Intellectuals: Responses to Islamism." *Journal of North African Studies* 13, no. 2: 157–173.

Magnuson, Douglas K., 1991. "Islamic Reform in Contemporary Tunisia: Unity and Diversity." In I. William Zartman, ed. *Tunisia: The Political Economy of Reform,* 169–192. Boulder, CO: Lynne Rienner.

Perkins, Kenneth J., 1986. *Tunisia: Crossroads of the Islamic and European Worlds.* Boulder, CO: Westview Press.

Silverstein, Paul, "Weighing Morocco's New Constitution." *MERIP,* July 5, 2011. Available at: http://www.merip.org/mero/mero070511. Accessed July 27, 2011.

Schwedler, Jillian, 2004. "Is Moderation a Myth? Islamist Parties in Comparative Perspective." Paper prepared for the "Roots of Radicalism" conference at Yale University, May 7–9.

Zghal, Abdelkader, 1991. "The New Strategy of the Movement of the Islamic Way: Manipulation or Expression of Political Culture?" In I. William Zartman, ed., *Tunisia: The Political Economy of Reform,* 205–217. Boulder, CO: Lynne Rienner.

Chapter 8

Islam and Politics in Sub-Saharan Africa

LEONARDO A. VILLALON

THE SETTING: THE MUSLIM MOSAIC SOUTH OF THE SAHARA

Reliable numbers are hard to come by, but a good guess might place the Muslim population of sub-Saharan Africa somewhere in the range of 30–40 percent.[1] As Table 8.1 below indicates, fully thirty-two of the forty-eight countries in the region have significant Muslim populations, ranging widely from 10 to 100 percent, and another ten have smaller but often important Muslim communities.[2]

Geographically, the regions of concentrated Muslim presence reflect the early historical expansion of the religion on the continent (Robinson 2004; Levtzion and Pouwells 2000). Stretching south across the Sahara, the vast savannah zone known as the Sahel is overwhelmingly Muslim until it reaches the forest belt of west and central Africa. Moving south from Egypt through the Nile valley, and across from the Arabian Peninsula, the Horn of Africa represents a second major zone of Muslim importance. And via contact with seafaring traders in the Indian Ocean, Islam came to dominate in what is now known as the Swahili coast, stretching as far south as

Table 8.1 SUB-SAHARAN AFRICAN COUNTRIES BY ESTIMATED
MUSLIM POPULATIONS

Predominantly Muslim countries (10) 85–100 percent Muslim	Comoros, Djibouti, Gambia, Guinea-Conakry, Mali, Mauritania, Niger, Senegal, Somalia, Sudan
Religiously divided countries (9) 30–70 percent Muslim	Burkina Faso, Chad, Côte d'Ivoire, Eritrea, Ethiopia, Guinea-Bissau, Nigeria, Sierra Leone, Tanzania
Significant Muslim minorities (13) 10–20 percent Muslim	Benin, Cameroon, Central African Republic, Ghana, Kenya, Liberia, Madagascar, Malawi, Mauritius, Mozambique, South Sudan, Togo, Uganda
Small Muslim minorities (10) 1–10 percent Muslim	Botswana, Burundi, Democratic Republic of Congo, Gabon,* Lesotho, Republic of Congo (Brazzaville), Rwanda, Sao Tome and Principe, South Africa, Zambia

Source: author's compilation from diverse sources and estimates.
*Primarily noncitizen residents, mostly West Africans.

Mozambique, and touching the island of Madagascar. From these areas, the religion spread gradually over the centuries, moving south and west into more tropical zones, following commerce and migration. This expansion continues today through various means; there are, for example, intriguing indications that Islam is drawing converts in zones of recent turmoil, including Rwanda following the 1994 genocide, and the eastern regions of the Democratic Republic of Congo.

Islam on the continent has been overwhelmingly Sunni, with the *Maliki* legal school dominating throughout the northwestern regions of the continent, and the *Shafi'i* school in the east.[3] Across the continent, Sufi forms of Islam have been key in the spread of the religion, and central to much of religious and social life—although there has been significant variation in what this has meant in practice (Brenner 2000; Piga 2006). Generally the expansion of Islam in Africa was accomplished with a high degree of adaptation to local cultures and societies. Thus Robinson (2004) writes of simultaneous processes of "Islamization of Africa" and of "Africanization of Islam." This fact, however, has also fed long internal debates on religious practice and persistent efforts at reform. Thus in West Africa themes of the reformist jihads of the eighteenth and nineteenth century are echoed in the critiques of Sufi practices by contemporary reformists, variously known locally as "Wahhabis," "Salafis," or simply "Sunnites" (Loimeier 1997, 2003; Sani Umar 1993; Miles 2007). Some scholars have labeled this dynamic tension a struggle between "African Islam" and "Islam in Africa" (Westerlund and Rosander 1997).

The rapid European conquest of Africa in the late nineteenth century drew colonial boundaries with little regard to social realities, and within less than a century these were to be inherited as the permanent borders of independent states. The result was a set of countries with a highly varied mosaic of languages, ethnicities, and religions. Consequently, Muslims in sub-Saharan Africa today live in strikingly different political and demographic contexts, resulting in very diverse patterns of religious roles in African political life.

The parameters of the role of Islam in politics in any given country south of the Sahara are thus shaped by several broad characteristics. These would include demographics (the relative size of the

Muslim population); the nature of the state (including both the colonial legacy and the subsequent historical transformation in the postcolonial period); and the religious landscape (as shaped by both dominant domestic religious actors and increasingly transnational religious influences). Given the sheer number of countries and their diversity, I cannot in what follows describe the specific dynamics of individual cases. I will, instead, describe some broad African patterns that result from variations in these characteristics, with references to some key cases.

THE ARENA: POSTCOLONIAL STATES AND MUSLIM SOCIETIES

The drawing of the colonial map over the broad zones of historical Muslim presence has meant that contemporary Muslims in Africa find themselves in very diverse demographic situations, with important consequences for the patterns of religion and politics. At the risk of excessive simplification, we can identify some central dynamics in different contexts.

In the countries of clear and strong Muslim dominance, debates about religion and politics have tended to center on the question "What impact—if any—should the fact that we are overwhelmingly Muslim have on our political system?" that is, "Does the fact of being a Muslim country mean that the political system should reflect Islam, and if so how?" This has been most notably the case in the francophone countries of the Sahel.[4] In those countries, with the exception of Mauritania, which is effectively 100 percent Muslim and was set up as an "Islamic Republic" at independence, the presence of Christian minorities has meant that the dominant answer to that question has historically incorporated a version of secularism, reinforced by a consistent discourse insisting on recognizing religious pluralism.

In the countries we might label demographically "divided," where Muslims may represent between 30 and 70 percent of the populations, the major political dynamics of religion tend to center on the competition for relative access to power for the different religious communities. Given the demographic uncertainties that characterize the continent, much debate actually focuses on competing claims concerning the actual size of religious communities. In countries such as Ethiopia or Tanzania, for example, there are widely varying claims of the relative importance of the Muslim population.

There are also significant variations in terms of whether such religious divisions become politically salient, a fact that points to the centrality of politics—and not religion per se—in defining these relations. Thus in the divided country of Sudan before partition in 2011, as well as in neighboring Chad, for example, much of postindependence history has been a conflict over Muslim control of the state. In a somewhat different pattern, Nigeria (by far the largest country on the continent with an estimated population of some 160 million) has also been marked by a rivalry between the Muslim north and primarily non-Muslim south. In most other divided cases, however, the most striking dynamic has been the relatively peaceful nature of interreligious relations and their relative lack of importance as political cleavages (Sanneh 1997). This is the case in such diverse countries as Ethiopia and Eritrea in the Horn of Africa, or Burkina Faso and Sierra Leone in West Africa. It merits noting, however, that contact and rivalry as both major world religions seek to expand, primarily at the expense of historical African religious traditions, as well as the new liberalized political contexts (which we shall discuss below), seem to be producing increased tensions in various places (Becker 2008).

In the large number of countries with Muslim minorities of various sizes, to the extent that religion has had any significant political impact at all, it has been primarily focused on efforts to ensure minority religious rights, often via the pursuit of specific legal or constitutional provisions granting Muslims autonomy in such areas as family law. This is the case in a number of countries with significant Muslim minorities, such as Kenya, Uganda, or Benin, as well as in the case of the very small Muslim community of South Africa (Hashim 2005; Twaddle 2003; Brégand 2007; Tayob 1999).

Beyond the demographic issue, the most important factor shaping the political role of Islam in Africa has been the state context. It is thus useful to consider briefly the nature and trajectory of African states as these have defined the possibilities for religion to assume a political role. With very few and only partial exceptions, African countries today are the direct heirs to a colonial legacy.[5] In addition, their accession to independence was largely driven by transformations in the international system, and that international context has continued to shape the possibilities for African statehood.

The young leaders of African independence movements in the late 1950s and early 1960s came overwhelmingly from the small elite who had received a European education, and they espoused nationalist ideologies centered on the colonial territories. Given the realities of African social pluralism and the strong centripetal forces that marked countries from the moment of independence, they placed strong emphases on policies of "nation-building," and had little tolerance for movements based on ethnic or religious identities. Islam, therefore, was most often fairly marginal to the independence movements. Thus with the exception of Mauritania noted above, set up as an "Islamic Republic" by the French but intended only to reflect a cultural reality and not a political agenda, secular states were the norm everywhere.

There was also, of course, variation, and the distinction between the French and the British colonies remains highly salient in Muslim Africa. However imperfectly applied, the French policy of "assimilation" produced a political elite deeply rooted in a French education, and strongly committed to French notions of *laïcité*, or secularism, with an enduring impact on understandings of constitutionalism and politics more broadly. By contrast, British "indirect rule" and the reinforcement of local authorities and chiefs, and in Muslim zones such as northern Nigeria a careful policy of shielding religion from outside influence, produced a much greater willingness to accommodate religious demands in law and politics.

Strikingly, however, across the continent the optimistic moment of independence and the promise of liberation through popular democratic systems was swept aside very quickly by the emergence of authoritarian regimes of various sorts. This phenomenon, reinforced by the Cold War context and the search by the superpowers for proxy regimes, resulted in military, single-party, or personalized patrimonial political systems in virtually every country. With very limited exceptions, the period from the mid-/late 1960s to 1990 was a time of authoritarian rule in Africa.[6]

The impact of this authoritarian landscape on the possibility for a political role for religion was mediated by dual impulses on the part of the state. The core imperative for African regimes was to maintain control, and hence they had little tolerance for alternative sources of authority, and allowed little space for religious action in the political sphere. On the other hand, there was the constant temptation to attempt to capture or claim religious forces in an effort to legitimize and lend support to regimes with little credibility. This second logic increased in importance in the late 1970s and 1980s, as economic crises and declining legitimacy in the face of the unfilled promises of independence put regimes on the defensive. An extreme example of this dynamic is that of Sudan under the military autocrat Jaafar Nimeiri, where the imposition of *Shari`ah* in 1983, in a deeply divided country, can be understood as a desperate (and ultimately unsuccessful) effort to legitimize the regime in the eyes of the Muslim majority at the expense of the large non-Muslim population.

A common response to these two contradictory impulses was the effort by states to create inclusive and official Muslim organizations that could be domesticated by state sponsorship while also, it was hoped, buying sympathy by such a demonstration of state solicitude toward Muslims. Thus in both Muslim majority and minority contexts, and in both francophone and anglophone countries, such structures were created in the 1970s; the Malian Association for the Unity and Progress of Islam (AMUPI), or the Islamic Association of Niger (AIN) in the Francophone Sahel, and the Supreme Council of Tanzanian Muslims (BAKWATA) or the Supreme Council of Kenyan Muslims (SUPKEM) in East Africa, are key examples (Constantin 1995; Villalón 2010). The important case of Senegal, it merits noting, was long considered exceptional precisely for having found a sociopolitical balance to these competing impulses via a system of symbiotic relations built on the strong collaboration of Sufi leaders with an officially secular and quasidemocratic state—a system that was largely inherited from the colonial period (Villalón 1995).

The "precarious balance" between state and society in Africa that some political scientists described in the 1980s was to become even more fragile and difficult with deteriorating social and economic conditions on the continent (Rothchild and Chazan 1988). In Muslim Africa, social change in the late 1970s and 1980s was to lead to a seeming "revival" or "resurgence" of religion, first in private life, but quickly taking on implications for public and political life

(Brenner 1993; Masquelier 2009). Under the influence of the Iranian revolution, with the increased presence and resources of the Arab Gulf states and Saudi Arabia, and other means of greater contact with the broader Muslim world (Hunwick 1997), we began to see some cases of increased Muslim political activity. These both fed on and contributed to increasing internal debates about Islam, translated in many cases as increased tensions between Sufis and reformists. Thus such movements as the Nigerian "Izala" (Jama`t Izalat al Bid`a wa Iqamat as Sunna; Society for Removal of Innovation and Reestablishment of the Sunna, founded in 1978), perhaps the largest reformist movement in Africa, were born in this context (Sani Umar 1993; Kane 2003).

The political, economic, and social situation of Africa was, almost universally, to continue to decline throughout the 1980s, and by the end of the decade persistent African crises had resulted in the extreme fragility of political systems across the continent. Facilitated by the international transformations marked by the collapse of the east bloc and the end of the Cold War, the examples of popular uprisings in a few countries quickly spread, and as the "third wave" of demands for democratization swept the continent, the political contexts of Africa were profoundly transformed, with equally profound consequences for the potential political role of Islam.

TRANSFORMATION: ISLAM IN THE PUBLIC SPHERE IN THE ERA OF LIBERALIZED POLITICS

In the early 1990s, then, African states found themselves at a critical juncture, facing the need to reconfigure political systems that were no longer functional, with the looming threat of disorder and collapse as the alternative (Villalón and Huxtable 1998). In sharp contrast with much of the Muslim world—and most strikingly with the Arab states—the vast majority of sub-Saharan countries embraced "democratization" as the way forward. Given the weakened situation of many states on the continent, and hence their inability to control social forces that were unleashed in the process, there were quickly significant variations in the consequences of this democratic turn on the continent. In the most tragic of cases we saw situations of complete state failure or collapse; the 100 percent Muslim country of Somalia represents the most important of those for our purposes. But in many others we have seen a real liberalization of politics, even if full and substantive democracy has proven an elusive goal for many. It merits emphasizing, in any case, that virtually everywhere on the African continent, regimes in the 1990s and the 2000s were far more liberal than those in most of the Arab world, resulting in a very different set of dynamics for Islam and politics. Most notably Senegal, as well as Mali from 1992 until the tragic collapse of the regime in March 2012, presented rare examples of functioning Muslim democracies.[7]

Islam and politics, of course, influence each other, and it is thus important to consider not only how religion has shaped politics, but also how these transformations in the African political landscape have affected religion. Once again, there is much variety in terms of what liberalization or democratization has meant for the political role of Islam, but also some broad similarities. In a major break from the period of authoritarian and corporatist regimes, the era of liberalization produced a veritable boom in voluntary social associations on the continent. These include the many associations that have been celebrated as part of "civil society," and they have also included many and varied religious associations. The flourishing of what we might call a "religious civil society" in many cases thus led naturally to a heightened political role for Islam (Cruise O'Brien 2003; Holder

2009). This religious assertion has been often interpreted (both domestically and by outside observers) as a "backlash" or challenge to liberalization, but I would argue that in fact the increased political role for Islam should be seen as the logical (and often even healthy) consequence of liberalization. The paradox of democratization is that it empowers groups to speak and make their case, even if they wish to challenge much of what others claim to support in the name of democracy. The challenge of democratization is not to suppress such differences, but to find procedures for reconciling them.

Thus in various African cases this has led to some very important and fundamental debates about the meaning of democracy in a given religious context. In ways analogous to debates on legalizing gay marriage in the United States or parts of Europe, the fundamental debate has been about whether "democracy" demands a specific answer to such issues, or whether it prescribes that the answer should depend on what most citizens would like. This discussion leads naturally to a questioning of the relationship between democracy and secularism, and the appropriate boundaries for religion in a constitutional order (An-Naim 2006). The debates about these issues have been intense in various places, and religious actors have at times been vociferously involved. What we have not seen, however, is any serious effort by Muslim (or other) religious actors in Africa to impose an answer to this question by capturing the state.

In addition to these core debates, political liberalization in Muslim Africa has produced several other effects. Breaking the monopoly of official state Islamic organizations, for example, has in some real senses resulted in a "democratization" of religion, with new claimants to religious legitimacy emerging to challenge established authorities. In virtually every Muslim community on the continent, then, the decades since the 1990s have been marked by increased and often intense disputes about who has the authority to speak in the name of Islam. In many cases this has taken the form of increased tensions between reformers (Salafists, Wahhabis, and others) and practitioners of the historical popular practices of religion, often Sufi in form or inspiration. In cases as diverse as Niger, Ethiopia, and Mozambique, these dynamics have been largely promoted by merchant communities and new economic elites (Meunier 1997; Østebø 2009; Bonate 2009). These religious debates themselves are shaped by local contexts, however, and thus transnational movements such as Salafism are themselves often "localized" in the process (Østebø 2008).

The new possibilities for claiming religious authority has also had the effect of empowering new social categories. Most significantly, perhaps, the liberalized contexts have given new voice to women, and Muslim women's movements of varying religious and political positions have emerged as significant actors in diverse settings (Alidou 2005; Augis 2005; Badran 2011). Given the increased social prestige associated with "modern" religious knowledge, particularly in settings where strong elite commitment to secularism had previously devalued religious training, people whose education had been primarily Arabic based (referred to as *arabisants* in the francophone countries) found themselves increasingly recognized and called on to comment on public affairs. This phenomenon is having in turn a significant impact on education, and there has been in many countries a significant expansion in religious as well as Arabic language education in both state and private schooling (Brenner 2001; Galilou 2002; Villalón 2012).

These general dynamics have varied significantly in different contexts, and the specific pattern of such transformations in any given case has shaped the resulting politicization of Islam in that country. Although we cannot do justice to the full range of such situations, it may be instructive to comment on a few important cases.

In the overwhelmingly (90 percent plus) Muslim countries of the Francophone Sahel—namely Mali, Niger, and Senegal—the democratic turn was very much led by a secular elite, with a conception of democracy rooted in the European experience and incorporating French notions of *laïcité*, prescribing a particularly strict distancing of the religious from the political (Villalón 2010). For religious groups the French term had strongly negative connotations, and in all three countries they thus initiated challenges to using it in the new constitutions. In Niger, in fact, it was ultimately replaced in the constitution by a statement about the "nonconfessional nature" of the state, although the term *laïc* remains in common usage to describe it. Gradually, however, the debate moved from whether there should be *un état laic* to what *laïcité* actually means. Almost universally, political actors have distanced themselves from secularism in the French mode to adopt something closer to an American understanding of secularism: freedom to freely practice religion includes the need for the state to make space for religious practice.

Liberalization in the Sahel also produced a rapid proliferation of new religious voices. In Mali and Niger the collapse of the old single official Muslim associations mentioned above led to veritable explosion of new associations, and a somewhat analogous process resulted from the declining authority of Sufi elites in Senegal. Brief efforts at founding religious parties by some Muslim groups were quickly aborted, but almost immediately religious voices began to protest that the "democratic" systems being proposed did not reflect the Muslim majority's views, and some began to question whether democracy was even desirable. In each country there were early clashes between religious and secular actors, some on symbolic issues (beauty pageants and the like), but others on more substantial ones—most centrally family law. Strikingly, however, the fact that democratization gave religious actors a voice they had not previously had was not lost on them, and they quickly moved from protests that democracy was not compatible with Islam to arguing instead that democracy in Muslim societies should reflect Muslim values and interests. In the cases of Mali and Niger this shift was particularly apparent in the debates about family law (Villalón 1996; Soares 2009). In both cases, French-inspired "family codes" that civil society activists insisted were central to democratization processes were stalled as religious groups argued—in the name of democracy—that family law should be publicly debated and reflect popular will.

In the process, the democratic debate moved from what seemed a two-sided struggle between "secular" and "Islamic" actors to a much more fluid and open debate about what the content of democracy should be in a Muslim society. And this included an internal debate among Muslims about what—in fact—was the "correct" position of Islam on any given issue. Should polygamy be banned? Is the death penalty acceptable or required? These and similar questions became not just subjects for contention between secularist and religious groups, but also internal debates within Muslim society. Democracy facilitated these debates, and hence was largely embraced by Muslim actors in these countries. Unsurprisingly, then, opinion polls have found that African Muslims are no less—and frequently more—supportive of democracy than non-Muslim Africans (Bratton 2003).

In many religiously divided countries, liberalization has produced intensified debates about the communal rights of Muslims, often inscribed in constitutional issues. Such dynamics have been particularly pronounced in Kenya and Tanzania, home to the most significant populations of Swahili-speaking Muslims, important minorities in each (although there are occasional Muslim claims to be a majority in Tanzania).

Muslims probably represent approximately 10 percent of the population of Kenya. At independence in 1963, there were provisions for special legal status for Muslims in the constitution, inherited from special colonial provisions that had been made and maintained as part of a deal with the Sultan of Zanzibar. In the single-party period that was to last through the 1980s, however, there were various state efforts to remove those provisions and to standardize family law across the country and much of Muslim politics were an effort to resist this. Thus the 1972 "succession act" eliminated special status for Muslim inheritance, and became a major point of contention, though it was never fully implemented.

As elsewhere, the 1990s saw a tense sociopolitical climate rocked by prodemocracy activism in Kenya. In this context, SUPKEM, which had been the sole officially recognized Muslim association since 1979, along with many other new Muslim civil society groups, were increasingly politicized, and agitated in defense of the interests of Kenya's Muslim minority (Oded 2000). In particular, Muslim groups were active participants in the ongoing debates on a new constitution for Kenya over the course of the 2000s. When a first draft was released in 2002, it in fact provided for Muslim *Kadhi* courts to deal with personal law issues. The ensuing controversy furthered an open politicization of Muslim-Christian tensions (Hashim 2005). The issue remained a point of contention in the subsequent rocky history of Kenya's efforts at democratization, marked by the rejection of the draft constitution in the referendum of 2005, and by an unprecedented wave of violence after the strongly contested elections in 2007. In the complex politics of building a coalition in support of the constitution, the *Kadhi* courts were ultimately included in the version approved in 2010, but the issue remains highly controversial. Among the many political tensions that mark Kenya are religious politics centered on Muslim efforts to maintain their special status and Christian efforts to resist this. It is clear that liberalization has brought these issues to the forefront, and that democratization must meet the challenge of balancing these competing claims.

In the United Republic of Tanzania, similar debates concerning the role of *Kadhi* courts for Muslims have centered on whether they should be instituted on the divided mainland, paralleling those that exist on 99 percent Muslim Zanzibar. It has also paralleled Kenya in an ongoing debate on family law and special constitutional provisions for religious communities (Hashim 2005). This has been complicated by—and contributed to—rising tensions between Muslims and non-Muslims, in part due to competing claims about who constitutes the majority.

Despite the fact that the successor to Tanzania's founding father president, Julius Nyerere, was the Muslim Ali Mwinyi (president from 1985 to 1995), Muslims in the country have expressed a growing sense of marginalization (Mbogoni 2004; Loimeier 2007). In February 1998, an unprecedented incident in which four Muslims were killed by state police sparked increasing tensions. Further complicating the situation is the fact that liberalization in the 1990s sparked a proliferation of religious voices even within the Muslim community, and resulted in rising tensions as BAKWATA—closely tied to the ruling single party until 1994—was challenged by Islamic reformist groups.

Religious tensions have thus been one complication of the democratic process in both countries, but they have by no means defined that effort. The challenge for both is to find means of balancing the concerns of separate religious communities while constructing a system that could be characterized as democratic. And they are by no means unique in Africa; there are similar challenges in defining legal and constitutional provisions for Muslim communities in the context of liberalization in various other countries, including

Burkina, Benin, Ghana, and the unique and particularly interesting case of South Africa.

Perhaps the most interesting, and certainly among the more important, African experiments with political Islam in liberalized contexts are presented by twelve Muslim majority states in the northern region of the Federal Republic of Nigeria. These may represent the most significant case in the world of *Shari`ah* adoption as part of a process of electoral democratization. Nigeria, Africa's most populous country, has a federal political system, constructed out of a long history of ethnoregional tensions, the seeds of which were sown in different British colonial policies and the incomplete merger of the north and south prior to independence. The tensions that marked the country at birth gradually took on a more religious coloration starting in the 1970s. In the late 1980s and early 1990s, the military ruler Ibrahim Babangida, maneuvering to stay in power, took a number of steps that politicized religion further, such as joining the Organization of the Islamic Conference (OIC) in 1986.

Following a failed effort at transition to democracy, a particularly repressive military regime under General Sani Abacha was to rule from 1993 to 1998, leaving little room for religious organizations in politics. Unsurprisingly, however, the return to civilian rule and holding of democratic elections in 1999 reopened possibilities for religious political mobilization. Seizing the opportunity, the candidate for governor in the state of Zamfara campaigned on the promise of adopting *Shari`ah* law, and quickly did so once elected. Other states promptly followed suit, and by 2002 twelve northern states (of Nigeria's thirty-six) had adopted *Shari`ah* law, with broad popular support. While the constitutionality of these actions at the federal level was challenged, the federal government had no effective power to challenge these moves.

The governments of *Shari'ah* states quickly undertook a series of symbolic actions intended to moralize society, such as bans on alcohol, gambling, and prostitution. They also adopted a number of criminal penalties based on Islamic, *hudud*, punishments. Quickly, two very high profile cases of young women sentenced to death by stoning for adultery provoked a major outcry, in Nigeria and abroad. Following intense debates, however, both of these sentences were eventually overturned by *Shari'ah* courts of appeal, on Islamic grounds. Reflecting this, what most significantly marked the first decade of *Shari'ah* in these states is the fact that rather than a mechanical imposition of established law, the process has rather provoked significant internal debate about the meaning of *Shari'ah*, a process that has had the effect of moderating application of stricter penalties (Ostien et al. 2005). These states thus represent an unexpected situation: the centrality of *Shari'ah* in the establishment of some measure of democracy.

We should be careful, of course, not to romanticize this experience; the *Shari'ah* and democratic experiment has coexisted with the continued periodic appearance of stridently radical Islamist movements in northern Nigeria, leading to occasional bouts of intense violence, and provoking in turn ferocious governmental retaliation. Much media coverage as well as scholarly attention understandably focuses on these episodes, the most significant of which have involved the so-called Boko Haram movement. But contextualizing the violent movements also allows us to note the more interesting face of the *Shari'ah* experiment, as an open political debate about what should be the legitimate government for Muslims situated within a broadly chaotic political environment at the national level.

As these cases demonstrate, Islamic political involvement within the liberalized contexts of post-Cold War Africa show interesting variation, and most importantly a wide range of possibilities for politics in Africa's Muslim societies, with potentially instructive lessons for the rest of the Muslim world.

POLITICAL ISLAM AND WEAKENED STATES IN THE AGE OF TERROR

The age of terror started in Africa before the events of September 11, 2001 in the United States; it began specifically with the simultaneous bombings of the US embassies in Kenya and Tanzania on August 7, 1998. These attacks left over 300 people dead, the vast majority Kenyans. For our purposes here, what was most striking is that these attacks were carried out by outsiders, and gained no popular sympathy in either country. As implied in my discussions of those countries above, these events also had relatively little domestic impact on Islam and politics. Despite this, however, they set the stage for what was to be an intense and growing anxiety in the West, and among some African elites, about the potential danger of "radicalization" of African political Islam. Many of the dynamics I have discussed above as phenomena linked to liberalization—religious discourse in the public sphere, increased demands for Islamic education, opposition to Western-inspired family law, and such—have been read as symptoms of this looming danger (Lyman and Morrison 2004; Rotberg 2005).

Two major zones of concern have been identified in this respect: the countries of the Horn of Africa and Sahelian (or more specifically Saharan) West Africa (International Crisis Group 2005). Northern Nigeria, although part of the Sahel, is also sometimes singled out for its unique dynamics. Elsewhere in the Sahel the concern was fueled by various violent kidnappings and killings, mostly in the open Sahara, and carried out by groups apparently affiliated with or inspired by the Algerian GSPC (Salafist Group for Preaching and Combat), reconfigured as Al- Qaʻida in the Maghreb (AQIM) in 2006, although certainly shaped by highly local concerns. These events placed significant pressure on governments in the region, and resulted in several major US-led initiatives to attempt to contain or defeat *jihadi* Islam in the region. While this complex situation remained difficult to sort out, the most striking fact has been the almost complete lack of support for such Islamist activities among local populations, among the materially poorest people on earth. Despite massive military efforts, however, it has proven extremely difficult to eliminate all such groups in the vast and largely ungoverned spaces of the region. Such *jihadi* activities thus seem likely to remain a thorn in the side of governments across the region, but also seem unlikely in themselves to be able to mount major offensives against states.

This precarious situation was abruptly disrupted by forces unleashed by the fall of the Qaddafi regime in Libya. The flow of arms and returning fighters who had been recruited from the Sahel to fight in Qaddafi's army, as well as refugees and returning migrant workers, placed extraordinary pressures on Sahelian countries in late 2011 and early 2012. In the particularly fragile situation of Mali the initial impact was to spark a new rebellion among the ethnic Tuareg population of the northern regions, feeding on historical grievances, but importantly with no religious agenda or motivation. In a complicated and still unclear sequence of events, government mishandling of this uprising provoked a military mutiny, which in turn ended in the overthrow of the government, abruptly ending Mali's twenty-year period as a much-lauded democracy in Muslim West Africa.

Most dramatically following the coup, both the Malian military and the Tuareg separatist movement quickly lost control of the northern half of the country, including the historical and important cities of Timbuktu and Gao. In their place, the region was quickly and opportunistically occupied by a shifting assortment of militant *jihadi* groups, including AQIM, an affiliated Tuareg-led group that took the name of the Ansar Ad-Dine, and eventually a new group calling itself the Movement for Unity and Jihad in West Africa (MUJWA). Terrorized local populations have shown no support for these small but well-armed movements, which seem to be drawing both resources and fighters from outside the region. Political paralysis in the Malian capital of Bamako, however, and the ambivalence of outside actors to intervene in a fragile political situation and an extraordinarily inhospitable vast desert region, have produced a stalemate whose ultimate resolution is far from clear.

An equally difficult and ambiguous situation has been presented by political Islamic movements in the Horn of Africa. Islamism as a political ideology has long been present across the region, perhaps more than elsewhere in sub-Saharan Africa, and its various ideological strains are genealogically linked to Egyptian and Sudanese Islamist movements (de Waal 2004). In the two divided countries of Ethiopia and Eritrea, countries that have in addition experienced significant strife and violence, what is most striking is the fact that despite deep political divisions Islam has not been politicized as a major force in either country, and in neither would the Muslim-Christian cleavage be considered a major force in national politics.

And finally, Somalia. What might appear in some accounts as the site of Africa's most politicized Islamic society, may on closer look appear as one of its least significant in terms of our analysis of Islam and politics—despite the deep and damning tragedy that it represents for the world community. Somalia's state, the most heavily armed and one of the most highly involved in Cold War rivalries for most of its independent history, collapsed into anarchy as the support structure for Africa's authoritarian regimes crumbled in the early 1990s. Two decades, a full generation, later, there is still no functioning state. Appearing in significant measure only in the second decade of this tragic picture of human suffering, political Islam in Somalia has been much more an epiphenomenal product of this history than a key factor in explaining the situation (Menkhaus 2004). Indeed, the one hope for Somalia in the mid-2000s was the de facto Islamic government known as the "Islamic Courts Union" (ICU), which effectively ruled much of the country until pushed out by Ethiopian troops, with US support, in late 2006. The ICU appears to have gained some significant legitimacy for the stability that it was able to impose, and its breakup following the Ethiopian invasion spawned a more radical set of smaller *jihadi* groups, "pirates," and other seeming threats to the international community. In this context it is extremely difficult to predict the fate of political Islam in the region, but it is also unimaginable that a stable government could be constructed without explicitly building on a religious identity and the legitimacy it would confer.

In the highly politicized global context of Islam in the age of terror, we see wide variations in the role of Islam in its multiple sub-Saharan contexts. The fate of individual states in Africa has clearly been central to setting the parameters for Islam's political role. And Muslim societies on the continent have demonstrated a capacity for innovation and significant experimentation with political models. Unfortunately Africa has been largely neglected in much of the voluminous recent literature on Islam and politics, and there is much that we still do not know about dynamics on the continent. But it is also clear that Africa presents important possibilities that need to be considered if we are to fully describe the multifaceted political roles of Islam in the modern world.

NOTES

1. Very few countries have carried out reliable censuses in Africa, and even in those few that have done so the political sensitivity of relative demographic importance means that the question of religion is usually not asked, or the results not released.

2. The partition of Sudan in July 2011 left the remaining north of that historically *divided* country as a new Muslim majority state (Sudan) and produced the new Muslim minority state of South Sudan. No reliable figures are available for the religious demography of either country, and questions of citizenship on both sides will no doubt long complicate efforts to count. Various informed sources suggest, however, that the resident Muslim population of South Sudan currently comprises a significant minority, perhaps in the range of 10 percent.

3. Very small Shi`a populations in some places are either primarily of non-African origin, or of relatively recent vintage as politically motivated movements.

4. Following the Africanist convention, "francophone" refers to the former French colonies where French has been maintained as the official language, although it is never spoken by the majority.

5. The commonly cited exceptions, namely Liberia and Ethiopia, were nevertheless heavily shaped by the broader colonial experience of the continent, both in terms of boundaries and by external influences on the elaboration of the state apparatus.

6. The rare exceptions that were presented at the time as indicators of the possibilities for democracy in Africa included the small island republic of Mauritius, and the cases of Senegal and Botswana, both stable and civilian regimes, but whose "democracy" was marked by significant limitations—namely the persistent hold on power of the parties that had led them to independence.

7. An ongoing research project on Muslim democracies, led by Mirjam Künkler at Princeton University, used various political datasets to identify only five democracies in predominantly Muslim countries in 2010: Turkey, Indonesia, and Albania, in addition to the two African cases named here. It merits noting that the collapse of the democratic system in Mali in 2012 was unrelated to religious issues, but rather attributable largely to a weakened state structure unable to withstand strong pressures resulting from the consequences of the collapse of the Qaddafi regime in Libya.

REFERENCES

Alidou, Ousseina. 2005. *Engaging Modernity: Muslim Women and the Politics of Agency in Post-Colonial Niger*. Madison: University of Wisconsin Press.

An-Naim, Abdullahi Ahmed. 2006. *African Constitutionalism and the role of Islam.* Philadelphia: University of Pennsylvania Press.

Augis, Erin. 2005. Dakar's Sunnite Women: The Politics of Person. In *L'Islam politique au sud du Sahara: Identités, discours et enjeux,* ed. Muriel Gomez-Perez, 309–326. Paris: Karthala.

Badran, Margot, ed. *Gender and Islam in Africa: Right, Sexuality, and Law.* Washington D.C.: Woodrow Wilson Center Press, and Stanford UP, 2011.

Becker, Felicitas. 2008. *Becoming Muslim in Mainland Tanzania, 1890–2000.* Oxford: Oxford University Press.

Bonate, Liazaat J. K. 2009. Transformations de l'Islam à Penda au Mozambique. In *L'économie morale et les mutations de l'Islam en Afrique sub-saharienne,* eds. Jean-Louis Triaud and Leonardo A. Villalón. *Afrique Contemporaine* (Paris), no. 231: 61-76.

Bratton, Michael. 2003. Briefing: Islam, Democracy and Public Opinion in Africa. *African Affairs* 102: 493–501.

Brégand, Denise. 2007. Muslim Reformists and the State in Benin. In *Islam and Muslim Politics in Africa,* eds. Benjamin F. Soares and René Otayek, 121–136. New York: Palgrave Macmillan.

Brenner, Louis, ed. 1993. *Muslim Identity and Social Change in Sub-Saharan Africa.* Bloomington: Indiana University Press.

Brenner, Louis. 2000. Sufism in Africa. In *African Spirituality,* ed. Jacob K. Olupona. New York: The Crossroad Publishing Company: 324–349.

Brenner, Louis. 2001. *Controlling Knowledge: Religion, Power and Schooling in a West African Muslim Society.* Bloomington: Indiana University Press.

Centre d'Etude d'Afrique Noire. *L'Afrique politique 2002: Islams d'Afrique, entre le local et le globale.* Paris: Karthala.

Constantin, François. 1995. Muslims and Politics: Attempts to Create Muslim National Organizations in Tanzania, Uganda and Kenya. In *Religion & Politics in East Africa: The Period since Independence,* eds. Holger Bernt Hansen and Michael Twaddle, 19–31. London: James Currey.

Cruise O'Brien, Donal. 2003. *Symbolic Confrontations: Muslims Imagining the State in Africa.* London: Hurst and Company.

De Waal, Alex, ed. 2004. *Islamism and Its Enemies in the Horn of Africa.* Bloomington: Indiana University Press.

Galilou, Abdoulaye. 2002. The Graduates of Islamic Universities in Benin: A Modern Elite Seeking Social, Religious and Political Recognition. In *Islam in Africa,* eds. Thomas Bierschenk and Georg Stauth, 129–146. Yearbook of the Sociology of Islam 4. Berlin: Lit Verlag.

Gomez-Perez, Muriel, ed. 2005. *L'Islam politique au sud du Sahara: Identités, discours et enjeux.* Paris: Karthala.

Hanretta, Sean. 2005. Muslim Histories, African Societies; the Venture of Islamic Studies in Africa. *Journal of African History* 46: 479–491.

Hashim, Abdulkadir. 2005. Muslim Personal Law in Kenya and Tanzania: Tradition and Innovation. *Journal of Muslim Minority Affairs* 25(3): 449–460.

Holder, Gilles, ed. 2009. *L'Islam, nouvel espace public en Afrique.* Paris: Karthala.

Hunwick, John. 1997. Sub-Saharan Africa and the Wider World of Islam: Historical and Contemporary Perspectives. In *African Islam and Islam in Africa: Encounters between Sufis and Islamists,* eds. David Westerlund and Eva Evers Rosander. London: Hurst & Company: 28–54.

International Crisis Group. Islamist Terrorism in the Sahel: Fact or Fiction? Africa Report No. 92, March 31, 2005. Available at: http://www.crisisgroup.org/home/index.cfm?id=3347&l=1 (accessed February 20, 2010).

Kane, Ousmane, and Jean-Louis Triaud, eds. 1998. *Islam et islamismes au sud du Sahara.* Paris: Karthala.

Kane, Ousmane. 2003. *Muslim Modernity in Postcolonial Nigeria: A Study of the Society for the Removal of Innovation and Reinstatement of tradition.* Leiden: Brill.

Levtzion, Nehemia, and Randall L. Pouwells, eds. 2000. *The History of Islam in Africa.* Athens: Ohio University Press.

Loimeier, Roman. 1997. *Islamic Reform and Political Change in Northern Nigeria.* Evanston: Northwestern University Press.

Loimeier, Roman. 2003. Patterns and Peculiarities of Islamic Reform in Africa. *Journal of Religion in Africa* 33(3): 237–262.

Loimeier, Roman. 2007. Perceptions of Marginalization: Muslims in Contemporary Tanzania. In *Islam and Muslim Politics in Africa,* eds. Benjamin Soares and René Otayek, 137–156. New York: Palgrave Macmillan.

Lyman, Princeton N., and J. Stephen Morrison. 2004. The Terrorist Threat in Africa. *Foreign Affairs* 83(1): 75–86.

Masquelier, Adeline. 2009. *Women and Islamic Revival in a West African Town.* Bloomington: Indiana University Press.

Mbogoni, Lawrence E. Y. 2004. *The Cross versus the Crescent: Religion and Politics in Tanzania from the 1880s to the 1990s.* Dar es Salaam: Mkuki na Nyota Publishers.

Menkhaus, Kenneth J. 2004. *Somalia: State Collapse and the Threat of Terrorism.* Adelphi Paper 364, International Institute for Strategic Studies. Oxford: Oxford University Press.

Meunier, Olivier. 1997. *Dynamique de l'Enseignement Islamique au Niger: Le cas de la ville de Maradi.* Paris: L'Harmattan.

Miles, William F. S., ed. 2007. *Political Islam in West Africa: State-Society Relations Transformed.* Boulder: Lynne Rienner Publishers.

Oded, Arye. 2000. *Islam and Politics in Kenya.* Boulder: Lynne Rienner Publishers.

Østebø, Terje. 2008. Localising Salafism: Religious Change among Oromo Muslims in Bale, Ethiopia. PhD diss., Stockholm University.

Østebø, Terje. 2009. Une économie salafie de la prière dans la région du Balé en Éthiopie. In *L'économie morale et les mutations de l'Islam en Afrique sub-Sahari-*

enne, eds. Jean-Louis Triaud and Leonardo A. Villalón. *Afrique Contemporaine* (Paris), No. 231: 45–60.

Ostien, Philip, Jamila M. Nasir, and Franz Kogelmann, eds. 2005. *Comparative Perspectives on shari`ah in Nigeria.* Ibadan: Spectrum Books, Ltd.

Otayek, René, ed. 1993. *Le radicalisme Islamique au sud du Sahara: Da`wa, arabisation et critique de l'Occident.* Paris: Karthala.

Paden, John N. 2005. *Muslim Civic Cultures and Conflict Resolution: The Challenge of Democratic Federalism in Nigeria.* Washington: Brookings Institution Press.

Piga, Adriana. 2006. *Les voies du soufisme au sud du Sahara: Parcours historiques et anthropologiques.* Paris: Karthala.

Robinson, David. 2004. *Muslim Societies in African History.* Cambridge: Cambridge University Press.

Rotberg, Robert I., ed. 2005. *Battling Terrorism in the Horn of Africa.* Washington: Brookings Institution Press.

Rothchild, Donald, and Naomi Chazan. 1988. *The Precarious Balance: State and Society in Africa.* Boulder: Westview Press.

Sani Umar, Muhammad. 1993. Changing Islamic Identity in Nigeria from the 1960s to the 1980s: From Sufism to anti-Sufism. In *Muslim Identity and Social Change in Sub-Saharan Africa*, ed. Louis Brenner. Bloomington: Indiana University Press: 154–178.

Sanneh, Lamin. 1997. *The Crown and the Turban: Muslims and West African Pluralism.* Boulder: Westview Press.

Soares, Benjamin F. 2005. Islam in Mali in the Neoliberal Era. *African Affairs* 105(418): 77–95.

Soares, Benjamin F., and René Otayek, eds. 2007. *Islam and Muslim Politics in Africa.* New York: Palgrave Macmillan.

Soares, Benjamin F. 2009. The Attempt to Reform Family Law in Mali. *Die Welt des Islams* 49: 398–428.

Tayob, Abdulkader. 1999. *Islam in South Africa: Mosques, Imams, and Sermons.* Gainesville: University Press of Florida.

Triaud, Jean-Louis, and Leonardo A. Villalón, eds. 2009. *L'économie morale et les mutations de l'Islam en Afrique sub-Saharienne.* Special issue of the journal. *Afrique Contemporaine* (Paris), No. 231.

Twaddle, Michael. 2003. The Bible, the Qur'an and Political Competition in Uganda. In *Scriptural Politics: The Bible and the Koran as Political Models in the Middle East and Africa*, ed. Niels Kastfelt, 139–154. London: Hurst.

Villalón, Leonardo A. 1995. *Islamic Society and State Power in Senegal: Disciples and Citizens in Fatick.* Cambridge: Cambridge University Press.

Villalón, Leonardo A. 1996. The Moral and the Political in African Democratization: The *Code de la Famille* in Niger's Troubled Transition. *Democratization* 3(2): 41–68.

Villalón, Leonardo A., and Phillip A. Huxtable, eds. 1998. *The African State at a Critical Juncture: Between Disintegration and Reconfiguration.* Boulder: Lynne Rienner Publishers.

Villalón, Leonardo A. 2010. From Argument to Negotiation: Constructing Democracies in Muslim West Africa. *Comparative Politics* 42(4): 375–393.

Villalón, Leonardo A. 2012. Rethinking Education in the Sahel: Democracy, Religious Change, and the Politics of reform. In *Governing Africa's Changing Societies: Dynamics of Reform*, ed. Ellen Lust and Stephen Ndegwa, 177–201. Boulder: Lynne Rienner Publishers.

Westerlund, David, and Eva Evers Rosander, eds. 1997. *African Islam and Islam in Africa: Encounters between Sufis and Islamists*. London: Hurst and Company/ Athens: Ohio University Press.

INDEX

Names starting with "al-" are alphabetized by the subsequent part of the name.